S0-ACA-226

GIVE ALL TO OREGON!

GIVE ALL TO OREGON!

Missionary Pioneers of the Far West

by

CECIL P. DRYDEN

HASTINGS HOUSE · PUBLISHERS

New York

Published simultaneously in Canada
by Saunders, of Toronto, Ltd., Don Mills, Ontario.

Library of Congress Catalog Card Number: 68–20254.

Printed in the United States of America.

CONTENTS

PART THREE

THE CATHOLICS ENTER THE FIELD

LIST OF ILLUSTRATIONS

(Following page 128)

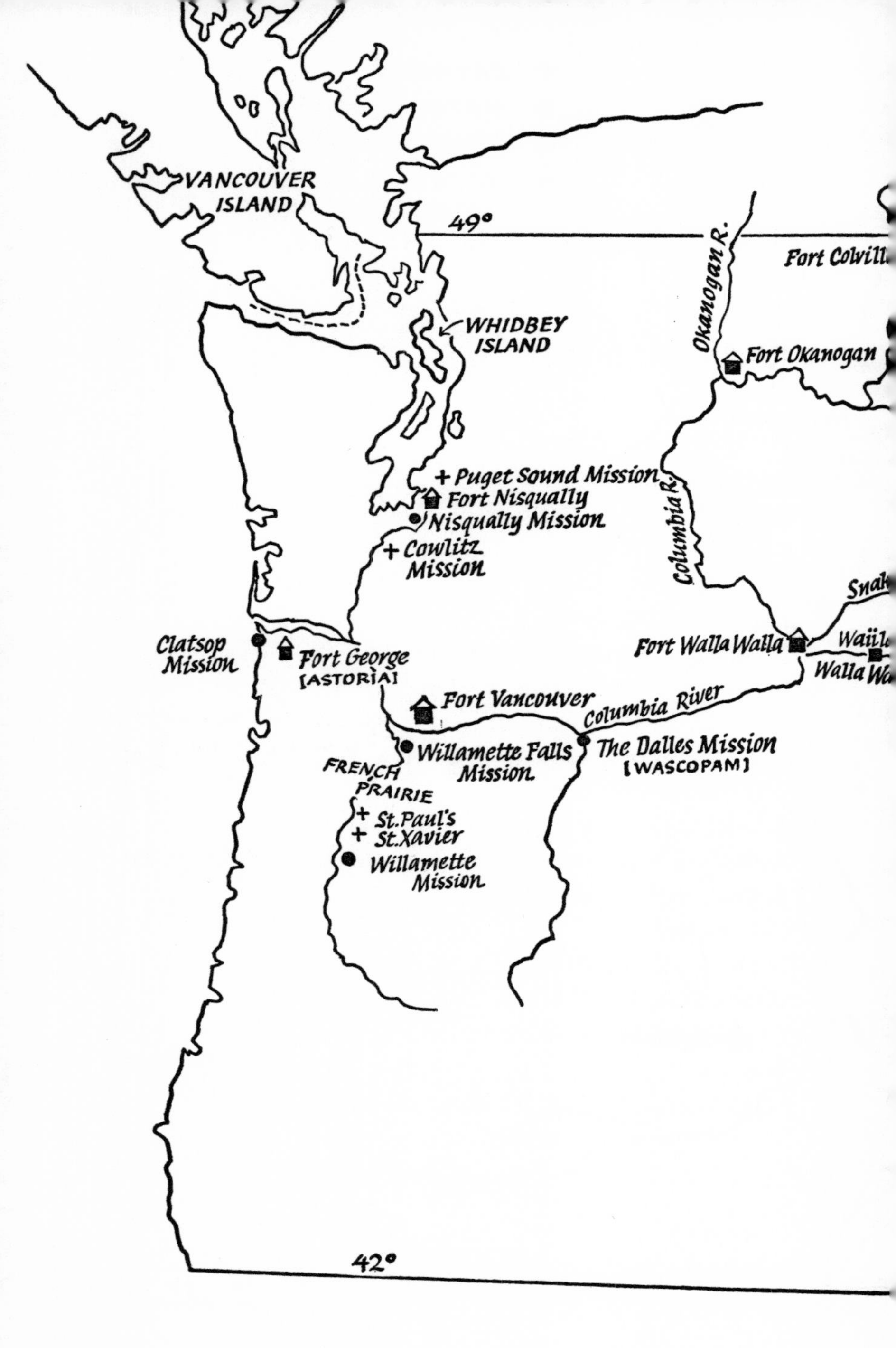
VANCOUVER
ISLAND
49°
Okanogan R.
Fort Colvill
WHIDBEY
ISLAND
Fort Okanogan
+ Puget Sound Mission
Fort Nisqually
Nisqually Mission
Columbia R.
+ Cowlitz
Mission
Clatsop
Mission
Fort George
[ASTORIA]
Fort Walla Walla
Walla Wa
Fort Vancouver
Columbia River
Willamette Falls
Mission
The Dalles Mission
[WASCOPAM]
FRENCH
PRAIRIE
+ St. Paul's
+ St. Xavier
Willamette
Mission
42°

CATHOLIC
METHODIST
AMER. BOARD
HUDSON BAY COMPANY POSTS
L. Pond Oreille
Mission
Fort Spokane
Lake Coeur D'Alene
Cataldo Mission
+ DeSmet
Flathead Lake
St. Ignatius
Clark Fork River
Bitter Root Mountain Boundary
Clearwater R.
Lapwai
Kamiah Mission
+ St. Mary's
Salmon R.
Snake River
Fort Boise
Portneuf R.
Fort Hall
Glenn's Ferry Crossing
Snake R.
0 25 50 75 MILES

PREFACE

This is a story about people, about those unsung pioneers who braved the dangers of trackless wilderness, mountain and turbulent river to carry the cross to the "heathen" in Old Oregon.

Much has been written about the fur trader, the mountain man and the settler, and their part in the opening of the Great West. But the missionary has remained practically a forgotten man. Except for Dr. Marcus Whitman and his wife, who suffered martyrdom in the cause, those devout men and women who volunteered their services in "reclaiming" the red Indian are scarcely known, even by name.

In 1831, there came to the ear of civilization a strange, appealing call from the Rocky Mountains. In that year, a delegation of Nez Perce and Flathead Indians arrived in St. Louis with a request for the white man's "Book of Heaven."

As soon as this fact was published, Christians everywhere felt a sense of guilt that they had so long neglected God's red children beyond the Mississippi. "When the heathen come knocking at our very doors," said the religious leaders, "surely it is time for the churches to awaken to their responsibilities."

The plea produced results. The missionary movement was begun, with the Methodists in the vanguard. In 1834, Jason Lee and his few helpers arrived in the Willamette Valley to build the first Oregon mission. In 1836 came the missionaries of the American Board, led by Dr. Marcus Whitman, and two years later the Catholics entered the field.

This is their story—the story of their sacrifices, their frustrations, their petty disagreements, their small successes, their woeful failures. If they did not succeed in converting multitudes of Indians to Christianity, they at least prepared the red man for the inevitable day of paleface domination. And in addition, they as pioneers played an important role in blazing a trail across the continent for the thousands of settlers who followed them.

PART ONE

JASON LEE AND THE METHODISTS

1 • *The Call from the Mountains*

WHEN WILLIAM WALKER STRODE down the streets of old St. Louis that autumn day in the year 1831 he had no notion of starting a missionary movement to the West. His mind was solely on a piece of business which included an interview with William Clark, co-leader of the famous Lewis-Clark Expedition of 1804–1806. Walker was a half-breed agent and interpreter from the Wyandotte Indian reservation at Sandusky, Ohio. The tribe was to be moved somewhere west of the Mississippi River, and he had been sent by the federal government to examine the lands under consideration.

Captain Clark was not hard to find in a small place where everyone knew the genial Superintendent of Indian Affairs. The interview was a pleasant one, and when it was over, Clark detained his caller, saying, "By the way, I've had some visitors—a delegation from the Rocky Mountains."

"Indians?" asked Walker, his interest aroused.

"Yes, three Nez Perces and one Flathead, as near as I can make out. And can you guess why they're here?"

"Just to see you, I suppose. You stopped among them when you were out there, didn't you?"

Clark looked serious. "Yes, but they're hunting something more important than me. They came to get the white man's Book of Heaven, and thought I might be able to help them."

Walker's dark eyes glowed. "I never heard of such a thing! Heathen coming for the Bible! Who told them about it?"

"Knowledge of our religion has been leaking into the mountains for some time. There's a few Christian Iroquois in the Rockies—brought in by fur traders. They've had contact with the Flatheads, who have always been on good terms with the Nez Perces. Then there's Spokane Garry, educated at the Red River Mission School in Winnipeg. He came home with a Bible."

"I see, Captain. They've picked up a little here and there."

Clark continued: "It seems that once upon a time some traders came upon Indians worshiping in their own primitive way. 'That's all wrong,' said the mountain men. 'You're displeasing the Great Spirit. The whites, living in the land that looks toward the rising sun, are the only ones who know the true way of worshiping God. They have a Book containing all the directions.' "

Walker listened attentively while Clark concluded. "The Indians, I hear, held a council to decide what should be done. 'If all this is true,' they reasoned, 'we must know more about it. We can't put it off.' "

"And so they're here," Walker mused. "It's stranger than any fiction I ever read."

"Since they came to see me," said Clark, "I felt responsible for helping them all I could, even though I'm far from being a preacher. I gave them the story of man from the time of Adam. I told them about Jesus, and how he would come again to judge the world. I showed them a Bible, took them around the town and pointed out the cathedral. That's about all a common soldier could do, I guess."

There was silence for a moment, and then Walker asked, "What do you think they'll tell their people when they go back?"

Clark shook his head. "I doubt that they ever get back. Come here." He arose and opened the door to an adjoining room. Stretched out on a cot was an Indian, ragged and emaciated, apparently unconscious. William Walker was as deeply impressed by the sight as he had been by Clark's story. He stared at the motionless figure until Clark closed the door.

"That's one of them," explained Clark, "and he's very bad off. He won't live long. He's called Daylight, or Man-of-the-Morning." After a pause Clark went on. "Another died a few days ago, and was buried by the priests in the cathedral yard. His name was

Speaking Eagle, or Black Eagle. There are only two left to tell the story."

There was nothing more to be said. His business in St. Louis being finished, William Walker went back to his agency at Sandusky, Ohio. Months passed. Occasionally Clark's story flashed into Walker's memory, along with the vivid picture of the dying Man-of-the-Morning. Then, on January 19, 1833, he felt impelled to write a letter.

If anyone had predicted that this letter would be the starting signal of a missionary crusade to Oregon, Walker would have smiled incredulously. He was not a man of importance, only a servant of the Wyandottes and the federal government. But he had education and ability, and what he wrote made sense. He gave a detailed account of his visit to St. Louis in the fall of 1831, and of the four men from the mountains who had visited Captain Clark. He described the one he had seen, Man-of-the-Morning, and drew a sketch from memory, showing the features and the shape of the head. He mailed the letter to a friend, G. P. Disosway in New York, then promptly forgot about it.

This was not the end, however. That letter was destined to make missionary history in America. It so happened that G. P. Disosway was especially interested in missions. He had financed the founding of the Methodist Missionary Society in 1819. Now he took the letter and hurried to the office of *The Christian Advocate and Journal* and said, "Publish that. It'll startle the world."

He was right. Soon the story of the Nez Perce-Flathead delegation to St. Louis was published in all religious journals. From person to person the word was carried, from state to state, even across the water to Europe. Christians, aroused to a new sense of their responsibilities, stood ready to support a crusade on behalf of the red savages of the Rocky Mountains. The time, they declared, was now.

"When the heathen come knocking at our very doors," cried the preachers, "can we longer delay?"

Speaking Eagle and Man-of-the-Morning had died in St. Louis. No-Horns-on-His-Head died on the way home. Rabbit-skin-Leggings made the long journey back to the mountains, but was killed shortly after his arrival in a fight with the Blackfeet. But the visit the four made to St. Louis started the missionary movement in Old Oregon and, indirectly, it had a profound effect on the political history of the whole Northwest.

William Walker had lighted the missionary torch. Now who would carry it?

2 • *Jason Lee*

AS SOON AS DR. WILBUR FISK opened his copy of the *Christian Advocate and Journal,* a quick glance discovered the story of the Indian visitors to St. Louis. He read it avidly, and after he had finished he said excitedly to his wife, "We'll have one, sure enough! We'll have a missionary there for those benighted red men!"

"That's a noble idea," she anwered, "but where's your man?"

"I know of one who is in every way fitted for such an undertaking." Dr. Fisk pushed aside a stack of letters and picked up a pen. "You know whom I mean—Jason Lee, my prize student at Wilbraham Academy. If I can get him, we have the answer."

"Yes, but aren't you too late, Wilbur?" his wife asked. "Hasn't Jason Lee accepted an assignment with the British conference in Canada?"

Ignoring her question, Fisk sat down and wrote a note to his former student, Jason Lee, of Stanstead, Canada. Within half an hour, his invitation was in the post. The next day, regardless of the gnawings of ill health, Dr. Fisk went out to begin an appeal for funds. Being an influential Methodist as well as the president of Wesleyan University, at Middleton, Connecticut, his ardent requests bore immediate fruit. Within a few days, he had raised between seven and eight hundred dollars for the support of a mission to the Indians of the Far West.

When the Methodist Board of Missions met, Dr. Wilbur Fisk was its leading spirit. He made his recommendations with zeal and eloquence. "We don't need a whole army of missionaries," he declared. "We can do wonders with only two men—men without families, men of courage, men with the spirit of martyrs to throw their lives into the work, to live with the natives, learn their language, preach to them, open up schools, start agriculture and, in general, teach all the arts of civilized life."

It did not take much persuasion to convince the Board that a mission should be started without delay and that Jason Lee was the man to head it. While they waited to hear from Stanstead, Canada, the zealots made further appeals for the support of the proposed mission. Dr. Fisk's words carried weight with laymen, as well as with the Board.

"Money will not be lacking," he promised. "I will be the bondsman for the church. All we want is men. Who will go? I would go joyfully if I were younger and in good health. But the honor is reserved for another. Bright will be his crown, glorious his reward."

A wave of missionary enthusiasm flowed over the land. Contributions to the fund poured in from all corners, from small as well as large congregations and from personally interested individuals. One man in New York City offered all his property to the value of $2000, provided that he himself were chosen chief missionary. "Sorry," said the Board, in effect. "You don't have the proper qualifications; besides, that honor has been bestowed upon Jason Lee."

In May, 1833 came Jason Lee's acceptance from Stanstead. Dr. Wilbur Fisk rejoiced. Half the problem of the mission had been solved, so far as he was concerned. He eagerly awaited the time when his appointee, his business affairs disposed of, should appear to make preparations for carrying out his assignment as first Missionary to the Flatheads. At that time, and for years afterward, it was generally believed that the deputation from the mountains was composed exclusively of Flatheads. Later research, however, revealed that three were Nez Perces, and that only one was probably a member of the Flathead tribe.

Jason Lee was the descendant of a long line of rugged Puritan pioneers, the son of Daniel Lee and Sara Whittaker and the youngest child in a family of fifteen. He was born July 28, 1803 at Stanstead, Canada, just across the Vermont boundary. He spent his youth and early manhood in this community, where farms were carved out the hard way from the forested lands.

Jason's father died in 1806, leaving his mother with only slender means of support. The lad spent most of these first years in the home of his oldest brother, Elias, whose son Daniel was to become Jason's missionary companion in Oregon. The attachment between Jason and his nephew, who was only three years younger, seemed to be one of the David and Jonathan variety. Young Daniel always retained a profound admiration for his uncle.

Lee attended the little Stanstead school, but beyond that had small opportunity for an education. He was compelled to earn his own living from the time he was thirteen. When Jason was twenty-three, a great religious awakening came to Stanstead. He was converted at one of the revival meetings.

"I saw, I believed, I repented," he said. "After that, old faces wore a new glory, old friends spoke a new tongue."

Lee's conversion did not change his occupation immediately, however. For three more years, he toiled on with ax and shovel, all the time planning for the day when opportunity would launch him fully in the Lord's work. It came in 1829, when he was twenty-six. That summer he registered in the Methodist academy at Wilbraham, Massachusetts, and from the first day, made a favorable impression on the principal, Dr. Wilbur Fisk.

Since Lee showed unusual interest as well as stability of character and success as an instructor, Fisk was not long in singling him out as special tutor for a group of the most promising students. Teaching, however, was not the career of Jason Lee's choosing. He was determined to devote the remainder of his life to the ministry. With this resolve in mind, he enlisted as a preacher of the Gospel under the supervision of the Wesleyan missionaries, hoping eventually to receive a call to some foreign field. He had started rather late, and with meager preparation, yet he was the man of all men, from the viewpoint of Dr. Fisk.

Jason Lee closed up his business at home, and early in the summer of 1833 appeared before the critical eyes of the members of the Mission Board. At thirty, he was a powerfully built man weighing 200 pounds, and standing six feet three inches in spite of the slight stoop in his shoulders. He had a mass of medium-blond hair combed back from a high forehead, a heavy jaw, thin, closely compressed lips, a large nose and eyes described by a friend as "spiritualistic blue." He had the warm heart and the deep humility of a sincere Christian, combined with the courage and self-confidence of a fighting crusader. Every fiber of the man seemed to say boldly, "Here I am. Send me."

The Board was as favorably disposed toward Jason Lee as was Dr. Wilbur Fisk. At the close of the long conference, the chairman said, "You'll need an associate in the field, a kind of second in command with whom you can work intimately. We've decided to permit you to do the choosing. Think it over, and let us know when—"

"I choose Daniel, my nephew," Lee interrupted. "We understand each other. We've worked together."

The Board readily sanctioned the choice and in due course Daniel Lee was presented to high missionary officials. If Daniel were ever to shine, it would have to be in the reflected light of some more aggressive personality. He had few ardent supporters and, by the same token, few enemies. He was always partially eclipsed by the powerful shadow of his uncle. Jason was the leader, Daniel the follower. Everybody saw Jason; few saw the slight form of Daniel seeking the wings and letting others have the center of the stage. Jason was large and well favored in appearance; Daniel was small in stature with a bony frame and irregular, homely features. But Daniel was a hard worker, dedicated to the cause and possessed of a plentiful supply of common sense. He was practical rather than idealistic. In a few weeks he would be ordained by the New Hampshire conference. Fully as emphatically as Jason, he was ready to say, "Here I am. Send me."

By August 1833, Jason Lee had received his official appointment as "Missionary to the Flatheads," and Daniel had been named as his assistant. Now began the campaign of preparation—days, weeks and months of hard work for both the missionaries and the Mission Board. At a meeting in October the Board appropriated $3000 for the Flathead mission, the largest sum that had ever been allowed for a like project. Further, the Board authorized the appointment of a teacher and two lay assistants to be chosen by Jason Lee at his convenience. After the organization was pretty well in hand, the Board said, "Now you must go to the people. We appropriate the funds, but in the end, the public foots the bill. Go out. Tell all the folks about the Flathead mission. Get their support, and great things will be done."

Accordingly, the Board arranged for the Lees to make a speaking tour of the country, and planned the details of the itinerary. There were no idle moments during those months when Jason and Daniel were traveling from place to place, holding missionary meetings and fervently presenting the needs of the Flathead mission. The response was gratifying everywhere they went. Jason Lee took time to look for a teacher to take charge at his mission. Accompanied by a fellow preacher, he went to interview Cyrus Shepard, who was teaching the village school at Weston, a few miles from Boston. Shepard had been highly recommended, and when Lee met this large handsome man with the pleasant face and charming manners he was completely won over. "Mr. Shepard's a born teacher, and a missionary to the core," said the townspeople. "If he can't convert the heathen, nobody can."

The interview was short. This was the chance for which Cyrus had been waiting and he promptly accepted. Jason Lee went back to his travels convinced that something vitally important had been done for the Flathead cause. Shepard's fiancée, Susan Downing, of course could not go, but she looked forward to the time when she would join Cyrus in Oregon.

As plans gradually took definite shape, each week in that busy autumn saw the missionary project nearer completion. But there was one problem that had not yet been solved. This was the lack of an escort across the plains from St. Louis. Jason Lee had made repeated inquiries about fur caravans leaving for the mountains, but no answer had been received. It was the custom of small parties—and they were few indeed—to attach themselves to some large fur outfit in order to receive protection against the Indians. This was the only safe method of traveling.

By the middle of November the missionaries had decided to make the journey alone if no escort presented itself. At least, they would go to St. Louis and take a chance on finding some supply caravan going to the rendezvous in the Rocky Mountains. Luckily for them, in a few days there came news of the return of Nathaniel Wyeth from the West, where he had tried unsuccessfully to set up a business for himself in Oregon. Faced with losses which could not be repaired, Wyeth hurried home to Boston with a new project in mind. He was convinced that Oregon was the place for a man to make his fortune. Within twelve days after his arrival in Boston, he had organized the Columbia River Fishing and Trading Company. He had been too late for furs—the Hudson's Bay Company had frozen him out—but perhaps fishing would pay the dividends he coveted.

Jason Lee knew little about Nathaniel Wyeth or his projects, but here was his chance to get protection for the overland journey. Wyeth gladly granted an interview and willingly talked for hours on Oregon, answering scores of questions and giving plenty of advice gratis. The Flatheads, he said, were a friendly people, but he counseled against building in a place so isolated, so far away from the protection of a Hudson's Bay post. These words caused Lee no little concern. He had been appointed head missionary to the Flatheads, and if he did not dare go among them where in heaven's name would he go? Money had been appropriated for a Flathead mission. How else could it be legally used?

Nathaniel Wyeth promised the missionaries the protection of his caravan over the Missouri plains, starting in April. He had already chartered the ship *May Dacre* and would begin loading at once. She would have room to carry all the supplies for the Oregon mission. For this amazing generosity, Jason Lee thanked the Lord as well as Nathaniel Wyeth. With more time at their disposal and a ship at hand, the missionaries were able to buy more goods. They could now consider purchasing such things as farm implements, seeds, a variety of clothing and certain nonperishable foods.

When departure time came, Jason Lee felt that everything was in order. It was hard to say good-by, perhaps forever, to relatives and friends, but he had dedicated his life to service among the heathen, and for him the only trail lay ahead. In ample time, he, his brother Daniel and Cyrus Shepard made their way to Pittsburgh, where they boarded the *Gate City* for St. Louis.

3 • Overland to Oregon

TIRED AND TRAVEL-STAINED, THE party arrived at Independence, Missouri, the "jumping-off place" to the Wild West. Now it is a suburb of Kansas City; then, it was the last outpost of civilization. But it was important even at that time as a depot of supplies. Here boats dumped off tons of merchandise to be picked up by the Santa Fe traders and the Rocky Mountain fur men. The town stood on a prominent point that overlooked a panorama of timbered hills through which the river cut its winding way. About fifty log houses straggled along in a slovenly line that bore some resemblance to a street arrangement. Independence was known as a frontier village with two very opposite moods, one of lazy indifference, the other of buoyant, even wild energy. When traders descended and took the place by storm, there was a sound of revelry by both night and day; when they made their roaring exodus, the fifty houses again drowsed languidly by the muddy Missouri.

"Independence," mused Jason Lee. "Not much to look at, is she?"

"No," laughed Daniel, "but something to listen to, Uncle."

The little supply depot was agog, as full of energy as a cataract. On all sides was the babble of voices—talking, yelling, jesting—as caravans were whipped into shape and bargaining in horses and mules went on at a profane pace. To add to the turmoil, a small contingent of troops maneuvered in the very heart of the village. Sentries paced their beats along the river front.

"What's the trouble—Indians?" Jason Lee asked a passing trader.

"It's them Mormons," answered the man, setting his stiff-brimmed hat on the back of his head. "We've drove 'em outa here, but they're aimin' to come back an' butcher us. Uncle Sam's keepin' a eye on 'em."

Cyrus Shepard soon appeared with a report on the purchases he had made for the journey. He brought a word of warning, too. "They tell me," he said, "that Captain Wyeth is like time and tide—he waits for no man. Just yesterday he said, 'So the dignitaries aren't here yet! If they preach around much longer, they'll lose their passage, and I won't wait a minute for them.' "

"I thought we'd have ample time," answered Jason Lee with a calmness that was characteristic of him. "We have a week and a day. I think we'll get everything done."

The missionaries soon found themselves a part of the bustle and roar of the place. While Jason Lee and Shepard spent hours in rigging halters, bridles and pack saddles, and in assembling equipment of assorted kinds, Daniel Lee went out into the neighboring town of Richmond to find two laymen to help drive the cattle and horses. "We probably should not have delayed so long in St. Louis," said Jason Lee one day, "but the Lord, I am sure, will raise up helpers for us."

Luck or the Lord was with Daniel. Three days before the week had expired, he came back with the needed men. Philip L. Edwards was a native of Kentucky, a well schooled man of twenty-two who was eager for adventure and the improvement of his health. From the first, he showed initiative and the ability to manage. Courtney Walker was employed simply as a hired man for a year. He knew Indians, the frontier and how to do almost any kind of work. "If he can drive horned cattle," commented Lee, "he'll be an asset, even if he doesn't profess to be a Christian."

The day before the "last week in civilization" had ended, two strangers appeared in Wyeth's camp, asking for escort across the plains. They proved to be the scientists, Thomas Nuttall and John K. Townsend, who hoped to seek information on the botany and ornithology of the plains and the Northwest. Being assured of protection, they joined the ranks with good nature and good will.

In the meantime, Wyeth had whipped his company into shape for the starting. There were about fifty-four men in all, not counting the missionaries and those belonging to the Rocky Mountain Fur Company, traveling under the direction of Milton Sublette. These men were typical representatives of the fur trade. There were seasoned veterans who long ago had ceased to be concerned about the lack of the comforts of civilization. There was a scattering of "tenderfeet" venturing for the first time into the rough but glamorous life of the plains and mountains; and lastly, a fair showing of semi-outlaws, tough as ash poles, who submitted to authority only grudgingly.

"These are your fellow-travelers," said Wyeth, casting a sidelong glance at Jason Lee. "I'll protect you from them as far as possible, but of course there won't be much I can do."

"They're a rough, cursing, ungodly lot," Lee answered. "Such profanity I have never before heard. May the Lord have mercy on their souls."

Wyeth agreed unreservedly. "I swear myself," he said simply. "But it's a bad practice, and I often thought I'd quit. Not that religion has anything to do with it, because I'm something of a heathen from your point of view. Swearing, I admit, is poor taste and useless. It brands a man as being uncultured."

These men might spend half the night carousing, but they would have never an idle minute during the day. Nathaniel Wyeth saw to that. There were animals to care for, bridles and pack saddles to make or repair, and a mountain of goods to be sorted and baled. Wyeth had made a bargain with the Rocky Mountain Fur Company to take a consignment of supplies to the rendezvous on his way to Oregon. So here in Independence were piled tons of merchandise. And a conglomeration it was: nonperishable foods, weapons, ammunition, traps, clothing, blankets, tobacco and thousands of trading trinkets such as beads, hawk bells, mirrors, bright strips of calico and other gewgaws appealing to the Indians. For days, the men had been at work baling these things. They were made up into eighty-pound bundles for convenience in handling, and were to be roped, two to each saddle, onto the backs of the pack animals.

The last Sunday of that last week in civilization, Jason Lee had an invitation to preach in Independence, but Daniel cautioned, "I don't think you'd better do it, Uncle. When Mr. Wyeth's ready, he starts."

"Perhaps you're right, Daniel. We might raise a little more money for the Flatheads, but we'd better not risk being left behind. Since leaving New York, we've collected one thousand, two hundred and sixty dollars, and we've spent one thousand and ninety dollars for supplies and equipment."

"Traveling on the Sabbath won't be to our liking, will it, Jason?" Daniel ventured again.

"No, but when Captain Wyeth gives the word, we must be ready to march. After all, it's the Lord's cause."

Early in the morning, April 28, 1834, the camp awakened like a bombshell exploding, and from that time until the caravan was lined up, there was commotion and constant din—horses neighing and stamping, men yelling and cursing. Yet there was no time wasted. Wyeth saw to that.

Out of what seemed to be howling chaos, the cavalcade formed itself, swung forward and began the march. There were now some seventy men and 250 animals. Abreast in the vanguard rode Captain Wyeth, and Milton Sublette of the Rocky Mountain Fur Company. Alongside paced the mounts of the two scientists, Thomas Nuttall and young John K. Townsend. In double file rode the men armed with rifles and hunting knives and with powder horns at their belts. As a special responsibility, each man led two pack horses with their 160 pounds of merchandise balanced evenly on both sides of the saddle. The missionaries with a small herd of horned cattle traveled on the flanks.

Everything was in order now. The pack animals had dully accepted their burdens, and the mounts, fractious at first, were content to keep steady step with each other. On their part, the men had joined themselves into a happy company. Uproarious bursts of merriment and lively songs were constantly echoing along the line. There might be difficulties and dangers ahead, but what did they care? The living present was what mattered.

All day they traveled across a rolling country dotted here and there with patches of wood. Making camp the first night was a new experience for some. The company was divided into "messes" of eight men. Each mess had its separate tent and a captain who was an old hand at the business. In the morning, the mess captain was given the daily rations for his group. Each mess selected a cook. The company had nine messes, although Captain Wyeth's consisted of only four persons besides the cook. Wyeth chose the location for the camp and told each mess captain where to pitch his tent. The men unloaded the merchandise and built a barricade or fortification around the camp grounds in the form of a hollow square. The horses were hobbled and picketed inside the inclosure. There was a guard of from six to eight men that changed three times during the night. The captain of the guard, who was generally a mess captain, called the hour regularly by a watch, and every fifteen minutes cried, "All's well!" The men composing the guard were expected to repeat the words "All's well!" in rotation. When a guard did not answer, he was promptly visited and, if found delinquent, would be sentenced to walking for three days. The missionaries formed a mess by themselves, and faithfully took their turns at guard duty.

The first sound heard at dawn was the voice of Captain Wyeth calling, "Turn out! Turn out!" In a few minutes, the entire bivouac would be touched with life. When breakfast was ready, the men all squatted around the fire Indian-fashion and "braced their stomachs" with coffee, sow belly and fried dough. "Catch up! Catch up!" When this command was bellowed, there was an orderly striking of tents, saddling of horses, packing, mounting and falling into line. The cavalcade was then in motion again, wending its slow way across the hills that rolled after each other in endless succession. After fording the Platte River near its mouth, they pushed due westward, following the river toward the mountains. The rate of travel was about twenty miles

liam Sublette, who had lately arrived at the rendezvous. Taken off guard, the fur trader acted like a schoolboy caught by one of his own tricks. Before he fully realized what was happening, he was seated in front of the tall missionary who was leading out on all questions pertaining to the fur trade—profits, hazards, rivalries, the picture for the future. Neither alluded to the ruffianly threat that had been made. In his diary that night Jason Lee wrote: *How easy for the Lord to disconcert the most malicious and deep-laid plans of the devil.*

Lee could never forget the rendezvous—this wild meeting with its obstreperous mirth, its unearthly shrieks, its gambling, its whisky-drinking bouts, fisticuffs and gun-flourishings, its motley throng of whites and Indians milling eternally over the stamping-grounds. Among the Indians were Nez Perces, Bannocks and Flatheads. The Nez Perces and Flatheads, always keeping each other company, paid Lee a visit one afternoon. Through an interpreter, they made it known that they were friends of the whites and would like to have teachers. There was nothing very definite about their request, and Jason Lee managed to put them off. He was still troubled about where to build his Flathead mission.

At the end of two weeks, all were ready to travel onward. The Wyeth camp broke up, and, though burdened with surplus goods, the party pushed forward. They entered the present State of Idaho at Montpelier, and continued through the Bear River country to Soda Springs, unique for its sulphurous fountains, its endless beds of white clay and its "dismal, deep, and frightful chasms." In a few days, they met a party of Hudson's Bay Company's Canadians and Indians under the leadership of Thomas McKay. The two fur groups traveled on together. Thomas McKay, stepson of Dr. John McLoughlin of Fort Vancouver, was a good companion—witty, affable, keen for action.

Seeing McKay's Indians gave Jason Lee certain twinges of conscience. He was reminded of the Flatheads whom he had put off twice, the first time at the rendezvous and again some miles from there. The last time, ten or twelve Indians had come to him, asking if the missionaries intended to stop at the Flathead camp.

Lee evaded the issue. He said he did not know where the Flatheads lived. "But," he promised, "if we don't go to your people this time, we will the next year, or the one following."

Jason Lee was tortured by indecision. He had been appointed missionary to the Flatheads, and yet he thought it impractical as well as dangerous to isolate himself in the mountains. Anyway, he intended to go the remainder of the distance to Fort Vancouver before making the final decision. He wrote in his diary:

> Could I but know the identical place the Lord designs for us! Be it where it may, even a thousand miles in the interior, it would be a matter of great rejoicing. . . . Oh, God, direct us to the right spot where we can best glorify Thee and be most useful to the degraded red men.[1]

Continuing on their way, Wyeth's party, plus McKay's Canadians and Indians, reached the narrow but charming little valley of the Portneuf, and on July 14 arrived at the junction of this lively stream with the Snake River, near where the modern city of Pocatello, Idaho, now stands. "Here it is!" announced Nathaniel Wyeth, and without asking permission of Thomas McKay, set his men to building a fort out of cottonwood logs. This had not been a part of his original plan but he had to do something about the problem of the surplus goods. He resolved to store his unneeded merchandise here at the new fort, and leave a man in charge. It would be christened Fort Hall in honor of the senior member of the firm that was giving him financial aid in his fish-processing project on the Columbia River.

Here at Fort Hall the missionaries had another opportunity to recuperate before going the rest of the way to Vancouver, headquarters of Hudson's Bay Company in Oregon. One Sunday Jason Lee figured prominently in a history-making event. At Wyeth's request, he consented to preach in a nearby grove to as many men as cared to listen. When the hour came, he was there with his Bible in his hand, watching the men file in and take their places on the ground. About sixty, including Indians, composed the congregation. Lee arose, offered prayer and, assisted by Cyrus Shepard and Daniel, sang the old hymn beginning, "The

Fort Walla Walla, from a sketch made by member of Wilkes Exploring Expedition, 1838–1842 (*B. Driessen*)

Lord of Sabbath let us praise." After reading the short fifteenth psalm he plunged at once into his text: *Whether therefore ye eat or drink, or whatever ye do, do all to the glory of God.*

The Indians, though not understanding a word, followed every movement in respectful silence, kneeling when the preacher knelt and rising when he arose. If Lee expected demonstrations of disrespect from the rough traders, he concealed the fact, and delivered his rebukes in a mild and affectionate manner. Here was the opportunity for which he had been longing. He looked each man in the eye, reproved him for his vulgarity and drunkenness and pleaded with him to turn to a better life. Jason Lee had preached the first sermon ever delivered west of the Rocky Mountains.

In his diary that evening, the young scientist John K. Townsend wrote:

> Mr. Lee is a great favorite with the men, and deservedly so, and there are probably few persons to whose preaching they would have listened with so much complaisance.

After the service, some of McKay's men staged a series of horse races in which Kanseau, a halfbreed, was thrown from his mount and fatally injured. At Thomas McKay's request, Jason Lee took charge of the burial service, which was attended by men of both companies. This was the first Protestant funeral to be held west of the Rocky Mountains.

After a two weeks' rest, the missionaries were ready to resume the arduous journey. They crossed the Snake River at Island Ford, later called Three Islands, and again at Glenn's Ferry. In a few years, this ford was to be made famous by the crossing of thousands of pioneers on their way to the Willamette Valley in Oregon.

Toward evening of September first, 1834, the tired missionaries rode up to the gate of Fort Walla Walla and were hospitably received by the Hudson's Bay Company agent, Pierre Pambrun. Here were accommodations and a chance to relax, but Jason Lee had important business ahead and was eager to be on the move. The livestock he had driven across the country posed a problem, but not for long. Pierre Pambrun, in the name of his company, accepted the three horned cattle, the ten horses and four mules and in exchange gave Lee an order for their equivalent to be obtained at headquarters, Fort Vancouver. This was better luck than Lee had hoped for, and he gave thanks for every favor. But the Flathead problem was still heavy on his mind. He had been appointed chief missionary to these mountain Indians, and it hurt his conscience to think that he was not going among them.

The barge carrying the missionary party left Walla Walla on September fourth, and by the ninth was approaching The Dalles, the great falls of the Columbia River. This was indeed a sight to view, for here the mighty River of the West crowded its turbulent waters through a narrow-walled gorge. Going down the river, the first ten-mile stretch of rapids was known as *les petites dalles* or the "little narrows." The next barrier to travel was a five-mile stretch of rapids, or the "long narrows," and finally came what all river travelers dreaded, the "Big Eddy."

Indians were waiting at The Dalles, and for a few trifles, they assisted in making the portage around the formidable barrier. This accomplished, the voyage was resumed, though greatly hampered by heavy rains and fierce head winds that blew spasmodically. Within five days, the boatmen were buffeting the tumbling waters of the Cascades, the last impediment to river craft on the long final sweep to the ocean.

On September 15, Jason Lee wrote *finis* to the log of his journey and closed the book with a line that paid a high compliment to the Columbia, the "grand and beautiful river." At three o'clock in the afternoon, the barge drew up to the wharf at Fort Vancouver. Here, waiting to extend a welcome, was Dr. John McLoughlin, tall, silver-haired and dignified, known to the Indians as "the white-headed eagle." By this first handshake, an enduring friendship was established between the powerful representative of Hudson's Bay Company and the first missionary to Old Oregon.

4 • *The Willamette Mission*

FORT VANCOUVER AT LAST! THE missionaries were soon behind its friendly walls, having accepted McLoughlin's cordial invitation to stay until they had settled upon a site for their post. The size and apparent prosperity of the establishment amazed the visitors. Fort Vancouver, the center of Hudson's Bay Company activities in the Northwest, had been growing for ten years. It was a port where ships came to pick up the furs brought in from the "Up Country," grain from the Cowlitz farms and occasionally a cargo of lumber cut in Dr. McLoughlin's busy sawmill near the post.

Vancouver was located on a gentle slope on the north side of the Columbia River, some five miles from the mouth of the beautiful Willamette. The fort itself was not imposing in appearance. It had the usual stockade about twenty feet high, but lacked the bastions common to all company forts in the interior. Within the inclosure, in a quadrangular arrangement, were the dwelling houses of the chief officials. Most conspicuous was the home of the Chief Factor. It was of French-Canadian architecture, painted white and adorned by a piazza with two flights of steps leading up from either end and into a central hallway. There were flower beds in front and grapevines climbing over a rustic trellis. Between the two flights of steps, a four-pound cannon pointed toward the gate; on either side of this fieldpiece were stationed two mortar guns. Also, safe within the fort yard were warehouses, stores and shops of various kinds. From a tall flagstaff the Union Jack fluttered at once a welcome and a defiance, while from its own tower a bronze bell chimed out the hours.

Fort Vancouver was no haven for idlers. The company demanded that all posts be self-sustaining and consequently there had to be a diversity of occupations. The smiths had a never-ending job in the repairing of tools, farm implements and milling machinery, and in the daily making of fifty axes and hatchets for the use of trappers and Indians. Three men in the bakery were hard pressed to provide bread for the landsmen and sea-biscuits for the crews of the coasting vessels. The furs in storage had to be beaten once a week to keep the moths out. The farms, consisting of several hundred acres, were sown to grain or given over to pasturage for sheep, horses and cattle. There were vegetable gardens that required attention and apple trees in full bearing. For the service of the inhabitants there were a threshing outfit and a grist mill operated by horsepower. On a little stream not far from the fort, a sawmill supplied local needs in lumber, and in addition turned out occasional shipments to the Sandwich Islands (the Hawaiian Islands of today).

On the slope between the fort and the river was a village of thirty or more houses strung out along a single street. Here lived the lower servants of the company—Hawaiians, Canadians, half-breeds and a few Orkney Islanders. The mistress of every home was an Indian woman, who supervised the household affairs as well as a bevy of halfbreed children.

All this growth had taken place since 1824, when Dr. McLoughlin began to build. Almost any chance visitor or wayfarer would be welcomed at the boat landing by the white-haired doctor and given the best entertainment the place afforded. The great hall was a paradise, but for men only, and the elite among visitors. Since native women were not considered the equals of the whites, the Indian wives and children were not permitted at the officers' tables. Lucky was the guest who was invited to participate in the feasts and storytelling contests around the doctor's hospitable board.

It was a temptation for some visitors to luxuriate here as long as the hospitality lasted—but not for Jason Lee. He had his mind on the mission post and on the prompt starting of the Lord's work. But where to locate? That was the question that haunted him. Every night he prayed for guidance in this most important undertaking. The appointed "missionary to the Flatheads" was hundreds of miles from the Rocky Mountains, and had no intention of going there. Nathaniel Wyeth had come from Fort Hall. His brig, the *May Dacre,* had arrived safely with all the mission goods. How, Lee asked himself, could this tremendous amount of supplies and equipment be taken to a mission in the mountains? And had not Wyeth himself recommended locating as close as possible to a trading post?

Jason Lee did not appeal to his associates for help in making the choice of the mission site. Daniel left everything to his uncle to decide; Cyrus Shepard was only a lay teacher, and a very ill one since his trek across two-thirds of a continent. He had recovered somewhat after the party's arrival, but was still too weak to participate in the rugged business of exploring for a mission site. Edwards was ready to do any work assigned but Courtney was only a hired man. Lee, then, relied upon the Lord to guide him, but in the last analysis Dr. John McLoughlin was the deciding force. The Chief Factor stressed the danger of an isolated location, and pointed out the obvious fact that to do the most good among the Indians a missionary should come into contact with as many as possible.

Lee listened to the doctor, as most people did. The natives, he argued, should be taught to cultivate the land and led gradually to abandon their nomadic way of life. The Willamette Valley, he believed, would be the ideal place for the first mission in Old Oregon. He offered needed provisions, canoes and the services of two guides. "Go and decide for yourself," he told Lee. "Don't take my word alone."

With the question of location turning now hot, now cold, in his mind, Jason Lee embarked with Daniel in a canoe, and dropped down the Columbia to the mouth of the Willamette, passing the large island (now Sauvie Island) on which Nathaniel Wyeth was preparing to build his fishing establishment. Here, the *May Dacre* was riding serenely at anchor. After paddling up the Willamette for a few miles, they stopped at the farm of Desportes McKay, who had been a member of Wilson Price Hunt's overland expedition of 1811. Here they exchanged the canoe for horses and set out across the rich Tualatin plains. They went as far as the Chehalim, a small tributary of the Willamette, then swam their horses across to the east side, where the settlement was located.

At the big bend of the river was attractive French Prairie with the humble log cabins of some dozen retired employees of the Hudson's Bay Company. These French-Canadians had a few acres under cultivation, horses of the native stock and cattle loaned to them by the company. All had Indian wives and half-breed children. They lived on good terms with the natives and had no worries about the upkeep of either church or state. Though professing Roman Catholics, these simple people gave the Methodist missionaries a cordial welcome. Joseph Gervais, one of the most prominent of the settlers, put up a tent for the missionaries in his melon patch and said, "Take your comfort, yes, and if you find anything you like, eat it."

"This reminds me," said Daniel Lee, "of a verse of Scripture which reads, 'A lodge in a garden of cucumbers.' "

Jason Lee was yielding to temptation, as he well realized. The missionary to the Flatheads had decided to build his station near to people of his own kind. "But," he said to Daniel, "a man must think of the future. This fertile valley could well furnish homes for thousands of Christian families."

The decision was made. The mission would be built at Chemaway, on the southern edge of French Prairie, about sixty miles from the mouth of the Willamette River and ten miles from Salem, the present capital of the State of Oregon. Pleased with their choice, Jason and Daniel Lee hurried back to Fort Vancouver to proceed with the business of moving equipment and livestock to the mission site. Cyrus Shepard was not permitted to imperil his health by living in the open, with the dampness of an

Oregon winter beginning to gather. He would remain at Fort Vancouver and teach the halfbreed children of the company employees until a suitable shelter had been built at Chemaway.

The two Lees, with their assistants and help lent by the company, immediately began the task of moving. The supplies from the *May Dacre* were loaded onto barges and started up the Willamette. About twenty miles from the mouth, falls obstructed the river, making a portage necessary. Horses, taken in exchange for the ones left at Fort Walla Walla, as well as eight oxen and ten cows loaned by the Hudson's Bay Company, were driven overland. It was October 6, 1834, when everything was finally assembled at Mission Bottoms, a beautiful spot on the east bank of the river. To right, left and rear stretched acres of rich grasslands, itching for the scratch of the plow; in front flowed the endless, shimmering waters past an unbroken fringe of cottonwoods, ash and white maple. Far to the eastward, beyond the valley, the country climbed up into hills which grew into mountains as soon as they were beyond the reach of human sight. To the west lay "the land where the sunsets go" and the restless waters of the Pacific.

When Jason Lee surveyed the promising scene, he envisioned thousands of farms, cities, industries, roadways, river transportation, even railroads. All these were in Oregon's horoscope, and it would be the duty of the missionaries to help bring them about. In fact, to do this became a part of his dream for Oregon.

Here at Chemaway, in an inviting little grove, the missionaries unloaded their barges and began to put their tools in condition, for tomorrow and many tomorrows thereafter they must toil. The rainy season was in the offing and a hundred tasks had to be accomplished before that time. In his tent at twilight of that first day on Mission Bottom, Daniel Lee wrote in his diary:

> Here the first blow was struck by the pioneer missionaries in Oregon, and here they began their arduous toil to elevate and save the heathen from moral degradation and ruin.

The first need was a corral for the animals, and to this end the men bent to the back-breaking task of splitting rails. The next need was a prime necessity before any building could be started. This was the yoking and training of the oxen, most of which were unbroken. To make the animals docile under the yoke and willing to haul the logs that were being cut in the nearby woods required all the strength and patience of the entire force. While they were going through this trial Daniel Lee made entry in his diary: "Man never worked harder, and performed less."

Although no one shirked, the building went on slowly, and in the midst of it came the first storm of the autumn with driving wind and drenching rain. Some of the goods were soaked through, and had to be spread out to dry when the weather cleared again. With this equinoctial flurry past, the four struggled unremittingly to complete their shelter before another attack by the weather. By the first of November the pioneer mission house was finished to a degree where it afforded fair protection. It was thirty-two feet long by eighteen in width. A partition divided it into two rooms. A large fireplace occupied the end of one of the rooms. There were puncheon floors of fir logs and doors that hung awkwardly on wooden hinges. Each room had two windows to let in the feeble light of endless cloudy winter days ahead. Jason Lee whittled out the window sashes with his pocket knife and the construction was all done without benefit of nails.

A roof over their heads was a necessity; tables, stools and cupboards were luxuries made and installed, little by little, as time permitted. This house, with its later additions, served the mission until 1841. The food at bachelors' hall was as simple as the dwelling place, consisting of salt pork shipped from Boston, unleavened bread made of flour from Fort Vancouver, barley and peas bought from their French-Canadian neighbors, milk from Hudson's Bay cows and occasionally a haunch of venison from the Indians.

Through the ordeal of building, the servants of the Lord did not neglect their spiritual duties. Jason Lee's first sermon was delivered September 28, before a congregation of company employees at Fort Vancouver. On December 14 a like service was held, at which seventeen children and four adults received baptism. From the first, Jason and Daniel held Sunday services at the home of Joseph Gervais, two miles down the river; occasionally, they met with the settlers at Champoeg, father down on French Prairie. A Sabbath School was eventually organized for the children of that locality. These one-day-a-week efforts were desirable and well worth continuing, but since they did not reach the needy heathen they could not be considered true missionary work.

Toward the latter part of December, Cyrus Shepard came from Vancouver to assume his full share of the responsibilities. The three men then talked over plans for the future, as well as for the immediate present. It was apparent that regular school could not be started as yet. The Indians would have to be approached and no doubt persuaded. It would be Cyrus Shepard's duty to care for and informally teach the children brought to the mission.

Along with preaching and teaching went another task—that of making the mission feed itself by the tilling of the soil, planting and harvesting.

It was not long until the missionaries discovered among the Indians, who were chiefly of the Calapooya tribe, a great deal of sickness and general misery. Parents had died, leaving innumerable orphans whom the bachelor preachers resolved to save, if possible. First to be brought into the mission home was a boy of fourteen or fifteen, ragged and ill fed. Given the name of John Mark, he was commonly known as John Calapooya. In a day or two they found John's sister, the last of the family, all the rest of whom had died of sickness.

"We'll call her Lucy Hedding," said Jason Lee, smiling. Elijah Hedding was the Methodist bishop who had ordained him as missionary to the Flatheads.

"You're right," commented Daniel. "We'll have to choose names that we can pronounce and remember. And what better names can be found than those of Methodist dignitaries?"

Lucy's clothing was of the most primitive kind. She wore a piece of deerskin over her shoulders and a fringe of the same around her waist. Jason Lee cleansed these waifs from their vermin and Cyrus began looking around for clothing. He found a piece of tow cloth that had been used in baling goods and from it made a smock. "Well, Lucy," he said, "it's not a very fashionable garment, but maybe later we can find something better."

Lucy was not well. She had scrofula, and Daniel Lee, who was delegated to look after this particular phase of mission work, was unable to do much for her. But she adapted herself to the new life and was contented. John Calapooya proved to be willing and able. He was put to work with the ax under the supervision of Courtney Walker. He did all kinds of menial tasks without complaint and grew strong on the better food provided by the mission.

Later on in the winter the mission door opened to another child, a boy of about seven. He was almost naked, and his face was caked with dirt and scabs. He had no one—neither parents nor brother nor sister. "I want to live here, too," he said in the Calapooya tongue. As one orphan after another was added to the mission family, it was soon apparent that the house could not contain all the needy. Unfortunately, however, the children did not live there long. A few refused to stay at the mission, and in some instances their parents came and took them away.

For the missionaries it was one continuous struggle against sickness and death. The Mission Book, started by Cyrus Shepard upon his arrival, is little more than a record of children received, their illness and finally their death and burial. The winter was rainy. Fog hung eternally over the broad valley. The river flowed on as in a haze and the trees by the mission house dripped moisture incessantly. But the roof of the mission house did not leak, and by the broad fireplace in the evenings the bachelor missionaries read their Bibles, prepared food, made clothing for the orphans and sharpened tools for the work ahead.

Spring came early. One day when the planting was just beginning an Umpqua Indian, whom the neighbors knew as Joe, came to the mission, bringing his little boy to be taught religion and labor. Though living quarters were already cramped, Jason Lee accepted the child. A few days later, Umpqua Joe's friend, a Tillamook, brought his son to be given the same opportunities.

"It might be," said Daniel Lee, his thin face growing more serious, "that these Indians are trying to shove their responsibilities off on us."

"Providence sends them to us," answered Cyrus Shepard, "and we must find a place for all who come."

The Tillamook boy was like a small wild animal in captivity. Unhappy and completely indifferent to all teaching, he was often observed looking longingly toward the west where the wild sea waves were forever lashing at the high headlands. He was a misfit and eventually his father was obliged to take the lad home. Umpqua Joe's son, on the other hand, was industrious and teachable. He was making gratifying progress in every way when he fell ill of tuberculosis and went into a rapid decline. He died in midsummer.

One experience with the Indians taught the missionaries a lesson they never forgot. A child became ill and died at the mission. His brother came in a rage and threatened to kill Daniel and Cyrus. Jason Lee explained and reasoned till at last the savage seemed convinced and pacified. After that, the missionaries always tried to notify the relatives whenever a child became sick.

Along with caring for the children went the work of planting and building, although the missionaries were not free from sickness themselves. First one and then another were stricken with intermittent fever that incapacitated them for several days, or even several weeks at a time. In addition, Daniel Lee contracted a form of throat trouble that annoyed him all through the winter and spring. In spite of ill health, however, the men drove ahead. In the spring of 1835 an extension was joined to the original house, making room for more boarding pupils. The missionaries wanted to reach as many Indians as possible and in as many different ways as they could. They hoped to teach the fundamentals in education, the truths of the Bible, honest labor—in fact, all the basic principles of Christian civilization.

"The goal can never be reached," Jason Lee declared many times, "until the Indians can be settled down in one place."

Farming, and that on as large a scale as feasible, was the second objective of the Methodists. The mission had to be in part self-sustaining, which would require hard and endless labor. There were the boarding pupils to clothe and feed. In addition the farm was expected to be a laboratory where the missionaries hoped to teach the Indians some of the arts of civilization: animal husbandry, gardening, grain production. By the first spring, 1835, they had thirty-five acres ready for planting and a much larger area fenced in. A sizeable barn was built with the assistance of the French-Canadian farmers.

The children who stayed at the mission were taught to work and gradually became accustomed to the routine set up for them. After the school was started in September 1835 half the day was devoted to studying and half to work in and around the mission. Cyrus Shepard supervised all these activities, while his companions did the building and farming and made contacts with the Indians outside.

Cyrus was a real shepherd to his flock. He was not famed for his superior qualifications and his name is less well known than those of many of the other Methodist missionaries. He had had no previous experience in mission work. Never in his life had he preached a sermon—yet he was the true missionary, with no personal ambitions and no political aspirations. He was filled with the spirit of Christ, and the Indian children loved and trusted him.

By the end of the first year Jason Lee had his doubts that the red children could be saved. He saw the Indians as a vanishing race. Before his very eyes sickness and death had taken a pitiable toll. He could not help thinking that the intellectual approach to the savage was almost time wasted. But not so Cyrus Shepard: he believed that the smallest thing done for the least of these benighted people was an important step in the advancement of the Kingdom of God among them.

Meanwhile the first year in the Willamette was slipping by. In April 1835 a French-Canadian farmer brought two Indian boys to the mission station to have them educated. The father of one soon came and took his son away but the other, Kenotesh, stayed on, an asset to the establishment. For Kenotesh, though, it was the old story repeated over and over among these Indians—sickness and eventually death. On August 19, 1835, Shepard made the following record in the Mission log:

> This morning, at fifteen minutes before three o' clock, the spirit of Kenotesh took its flight to the invisible world. He was a youth of good promise and amiable disposition.

In a few days, the brother of Kenotesh came to the mission and stayed all night. At his request, the remains of Kenotesh were disinterred so that he could see how the boy had been buried. He went away, apparently satisfied.

About this time, a Calapooya chief brought his small daughter, Lassee, to the mission to be taught to read and write. He was an elderly man and in poor health. His lodge was more than a mile from the mission but the child was frequently taken there to see him. Shortly before his death Lassee went for a last visit. The old man's love showed through his tears as he fondled her, saying in a low broken voice, "Ni-kah-ten-as!" (My little one). He died soon after this, comforted by the knowledge that his daughter would be given good care. But Lassee's constitution was weak, and in a few months she followed him to the grave.

In September Louis Shangrette, a farmer living in the Vancouver area, died suddenly, leaving three halfbreed orphans, and five Indian slaves. Dr. McLoughlin asked Jason Lee to take care of the family in return for the property left by Shangrette. Lee consented, but only on condition that the slaves be considered free. The Mission Book for October 1835, recorded the arrival of the eight wards, and closed with the statement: "They pass our threshold and their shackles fall."

This addition to their family greatly increased the burden of the bachelor missionaries, but not for long. Two of the new arrivals promptly ran away and could never be found. "Well," commented Daniel Lee, "that's a relief, since there was so little to hope for." Before long, three of the others, including one of Shangrette's own children, died. A fourth developed a scrofolous condition, lingered a few months and then followed the others in death. This left only two of the original number inherited from Shangrette.

Cyrus Shepard acted in the capacity of steward, housekeeper, nurse and teacher. From the time of his arrival at Chemaway he had been making plans for the starting of a school. He realized this ambition in the fall of 1835, when in September he began giving daily lessons under a mountain of handicaps. All teaching was done in English, which made for painfully slow progress. The missionaries were not familiar with the Indian language and there were few to give aid in interpreting. In conversation the Chinook jargon filled a very great need. Shepard had brought from the States a few slates and old textbooks which he put into good use. The attendance at the school climbed from a mere handful to nineteen in a few months. The curriculum included reading, spelling, the singing of hymns, the learning and reciting of catechisms and useful labor. On Sundays Cyrus Shepard got breakfast and washed the dishes, then with the assistance of his colleagues set up the benches for Sabbath School. The first year saw fifty-three Indians in attendance, though not all on any one Sunday.

As the year was drawing to a close, Philip L. Edwards, the assistant, said he would like to leave the mission. His health had improved and he had seen Oregon. Further, he had gained experience by teaching school for a few months on French Prairie. He was ready now to go back and continue his law practice. Jason Lee regretted the loss of such a valuable helper but of course gave consent. Edwards engaged passage on the Hudson's Bay Company's ship, *Ganymede,* and left for Fort Vancouver in ample time to make his sailing. Daniel Lee, whose throat had been troubling him ever since his arrival in the Willamette, decided to consult Dr. McLoughlin and went with Edwards in the barge to Fort Vancouver.

McLoughlin suspected the beginnings of tuberculosis and advised Daniel to go to the Sandwich Islands for a year. "For a year?" Lee was stunned. How could he leave the mission work to just two men, his uncle and Cyrus Shepard? Courtney Walker, hired for a year, had already taken up service with Hudson's Bay Company. Edwards was conscience-stricken, as well as stunned. Leaving the mission short-handed would be a selfish thing to do. Although bitterly disappointed, he canceled his passage on the *Ganymede* and went back to Chemaway.

When the brig sailed, it was Daniel Lee instead of Philip Edwards who took passage on her. The scientist, Thomas Nuttall, was also a passenger. He had finished his botanical studies in Oregon and was on his way to California. John K. Townsend was spending another year in the area.

The first year of the Willamette Mission was at an end. The Book closed December 31, 1835, with the words: "Surely goodness and mercy have followed us."

5 • *Females—"Pious, Industrious, Intelligent"*

AT THE END OF A YEAR DANIEL Lee returned from the Sandwich Islands, much improved in health and filled with enthusiasm for the work he had been forced to leave so abruptly. He saw many changes, most of them encouraging. Forty-five acres had been put under the plow and that year had yielded 700 bushels of wheat and 300 bushels of potatoes. Also, Jason Lee had, singlehanded, salted and packed six barrels of salmon.

"Fish is still our main standby," he said to his nephew. "Thank the Lord for fish."

Daniel found the mission crowded with thirty children, the sick among the well. The house was, in fact, a hospital with not enough beds—many patients were lying on mats on the floor.

Something else was different in the picture. This was the presence in Oregon of a good many American settlers, most of whom were beginning to build homes in the Willamette Valley. "You can't keep people out of Oregon," Hall J. Kelley, the Boston schoolteacher and journalist, had been saying for several years. Kelley had flooded the East with pamphlets describing the beauties of Oregon and playing up her enormous possibilities. He had gone to Congressmen, urging them to take a stand against England and the Hudson's Bay Company and claim what was ours "by right."

"You can't keep settlers out of Oregon forever," was what Dr. John McLoughlin had been saying to himself. "Wheat will grow here, and where wheat will grow, men will go." He knew that would mean the end of furs and the rule of a fur company, but it was a fact which eventually would have to be faced.

"No, you can't keep them out of Oregon," Jason Lee often said to Cyrus, as they sat by the mission fire after the children had gone to bed. "Americans—thousands of them—are going to find their way here. It's too fine a country to be lost."

Lee was right. They were all right. Oregon was fast becoming a land of fascination for those whose feet itched to be on the march to new and better places. Singly and in small groups American adventurers and home-seekers were straggling into the raw but beautiful land by Pacific shores. And circumstances contrived to draw the missionary, Jason Lee, closer and closer to the center of affairs that were more political and economic than spiritual.

In the East the demand for the ownership of Oregon became so strong that President Andrew Jackson decided to make an investigation of the Columbia River area. He chose William A. Slacum of the United States Navy as his personal envoy, with instructions to collect all the information that would be in any way valuable to the government. In due course of time the brig *Loriot,* chartered by William Slacum in the Sandwich Islands, passed the bar at the mouth of the Columbia River and on December 23, 1836 was advancing up the big river.

William Slacum, as special envoy of the President, was to make observations and acquire a rather complete knowledge of the country without arousing the suspicions of the Hudson's Bay Company. His instructions included the taking of a census of both Indians and whites in the Willamette. Jason Lee accompanied him on all of his trips. He did his work with a high degree of thoroughness, adding to the value of his information by making charts of the Columbia River and locating all the Indian villages. Slacum could see for himself the wonderful agricultural possibilities of the Willamette Valley. He was impressed by the abundance of natural grass, indicating ample rainfall. "This is the finest grazing country in the world," he reported to his government.

Slacum and Lee had many conversations concerning this fair land and its future. Together they formulated a plan—certainly not spiritual, and beneficial to the natives only in a very remote way. Slacum was convinced that the principal lack for settlers of the valley was cattle. He reported to Washington, D.C. that the Hudson's Bay Company held a monopoly of the cattle business in Oregon by refusing to sell, either to missionaries or to settlers. It did, however, lend work oxen and milk cows, while keeping close control over cattle used for breeding purposes. Now was the time, he emphasized, for Americans to free themselves from the restrictions imposed by a monopolistic company. And how? Why, that was simple. Get cattle—and plenty of them—from California.

Jason Lee agreed with Slacum. A meeting was called at the Mission house January 12, 1837 that resulted in the formation of the Willamette Cattle Company. Money in the amount of $2700 was raised. Of this amount, Dr. McLoughlin invested $900, Jason Lee $400 for the mission and Slacum $500 in his own name. The settlers contributed the balance. Some of the French-Canadians were at first undecided, but Slacum assured them that the titles to their lands would be secured when the United States took possession of Oregon.

The next step was to appoint men to go to California to buy Spanish cattle, which could be obtained at three dollars per head. Again, William Slacum made himself useful. He offered free passage to California on the brig *Loriot* to as many as wished to go. He had finished his business in Oregon and was ready to sail for home. Slacum and the eleven men chosen boarded the brig January 21, 1837 and, with Jason Lee presiding, spent a short season in prayer for the success of the enterprise. They felt that these prayers had indeed been answered when 630 head of cattle were brought from California and distributed according to shares purchased. The price paid by purchasers was $7.67 per head.

Right or wrong, the Methodist mission could not be separated from cattle, politics, settlers—and still more settlers. The introduction of cattle ushered in a new era for Oregon. It paved the way for the real colonizing movement which was soon to begin. Upon his return to the States, William Slacum gave a glowing report to Congress containing a strong recommendation that the government be on the alert to seize opportunities in Oregon. Jason Lee's pleasure at the success of the Willamette Cattle Company was reflected brightly in his letters to the East. He looked upon this as the beginning of prosperity, an important milestone in the development of the country. It was well worthwhile, he thought, even if nothing else resulted from his efforts in Oregon.

When William Slacum went home, he carried something in addition to his report about the country. He carried a petition written by Jason Lee and signed by several of the settlers, asking the United States to establish a territorial government for Oregon. They did not seem to realize that this would have been a dangerous step to take, since at that time a joint-occupancy agreement between the United States and England was in force. Pressure continued to be exerted, however, and other petitions were later presented. Public sentiment in the United States for the possession of all Oregon was flowing like an undammed stream, and Jason Lee was moving with the current.

While worldly affairs in the Willamette were turning a bright side toward the missionaries, the same could not be said of the spiritual. Jason Lee's letters to the mission board and to his old friend and teacher, Dr. Wilbur Fisk, revealed what there was of hope, discouragement and almost complete frustration. A few months in the mission field had convinced the superintendent that the work was too great to be borne by three men, and bachelors at that. He requested helpers, principally women—"pious, industrious, intelligent females." He asked as a particular favor that Daniel's fiancée be included in any reinforcements that might be sent. "And I could dare to wish," said Cyrus Shepard, "that my Susan might also be chosen."

When optimism surged strongly within his being, Jason Lee told himself and the mission board that an adequate force of devoted men and women, and a large school, would do wonders toward reclaiming the natives. "Send us doctors," he wrote. "Send teachers and blacksmiths and carpenters and farmers. We need many helpers."

The spiritual progress of the Indians, Lee had to admit, was hardly noticeable. At first some of them seemed eager to learn how to pray, but the novelty soon wore off. In the beginning, they believed that material things would come as the result of prayer, and when they were disappointed their interest flagged. They hoped to obtain food and clothing through prayer, and not by the sweat of their brows. "It is truly discouraging," Lee wrote, "to feel that we have no proof that we have been instrumental in converting one soul since crossing the mountains. But we are helping a few to live more like human beings, and we're making the last days of many a trifle more comfortable."

Then, from the East, came a direct question that Jason Lee had to answer. Why, the Methodist Board of Missions wanted to know, was he spending so much time on secular things? Lee was sensitive on the point, and replied that he considered it expedient to do so. There was so much physical work to do, and no competent help to be had at any price. Farming was a job in itself but, lacking a doctor and housekeeper, Lee himself was often obliged to leave outside duties in order to make bread, do the laundry or wait upon the sick. Providing for the immediate needs of the flesh came before administering to the soul when a choice had to be made. "And how," he asked, "can the spirit give heed to Christian teaching when the miserable body is mortifying?"

"Send us help." This was the theme that ran through Lee's letters to Methodist leaders in the East.

On the afternoon of May 17, 1837, the *Diana* edged her way past the treacherous sandbar at the mouth of the Columbia River and stood in toward her destination, Fort Vancouver. She carried more missionaries for Oregon. In response to Jason Lee's request, the Board had sent a sizeable group known as the first reinforcement party. Here came two married couples, five children, one single man and three female teachers who were destined, if things went well, to be the brides of the missionaries in the Willamette.

There was gaiety on shipboard that May day, laughter and good-natured banter. Ten months after their departure from Boston, all were eager to set foot on the soil of Oregon. This extended voyage had allowed ample time for the members of the missionary party to become well acquainted—to find out each other's faults as well as virtues. The appointed leader of the group was Dr. Elijah White, physician, whom the whole party called "Father." White himself was a self-confident young man with ambitions to make a name for himself in Oregon. Being personable and gregarious, he was popular on shipboard from the first, especially among the women. Some of his associates regarded him as a serious Christian; others said frankly, "He may be a good doctor—and heaven knows we'll need one away out there in the wilderness—but he's really not as pious as he might be."

Luckily, "Father" White proved himself a good coordinator, and generally kept the passengers in high spirits, even though the drinking water on shipboard was stagnant and the sea-biscuit as hard as flint. Mrs. White was the typical wife of her day—gentle and submissive and devoted to the care of her year-old son, Silas. Another member of the White household was George Stoutenberg, an adopted boy of about fourteen. Mrs. White good-naturedly objected to being "mother" to all on board but her protests were disregarded by the young ladies who looked upon her as a chaperon.

In that small group was a variety of personalities. Alanson Beers, blacksmith, was a thoroughgoing Puritan, well versed in the Scriptures; he was not a general favorite on shipboard, though, because of his extreme irritability. The most popular person on the deck of the *Diana* was William H. Willson, former ship carpenter, who had sailed on many whaling voyages. When the days dragged out in their monotony the passengers loved to gather around Willson and listen to the sea yarns he could spin interminably. During the voyage, he studied medicine under Dr. White and by the time he reached Oregon most of the party were addressing him as "Dr. Willson."

The three women teachers naturally received their fair share of attention. Elvira Johnson had few thoughts for anything but Bible reading and prayer in her cabin. She had a slavish devotion to duty and her missionary zeal came out in every conversation when she said over and over, "Oh, I pray the Lord that I may make myself useful in Oregon." Little Susan Downing, fiancée of Cyrus Shepard, was universally liked. She had a charming personality, an elegant figure, dark hair and beautiful blue eyes. When she was amused, her laugh came from the depth of her soul and never failed to infect all those around her. Her taste in dress was the envy of all the other women.

Although Susan was the most popular of the schoolmistresses, the one whose name was on every tongue was Anna Maria Pittman, sent by the mission board as the prospective wife of Jason Lee. When the Methodists sent an unmarried woman into the mission field it was always with the thought that she should find a mate among the missionaries who were there, or who would arrive later. Anna Maria Pittman was the educated daughter of a well-to-do New Yorker. She was tall, dark and serious-looking, with a dignity that well became her thirty-three years. By nature, she was conscientious and persevering and, above all, pious. To her, religion was the "breath of life itself." She was fond of expressing herself in poetry and some, including Dr. Elijah White, thought she had considerable poetic ability. Probably Miss Pittman knew what was expected of her—that she become the wife of Jason Lee—provided, of course, that the two found themselves congenial. Although she never once alluded to this, all her associates had their suspicions, and she was obliged to submit to constant teasing throughout the voyage.

Meantime, the *Diana* plowed her slow way up the great river, the pilot's barge, carrying Dr. White and his family, guiding the course. Long before the brig had docked at Fort Vancouver the news had spread among the company's employees, and by the time the missionary party began to land a host of curious persons had assembled to stare at the strange creatures known as "white females." Dr. McLoughlin gave them a cordial welcome and immediately dispatched a messenger to Chemaway, informing Jason Lee of the arrival of the reinforcement party.

The following afternoon the missionaries rested on the piazza of the Chief Factor's house. All around was the forest, bright in its summer green. A few white clouds, like patches of frothy meringue, idled across a pale blue sky; in front rolled the majestic river. While they were talking, Dr. McLoughlin, with the aid of a telescope, located two barges straining against the current. When they drew up to the landing he said simply, "Mr. Lee has arrived." At once, the conversation assumed a livelier tone as all eyes were directed toward Anna Maria Pittman. That lady maintained her dignity, with no sign of changed emotion registering in her long, serious face.

It was Susan Downing who nudged her, saying slyly, "Look,

Anna Maria. See if you can tell at this distance whether you'll find yourselves compatible."

Under the eyes of eager watchers the canoes were beached and in a short time Jason Lee's tall, stooped figure was climbing the gentle incline with long, ungainly strides. As he came nearer Miss Pittman's friends let loose such a flood of low-spoken banter that she became quite flustered, but when the introductions were begun, all fell into discreet silence. Dr. McLoughlin presented Dr. Elijah White, who in turn introduced other members of the party. He reserved Anna Maria Pittman until the last. When finally she met Jason Lee face to face, a slight flush softened the severity of her countenance.

The following afternoon the party was ready to leave for the Willamette Mission. Everybody was in good health and better spirits. Each person was assigned to a place in the barges and Anna Maria found herself, by accident or design, in the last boat with Superintendent Lee. For two days, she was to be his only companion, except for the native paddlers. No one knew who had made the arrangement but there were knowing smiles on every face as the barges pushed off from the landing on that perfect day in May. "The courtship begins," whispered one to the other as the oars began to splash in the sunshine.

It was like a holiday excursion, with good-natured raillery, laughter and song to accompany the measured sweep of the paddles. Among so many excellent oarsmen, there was a temptation to vie for honors in occasional bursts of speed. Then it was nip and tuck, with first one barge and then the other in the lead, the boats passing and being passed so close that the passengers could touch hands.

Night encampment was made at Oak Grove. Supper, consisting of bread and butter, tea, salmon and potatoes, was eaten with relish. At eleven o'clock the following morning, they arrived at the falls of the Willamette, a beautiful spot and romantic. Jason Lee, however, saw something else. Pointing to the enormous volume of water charging over the precipice, he said, "Wonderful horsepower there! Splendid place for a settlement!"

With the assistance of Indian carriers, the portage was made without difficulty, and the barges now began laboring against the current. Going up the Willamette River was quite a different story from floating down the Columbia. At Champoeg on French Prairie the boats were exchanged for horses. About noon the party approached the mission house, which was almost hidden by trees at a sharp bend in the river. A tall, handsome man in plain brown attire and a surprised look on his face met them at the door.

"So we got here sooner than you expected," laughed Jason Lee. "But too late to retreat, Cyrus. Too late to put on your cravat!"

Laughing in reply, Cyrus quickly wiped his hands and ran to assist Susan Downing from her horse. What did it matter if they presented a striking dissimilarity in appearance—he in his kitchen garb and she in her most attractive frock? Susan had crossed some twenty thousand miles of water to be his helpmeet. It was enough that they were together at last.

When the bachelor's dinner was ready, the new members of the mission family were initiated by being seated at a rough table with a brown homespun cloth and bright tin plates. Cyrus Shepard had prepared a meal that brought squeals of delight from the women and comments of wonder from the men. There was fried venison, along with cheese sausages, wholewheat bread, fried cakes and generous dishes of wild strawberries. While they were arranging themselves at the table, Daniel Lee suddenly made his appearance. He gave all a welcome, at the same time apologizing for not being on hand when they arrived.

"Had a hard night," he explained. "So many sick that I didn't get any sleep. I went out to fill my lungs with fresh air, sat down and soon dozed off."

Daniel suffered a bitter disappointment. His fiancée had decided not to come to Oregon, after all, and what was worse she was planning to marry someone else.

After dinner, Jason Lee took the new helpers through the garden filled with flowers and vegetables. "Thank Cyrus for this," he said. "He's a real lover of nature—loves to see things grow. There's a friendly rivalry between him and Dr. McLoughlin. Sometimes the doctor sends up a new variety and challenges Cyrus to match it."

Turning from the garden to the sick room gave pain to all. In one room, set up as a makeshift hospital, were Indian children of different ages. The bunks, made like shelves against the wall, were full, with the overflow stretched out on blankets or mats on the floor. "Poor accommodations," said Lee, "but it's the best we have up to date."

"How many have you here?" inquired Dr. Elijah White, casting disapproving glances around the crowded stuffy place, strong with the odor of sickness.

"Thirty-eight at present, including the few well ones that you see. Meet Wilbur Fisk"—Lee smiled as he recalled his old friend and teacher—"William Brooks and Nathan Bangs."

"How can you convert them in this state?" asked the zealous Elvira Johnson.

"We can't," Lee answered. "About all we can do is to try to heal their bodies. And it's hard—even at the best—to tame their wild nature. Some escape from us and return to their filthy lodges—and we never see them again."

In one corner was Sally Soule, slowly dying of tuberculosis. She was trying to make a doll dress under the direction of Cyrus Shepard. When the strangers approached she looked up with sad, listless eyes, then went back to her stitches. "The other children don't like her," Cyrus whispered. "She doesn't like to hunt wasp nests, or to eat the roasted insects which her people consider a delicacy. They tease her and call her 'the old maid.' "

Dr. White was aghast at the sight of the sick Indians. "And what is done about medical aid?" he asked.

Daniel Lee and Cyrus Shepard exchanged glances. "We all do the best we can," Jason Lee answered. "Some cases we take to Dr. McLoughlin, but the trip's hard and few survive it. Now with you here, we feel greatly relieved.

There was a large family at the mission now—fifty-four, including the Indians. Jason Lee was somewhat perturbed. Now that he had received the aid requested, he was hard pressed to find accommodations for them. Nor had he made definite plans for the extension of missionary work among the Indians.

Finding the cause of so much fever in the area became the

chief concern of Dr. White. It was his theory that the trees so close to the mission house produced a constant dampness that was detrimental to health. "I hope you won't have to destroy our beautiful green grove," Jason Lee said, as Dr. White began directing the Indian boys to climb the trees and do some thinning. "If it's ruinous to health," the doctor replied, "it must be sacrificed."

Lee believed that there must be some other explanation for the intermittent fevers that plagued natives as well as whites during any season of the year. Without sacrificing the grove, Dr. White succeeded in thinning it a great deal by careful pruning. "Now," he said when the job was finished, "that will allow for a freer circulation of air." But Jason Lee still had his doubts.

That picturesque bit of greenwood became almost a sacred grove to some of the mission family after the memorable Sunday, July 16, 1837. On that day, practically the whole community assembled to observe communion and to witness the marriage of Susan Downing and Cyrus Shepard. When all were seated—some on the ground, others on crude benches—Jason Lee announced the hymn, "When all Thy Mercies, O my God." After this the superintendent, in his best ministerial tone, gave a short talk on marriage, its obligations and its benefits. He ended rather abruptly and, in a conversational manner, said to the congregation, "Now, my friends, I'm going to prove to you that I'm willing to put into practice the things I have recommended."

Before blank faces and wondering eyes he stepped forward, took the hand of Anna Maria Pittman and led her to the makeshift altar. At the same moment, Daniel Lee arose from his place, took the Bible and proceeded with the marriage ceremony.

With serious faces, the couple stood before the little group of friends. Their courtship had gone on quietly and only Daniel had been told of their intentions. Jason was thirty-four, and she was past thirty-three. Both considered that it was God's will for them to marry. He had met Anna Maria in New York several years previous and had not been favorably impressed. "I've always said," he wrote to a friend, "that a lady might travel the world over to me, and I would never marry her unless we were suited to each other, and it was to the glory of God."

When Daniel Lee united his uncle and Miss Pittman in the bonds of holy matrimony he performed the first ceremony of its kind in the Oregon country. The vows having been said, Jason escorted his bride back to her seat, then took his place behind the altar to perform a similar rite for Cyrus Shepard and Susan Downing. A few days after the double wedding, Lee and Shepard, with their brides, went to the Coast on horseback for a brief honeymoon. For two weeks they camped in the peace and quiet of the sunset shores, removed from the dangers of the "most sickly season" in the Willamette Valley.

When the four returned, a complete reorganization of the mission was effected for the purpose of dividing the labor on as equitable a basis as possible and at the same time utilizing the particular talents of each. Susan Shepard became "mistress of the wardrobe," thus relieving Cyrus. Anna Maria Lee and Mrs. White took over the cooking and housekeeping, while Elvira Johnson spent all her time in teaching. Cyrus Shepard was headmaster. Daniel Lee and his band of Indian boys managed the garden and the fields until harvest time, when all the men were drafted. Alanson Beers was the blacksmith and William ("Dr.") Willson, the chief carpenter. Work was begun immediately on cabins for the families of Dr. White and Alanson Beers.

The housing problem had scarcely been solved when, on September 10, 1837, another group of assistants arrived. If money and human help could save the Indians in Oregon, the Methodist Board of Missions did not intend to be found wanting. Here came the Reverend David Leslie, a man of about forty, with his wife and three young daughters. The other preacher was H. K. W. Perkins, who expected to find a wife among the pious teachers of the Willamette. Miss Margaret Smith, teacher, also hoped to find a mate from among her associates.

With these additional seven, the mission family now totaled sixty, about half of whom were Indian wards. What would Jason Lee do with so many helpers? This was the question asked by some of the settlers. It seemed to them that there was about one civilizer to every savage. The missionaries themselves began to wonder what their assignments would be. The Indians, according to Superintendent Lee, were a scattered degraded race, fast disappearing. But he would find work for all his reinforcements, he told himself.

When winter came all were comfortably housed. Winter was the season when fogs hung low and rain fell dismally on the gray landscape. The river, like a weary serpent, wound its slow way between banks fringed with naked trees. But to the missionaries, winter meant something more than sitting around waiting for springtime. The men went to work and in a few months had completed a good-sized hospital where the sick, both Indians and whites, could be cared for. On Christmas Day a missionary meeting was called to which the settlers were also invited. Each man pledged a small amount and the sum of $400 was raised to start a mission farm for the benefit of the Calapooya Indians. On this farm the natives were to be taught how to build comfortable cabins, how to cultivate the land, plant crops and harvest them.

The project was actually begun. Men went eagerly out to the lodges to persuade their Calapooya neighbors to come and learn. They got little response. Some Indians refused to listen and others were completely apathetic. The missionaries gave their all. Settlers who themselves used deerskins for windowpanes made sacrifices in order to provide something as good for their red-skinned brothers. Small wonder there were discouragements.

The scheme did not work out. Either the Indians were not teachable or the missionaries were not skilled in the art of persuasion. The question of what to do next was discussed at many missionary meetings during that winter of 1837–38. If these Indians could not be taught, of what use were the several ministers who had been sent to Oregon at great expense?

"It's plain we can do little for these Indians," Jason Lee said with conviction. "They can't be converted in the usual way. They can be changed only through long association with Christian people who are, at the same time, thrifty, energetic and enterprising. We must build a Christian community here, with churches, schools and businesses. It will be the nucleus of a great settlement."

"But we must give some kind of an account to the Methodist Board," answered Dr. Elijah White. The doctor had been critical of Jason Lee almost from the day of his arrival. He had made sarcastic comments on Lee's courtship and marriage and had charged him with indecision and inefficiency in the management of the mission.

Lee's answer revealed what had been on his mind for many months. "We'll set up branch missions," he said, "and they must be built at strategic places throughout western Oregon—places where people are coming and going, attractive places where settlers can make a good living."

Lee's associates looked at him wonderingly. Had he turned his attention from missionary work to colonization? His concluding statement, however, put their minds to rest. "Our main purpose," he explained, "is to Christianize the red people. But there can be no harm in a secondary purpose which dovetails into the first."

The outcome of these winter meetings was the decision to build branch missions as soon as feasible. The first was to be at The Dalles on the Columbia River. This had long been a rendezvous for Indians. Hudson's Bay barges passed and re-passed in the business of the company. White men would one day settle here. Why not let the Methodist missionaries pioneer a path for them? A settlement here would help secure the territory of Oregon for the United States. The Dalles was about 140 miles from the Willamette Mission—not as the crow flew but as the rivers flowed.

Daniel Lee was chosen to take charge of the new project and the Reverend H. K. W. Perkins was named as his assistant. Perkins had by now married the zealous missionary teacher, Elvira Johnson. During the winter plans for the new post took shape and by February 1838 all was ready.

From this time on, Jason Lee thought a great deal about his expanding plans for Oregon. He had planted one Christian settlement and now he wanted to sow the seeds for a great empire. He would win the whole Northwest for the United States, not by force of arms but through immigration. Such a promising country as Oregon should not fall into the hands of a fur corporation. It was the Lord's will that American settlers, industrious and pious, should occupy the land. To carry out this scheme of Christian colonization Lee would have to request more assistants—more teachers, more doctors, more carpenters and a few more preachers.

But how would the Board of Missions react to such a proposal? Had he not said that the Indians were a diminishing race, only slightly impressed by the white man's religion or his way of life in general? Would the readers of his written request—even Dr. Wilbur Fisk—understand the problem as set out in cold words on paper? The more Lee pondered the matter the greater was his conviction that he should go east and personally lay before his board the needs of the mission and its plans for expansion.

His mind was made up. He talked the matter over with his associates. Some favored the idea, others opposed it. "But you're needed here," protested one of the objectors. "Your trip will take the better part of two years—one to go, the other to return."

"The work will be well laid out," Lee answered. "Daniel and Mr. Perkins will go to The Dalles as planned, and Mr. Leslie will be acting superintendent in my absence. There will be enough to keep everyone busy."

The latter part of February—the weather being favorable—Daniel Lee and Mr. Perkins loaded barges with supplies and set out for The Dalles. Jason Lee would start on his trip to the East within a few weeks.

One day in March an important meeting, attended by Americans and Canadian sympathizers, was held at the mission. The purpose was to draft a memorial or petition to the Congress of the United States asking that a civil government be set up for Oregon. Philip L. Edwards, who could qualify for almost any job, drafted the document. This petition had strong bearings on the future history of the Oregon country. It set forth the advantages of the region, including its climate, its adaptability to agriculture and stock-raising and its possibilities for trade with China. American settlers, the document stated, had been well treated by the Hudson's Bay Company but there were many disadvantages in being ruled by a foreign corporation. "We flatter ourselves," said the signers, "that we are the germ of a great State, anxious to give an early tone to the moral and intellectual character of its citizens. Our interests are identical with the country of our adoption—for these many reasons we are convinced that the Government should take formal and speedy possession of Oregon."

When the document had been read aloud to the eager listeners, thirty-eight men—about three-fourths of the male inhabitants of the Willamette Valley—affixed their signatures to it.

Many were the evenings that Jason Lee and his wife talked over his projected trip. She was six months' pregnant and he was sorely distressed at leaving her, but she insisted that he do his duty. She had married him to be a help, not a hindrance. Her part would be to continue her tasks at the mission with unflinching courage.

By March 25, 1838 all plans had been made. Philip L. Edwards would be Lee's companion. Following the example set by Nathaniel Wyeth, Lee decided to take with him two promising Indian boys to use as drawing cards at missionary meetings in the East. He chose Thomas Adams and William Brooks, lads of about fourteen or fifteen years of age.

While the barge floated easily down the widening Willamette, fringed now by budding trees, Lee took Anna Maria's last message from his pocket and read:

Must my dear companion leave me,
Sad and lonely here to dwell?
If 'tis duty thus that calls thee,
Shall I keep thee?—No, farewell,
Though my heart aches
While I bid thee thus farewell.

He folded the sheet and put it back in his pocket. "Thank the Lord for such a wife as Anna Maria—too brave to admit any sense of fear; too unselfish to ask me to stay when duty plainly calls." Although Lee was concerned about her health he had complete confidence in Dr. White.

Jason Lee and his party spent six days at Fort Vancouver, then went on to The Dalles, where Daniel and Mr. Perkins were hard at work building their mission house. The next destination was the Whitman mission at Walla Walla, and following that, a short stay with Henry Harmon Spalding on the Clearwater. On May 12, 1838, they joined a party of Hudson's Bay trappers bound for Fort Hall.

Meanwhile, back at Chemaway, Anna Maria prepared to

make the best of her situation. When her husband's barge was lost to sight around the bend she felt so weak that she lay down for an hour or more to gain strength and to pray for his safe return.

The farther her husband journeyed from her, the closer came her hour of trial. Dr. White now told her to expect it sooner than had been formerly predicted. On June 21 her labor pains began. They grew so intense that the doctor was obliged to use instruments to effect the delivery. On June 23 she gave birth to a son pronounced "fully formed and handsome." Mrs. Lee's condition seemed good, but Dr. White shook his head over the child, who lived but a few hours. Shortly, complications set in for the mother, and in two days after the death of her son, Anna Maria breathed her last.

The women of the mission could do no more than weep. This was the first time that death had visited them. Anna Maria's marriage had been happy. She had enjoyed her work at the post and was well liked by all. And she died as she had lived, confident in the belief that the will of the Lord was right. The Reverend David Leslie preached the funeral sermon and on June 27, 1838 Anna Maria Lee was buried in the picturesque grove where, a little less than a year before, she had been married. The first white woman to be married in Oregon was now the first to be buried in that far-off "land where the sunsets go."

The problem now was how to get word to Jason Lee. Hudson's Bay Company came to the rescue by sending a fast express to Spalding's mission on the Clearwater River. Spalding, in turn, dispatched six Indians with the message to Fort Hall. This required sixteen days and by that time the Hudson's Bay brigade had left for the rendezvous. It so happened that William H. Gray, bringing reinforcements to the Whitman mission, was at Fort Hall. He took over the responsibility and hired two hunters to cross the plains with the death message. He gave them an order on the American Board of Missions for $150. This was later repaid by the Methodists.

6 • *Recruits for a New Oregon*

THE MESSENGERS CAUGHT UP WITH Lee at the Shawnee Mission on the Missouri River September 9, 1838. Lee read the communication, trembling and pale, then went to his room. The night closed around him in his sorrow. He reviewed again and again that brief but happy life he had known with Anna Maria. "I was traveling joyfully along," he later wrote to Dr. Wilbur Fisk, "thinking that by now I would be a father. I wanted a child to call my own. . . . But no—I am a lonely widower and a bereaved father."

As he sat in the darkness with bowed head, he felt a desperate need for divine aid. After intensive prayer he was able to hold up his head and say, "The Lord gave, and the Lord has taken away. Blessed be the name of the Lord." There was no turning back, even though his family was gone and his personal happiness destroyed. The Lord's business was still upon his shoulders. He had "put his hand to the plow," and there was no retreating. His path was clear, he must go on.

Lee's next stop was at Alton on the Illinois side of the river. Here, at a well attended meeting, he pleaded the mission cause and, in addition, played up the amazing opportunities that Oregon offered to American settlers. At Peoria, the Willamette Indian boy, Thomas Adams, affectionately known as "Indian Tom," created a sensation all his own by telling in broken English about his home in the valley, about the salmon in the streams and the game in the hills. The boy fell ill here and Lee, not wishing to be detained indefinitely, found good nursing care for his charge and continued on his way to Chicago and thence to Detroit, Buffalo and finally New York City.

It was October 3, 1838 when he ended his cross-country journey. In due time, he was standing before the Methodist Board of Missions with the story of his accomplishments in Oregon and his appeals for further assistance. He made it clear that he preferred pious laymen—doctors, teachers, carpenters, farmers, mechanics —to preaching missionaries. The board gave careful consideration to the requests and by December 5 was ready to appropriate $40,000 for expanding the mission work in Oregon. Lee was overruled on some points; nevertheless he was overwhelmed at the enthusiasm with which his proposals were supported. He asked for two preaching missionaries; the board provided five. The lay members included a stewardess, four women teachers, a doctor, a blacksmith, two carpenters, a cabinetmaker and a business manager. In addition, the board allowed for farm machinery, mill equipment and seeds. Merchandise in the amount of $5000 was voted.

The money for the ambitious undertaking had been appropriated. Now it was Lee's duty to travel over the country, holding missionary meetings and raising funds. He gladly started out, taking the intelligent and witty Indian lad, William Brooks, as a powerful attraction. For six months he was on the road. He visited the New England States and Canada, and even went as far south as Virginia. In all he made eighty-three missionary appeals.

At first William Brooks tired easily but as he became accustomed to crowds he rose to every occasion, adding his bit in colorful phrases that brought smiles, cheers and a generous contribution from the congregation. One of William's first speeches was prompted by the sight of a blind Negro in Baltimore. Said the boy:

> I saw something. I never forget. He colored man. Can't read. Can't see nothin', but he see Jesus Christ. He be very happy. Oh, I love that old man because he love Jesus Christ. Some rich man die, and where they go? That old man go to Heaven. I shall never forget him again.[2]

At another place, young Brooks took occasion to censure people who carried liquor to the Indians:

> One thing, my friends, I must put in paper that no more these Americans they carry rum in my country—spoil all Indians. He make it himself, he must *drink* it himself—these Yankees.[3]

A curious lady once called him to task for what she called the "outlandish practice of head-flattening." William made answer:

> All people have his fashion. Chinese make little his foot. Indian make flat his head. You—he looked at her drawn-in waist, at the same time trying to encircle his own with both hands—you make small here.[4]

While in the East Jason Lee suffered another bereavement in the death of Dr. Wilbur Fisk, the man who had been most influential in starting the Oregon mission.

Under the excitement and strain of his speaking tours, Lee did not forget the petition he had helped to frame in the Willamette. When he was in Washington, D.C. in December he sent the petition to Senator Linn of Missouri. The senator introduced it on the floor of the Senate where it created something of a sensation. The Americans at last were becoming aroused to the desirability of possessing this far western territory which all travelers were praising to the skies. By many Oregon was looked upon as a plum ripe for the plucking.

Jason did not intend to go back to Oregon without visiting family and friends in Canada. On his way to Stanstead in February 1839 he stopped off at Newbury, Vermont, to call on Osmon C. Baker, a classmate and friend of academy days. Mr. Baker was in charge of Newbury Seminary, a growing Methodist institution. In his visit with Lee, Baker referred repeatedly to one outstanding student, the valedictorian of the November class. At first, Jason listened only out of courtesy but before long he found a new interest growing within him.

"She's Miss Lucy Thomson," Baker explained, "and she is now about twenty-eight. She's mature in her thinking, highly intellectual, refined and a staunch Christian—and further, Jason, she wants an opportunity to do missionary work among the Indians."

Lee's interest was kindled to the point where he made up his mind to meet Miss Lucy Thomson, to woo her and if possible win her for his wife. Jason Lee was a man of few words where his own personal affairs were concerned. He did not confide in his friend, Baker, but went to Barre, Vermont, where he met Lucy

Thomson and her family. The courtship was short, for Jason's business called him to Canada, then back to the States to make final plans for the return to Oregon.

The last of Lee's scheduled meetings was held at Schenectady, New York. Here to create interest were the two Indian boys, Thomas Adams having just arrived from Illinois where he had been detained for six months by his illness. On this occasion, the congregation missed the wit of William Brooks, for the boy was sick and able to say only a few words. In a very few days, Jason Lee realized with alarm that William was not long for this world. He sank rapidly and Lee remained at his bedside until the end came on May 29, 1839.

"I want to go home," the youth said, a short time before he died.

"Yes," his protector answered with regret in his voice; "to your home in Oregon."

"No," insisted William, "my Heavenly home."

William Brooks was buried in the cemetery of the Bedford Street Church in New York City.

For another five months Jason Lee was busy with the burdensome details of preparation for the voyage to Oregon. A great variety of things was to find storage in the hold of the *Lausanne:* machinery for sawmills and gristmills, farming implements, carpenters' tools, household necessities, window sashes, clothing for the mission stations, as well as thousands of articles donated to the Indians. In July Jason slid out from under his burden and made a trip to Vermont. Here, on the twenty-eighth of the month, 1839, he was married to Miss Lucy Thomson. The young lady made no profession that this was love at first sight, or indeed love at all. Jason Lee, she declared, was the kindest of men, and altogether worthy of her respect and confidence. She acted from conviction of duty, and firmly believed that Jesus meant what he said when he gave the command, "Go ye, therefore, and teach all nations." For her, the command was as imperative as when it was delivered to the disciples.

A few days before the time for sailing, the missionaries began assembling in New York. On October 9, 1839, they boarded the lighter that conveyed them to the *Lausanne,* riding calmly at anchor in East River. There were fifty-one persons in the party, including Mr. and Mrs. Lee and the Indian boy, Thomas Adams. Among the teachers was Maria Ware, the affianced bride of Daniel Lee, who had made her acquaintance through correspondence. The *Lausanne* carried an unusually large reinforcement party. The Board of Missions, however, made it clear that this was not a colonizing enterprise.

"We have nothing to do with planting a colony in Oregon," declared the Reverend Dr. Bangs, corresponding secretary. "The primary object of the enterprise is the salvation of the souls of the people in that region."

After the *Lausanne* was well under sail, Jason Lee felt impelled to write a letter to Mrs. George Pittman, the mother of his first wife. Her chidings and sharp criticisms had rankled. She had accused him of being indiscreet in his actions and secretive as to his intentions. He should have told her about his plans for a second marriage. She did not object to his remarriage eventually, but common decency should have told him to wait, at least until after he had looked upon the grave of his first wife. If Lee interpreted Mrs. Pittman's words correctly, she was more interested in conventionalities than in trying to understand his position. He now re-emphasized what he had said at their last meeting. He still loved Anna Maria, and could not think of her without pain. He meant no disrespect to her memory. Friends, he explained, had approved a second marriage, and even his superiors, including the chairman of the mission board, had advised him not to go back to Oregon without a wife.

Jason Lee told Mrs. Pittman that he was willing to be considered thoughtless and indiscreet. He asked only that she try to think kindly of Lucy, who had done nothing to merit persecution. He wrote at length, trying to pacify the lady. However, he gently refused to return all of Anna Maria's things. The spoons his first wife had bought with her own money and which they had used together he would not surrender. "The things you ask for, my dear mother," he wrote, "are the ones I cannot part with." He did not tell Mrs. George Pittman that the *Lausanne* carried an engraved marble headstone for the grave of Anna Maria.

As the voyage lengthened, Jason Lee was forming opinions

about the various members of the missionary party. While the ship was at anchor in Valparaiso, Chile, he wrote the following letter to Dr. Nathan Bangs:

> I have been watching our reinforcements in order to discover their traits and character, and I trust we shall be able to turn them all to some good account in that dark land; but I am persuaded that it is one thing to be a good missionary on the *Lausanne*, and another to be a good one in Oregon.[5]

The long voyage was made without accident, and on June 1, 1840 the *Lausanne* landed the "Great Reinforcement" safely at Fort Vancouver, where Dr. McLoughlin received them with his usual hospitality. Anticipating the arrival of the ship, Daniel Lee had come down from his post at The Dalles to meet his uncle and his fiancée, Maria Ware. Wednesday, June 3, 1840 was an important day in the history of Oregon. It marked officially Jason Lee's program of expansion—the combination of a missionary with a colonizing enterprise.

Word of the arrival of the ship had been sent to the Willamette, and in the evening of that memorable day, most of the members of the mission met in the big room provided by Dr. McLoughlin. Lee had had many months in which to think over his plans in all their details. In endless conferences with the Lord he had been assured that he had been called to play an important role in preparing the great Oregon country for Christian civilization. Now, while he unfolded his scheme for the planting of branch missions at all strategic places, his associates listened with eagerness, if not with one-hundred-per-cent approval. The Dalles Mission, started in the spring of 1838 by Daniel Lee and Mr. Perkins, was making gratifying progress. To assist in this work, Lee appointed Dr. Ira Babcock, physician, and Henry Brewer, farmer. Both had wives and the Babcocks had one child.

Since the mouth of the Columbia was considered strategic, Joseph Frost and his wife were given the assignment of starting a mission on the Clatsop Plains, back of Fort George (formerly Astoria). Dr. J. P. Richmond with his wife and three small children would go immediately to Puget Sound and build near Fort Nisqually, a Hudson's Bay post. His assistants were William Willson, carpenter, and Miss Chloe Clark, teacher. The Reverend Gustavus Hines was given the difficult task of winning the hostile Umpquas in lower Oregon. W. W. Kone and wife were appointed as assistants. The Reverend Alvin Waller, stationed at Willamette Falls, was given as assistant George Abernethy, business manager for the entire mission enterprise.

Not all the missionaries were pleased with their assignments, particularly the wives. The Richmonds voiced a complaint about being sent so far into the wilderness without having had even a look at the parent mission in the Willamette. Some could not make adjustments to raw conditions and others believed that Jason Lee's schemes were those of a visionary colonizer rather than those of a missionary to the heathen. Perhaps Jason Lee anticipated such reactions while the *Lausanne* was making her 20,000-mile voyage. If he did he staunchly decided to cast all suspicions aside and act on the assumption that the great plan he had formulated would be carried out to a successful conclusion.

7 • *Flood Tide at the Willamette Mission*

IT WAS JUNE AT CHEMAWAY, with all the trees in full leaf, wild flowers in bloom and a sea of grass billowing over the broad valley. Jason Lee was back after more than two years of absence—back for a bigger and better work for the Lord and the cause of Christian civilization.

Lee had given the mission group a surprise from which many could never recover. Without any previous announcement he had walked in with a new wife. They had imagined him grieving his heart out for the one who was now sleeping in peace in the picturesque little grove and they had been wondering how to console him. Coming with a new bride and a gravestone for the first!

What strange things happen! Jason Lee was not a heartless man but a practical one. He had human feelings, to be sure, but he also had work to do for God. When he was free he went alone to the sacred grove and stood with bowed head at the grave of Anna Maria, where the winds sang both a bridal song and a funeral dirge.

Two years had brought tragedy to others as well. Here in the grove lay the remains of George Stoutenberg, the adopted son of Dr. Elijah White—drowned in the Willamette while attempting to cross on horseback. And here, too, under a mound identified as "White," rested Jason Lee, the infant son of Dr. and Mrs. White —drowned in the Columbia when a canoe capsized. When Jason Lee moved over to another longer grave he shed tears as he had done over the mound of Anna Maria. Here lay Cyrus Shepard, patient shepherd of a heathen flock. He had been resting here for six months, having died January 1, 1840.

Cyrus Shepard had not been blessed with physical endurance, although his appearance belied the fact. For the first two years in Oregon, he suffered from repeated attacks of fever combined with influenza. In the spring of 1838 he developed a white swelling of the knee. At first he ignored it but the affliction grew steadily worse. Dr. White pronounced the ailment scrofula and began treatments. There was temporary improvement and Cyrus struggled on in pain for eighteen months, still doing full duty. In the fall of 1839 he was forced to take to his bed. After twenty days of intense suffering he decided to submit to an amputation of the leg. Dr. White performed the operation without benefit of anesthesia. It was torture to Cyrus but he could endure it because the Lord and Susan were his strong supports.

Cyrus survived, and with his usual cheerfulness and fortitude. When he was well enough, he wrote letters to Daniel Lee at The Dalles, describing his condition and praising the skill of Dr. White. He thought he was rid of the affliction, but the pain returned to plague him Then, in a letter to Daniel, he spoke of the indescribable torture. "When I feel like screaming with pain," he wrote, "I turn my voice in praise to God." The closing lines of that last letter were a comfort to Daniel to the end of his long life. They read:

> I would say to you such has been the abundance of peace given, that not a rising of impatience or fretfulness, nor a murmur of complaint has ever been felt by me during my sickness. Farewell! The God of all peace, grace and consolation be with you continually.
>
> Signed
>
> A part of Cyrus[6]

The stump of the leg seemed to heal satisfactorily but shortly afterward an abscess formed in the hip. Hopes faded, for this responded to no treatment. Shepard died on the first day of the year 1840, leaving Susan and two infant daughters. With his death, the mission community suffered a hard blow. What would now happen to the school? He had fathered it and nurtured it through its discouraging beginnings. When illness forced him to quit, it had an attendance of thirty-six, with immediate prospects of more. The Sunday School, which was an adjunct of the day school, had an attendance of forty-six.

After the death of Cyrus, acting superintendent David Leslie was faced with the problem of finding someone to fill the place of the most devoted of the missionaries. Fortune, however, sent a substitute in the person of William Geiger, who had given some service to the Whitman mission and was now on his way to California. He was persuaded to take charge of the school until Jason Lee's return from the East. Said a commentator years later, "With Shepard died all the interest in the hopeless scheme of educating the native children of the Willamette."

Jason Lee returned from the grove of sorrows to his own plans, in which dreams for the future of Oregon were to be transformed into realities. During his absence things had changed radically in the valley. The white population was increasing, but the red was diminishing at an alarming rate. "Where are all our Indians?" he asked, appalled at how few they seemed.

"Dead and gone," was the answer. It was literally true. Many had died; others, following their roving instinct, had gone to live elsewhere.

"But the French-Canadians?" Lee asked. "They used to be a part of our congregation. Where are *they?*"

He was informed that, in his absence, the Catholics had come to claim their own. In 1838 Fathers Francis Blanchet and Modeste Demers had arrived from Canada to missionize the Indians and minister to any whites and halfbreeds who were once professing Catholics. Father Blanchet had built a mission at St. Paul's on French Prairie and services were being held in the little log chapel.

In the summer of 1840, Jason Lee began plans for moving his mission from the old "Bottoms" to a more healthful spot ten miles farther up the Willamette River. He chose a site on Mill Creek at Chemeketa, an Indian word meaning "our old home" or "here we rest." Here he built a sawmill and a gristmill. After long labor, the machinery that had been brought on the *Lausanne* was installed. It was unloaded at Fort Vancouver, taken apart and carried on barges to its destination at Chemeketa. Lee's next project was the building of the Manual Labor School for Indians. This called for the expenditure of $10,000 approved by the mission board. For its day it was an "imposing structure," being three stories in height and topped by a belfry. It was three years in the process of construction and never had a very large attendance of Indian pupils. The first residence built at Chemeketa (later, Salem) was the parsonage. It was of typically New England architecture, painted white and ornamented by green shutters. This house was the admiration of the entire community.

Not all the recruits co-operated wholeheartedly in bringing about the new day for Oregon. There was a diversity of attitudes toward their superintendent, toward the work assigned and toward the "big plan" in general. Upon seeing the woefully small number of natives, some felt that Jason Lee had misled them. "There are just about twice too many of us," they said, "for the work there is to do."

Others declared, "We came out to convert the heathen, and now we find ourselves preparing to serve the whites. Is this the reward we get for sacrificing good positions in the States?"

"This reinforcement party," said the business manager, George Abernethy, "is too large to be absorbed. Mr. Lee has manufactured positions in remote places to take care of the surplus. Gross mismanagement!"

Jason Lee heard the murmurings but made no explanation.

The center of dissension seemed to be Dr. Elijah White, judged by some of his contemporaries to be "presuming," "egotistical" and ambitious to make a name for himself in Oregon. In the summer of 1840, a disagreement between the two men resulted in Dr. White's leaving the mission. Because of what he called "an honest difference of opinion," White resigned and went east, resolved to lay the whole matter before the mission board. After this, in all his references to Jason Lee the doctor spoke in slighting terms.

On January 17, 1842 Jason Lee called a meeting at his residence to discuss the possibilities of building a school for the white population of the valley. Out of this meeting and several others came a plan for the construction of the Oregon Institute. This project was not undertaken in the name of the mission nor did it involve mission funds. It was the work of individual persons who pledged themselves to raise the necessary amount. They had full faith that the United States would soon take over all of Oregon. The funds were raised and a carpenter hired; in a short time, the framework of the Oregon Institute took shape on Wallace Prairie. This was the beginning of the present Willamette University, which stands today as a memorial to the foresight and energy of the Methodist missionaries, especially Jason Lee.

On February 28, 1842, a daughter was born to the Reverend and Mrs. Jason Lee, and three weeks later the mother died, presumably of pleurisy. The benumbing effect of Lucy's death upon her husband and the rest of the mission group has been written in the following words by the Reverend Gustavus Hines:

> Her sickness was brief and not considered dangerous, though attended with a cold and expectoration. On March 20, she coughed. Mr. Lee who was standing by her side, raised her head upon his arm. One gasp, and all was over. A sadder husband, a sadder group, never surrounded a missionary's deathbed. When a few hours later, they laid away her remains by the side of his former companion, they laid away the casket that had borne one of the purest gems that ever blazed in the dark night of Oregon. As Mr. Lee, folding the infant daughter, then but three weeks old, to his heart, turned from that grave under the oaks of Lee Mission Cem-

etery, another golden strand was braided into the chain that would bind his heart forever to the vales and skies of Oregon.[7]

Lee bore his grief with heroic fortitude, as shown in his letters to relatives and friends. A second time he had lost the main prop of his life. Now his wives were sleeping side by side in a land far from the home of their childhood. That he loved them both devotedly cannot be doubted. The child that was left to him, Lucy Anna, was to be a living memorial to both wives. In a letter to his friend, Osmon Baker, Lee gave the details of his wife's last illness and death, and closed with the following paragraph:

> No, my brother, discouraged I am not. In heaviness I cannot be, while the grace of God, as hitherto, bears me entirely above that region. I feel it would be sin to waste my energies in fruitless grief, or unavailing sorrow, and yet I am aware that it is the sustaining grace of God in me that preserves me from it. Glory to God in the highest! I can exult in the midst of the furnace. One like the Son of Man is with me, and I expect to come forth without the smell of fire upon my garment.[8]

Lucy Anna was cared for in the home of the Reverend Hines, and Jason Lee plunged anew into his efforts to bring about that promised day for Oregon.

The coming of additional American settlers created more of a need for a civil government in Oregon and less for the protection afforded by a fur company. Much credit must be given to the missionaries and other settlers for maintaining a community well controlled, cooperative and free from crime. Yet Jason Lee longed for some incident that would persuade the government of the United States to take a bold stand on its claim to all of Oregon. Said one writer concerning Lee's ambitions:

> The mission might not Christianize the Indians, as they were becoming extinct, and what were left were inert and worthless; but he looked to a future that could recognize Lee as the moving spirit that planned and commenced an era that was to be permanent and great for national events; he wanted his name to go echoing down the aisles of time in connection therewith.[9]

Jason Lee was indeed the moving spirit in the effort to secure civil government for the community centering around the mission at Salem. Irked by the silence of the United States Government—even after two petitions had been sent—and faced with problems only a legally organized group could solve, the settlers created their own government. It was a great day when missionaries and other settler voted the acceptance of the Provisional Government, which a committee had laboriously drawn up. This was in May 1843. With the arrival of the large immigration of that summer, American power in Oregon rose to its peak. It placed the new government on secure foundations with an overwhelming American majority.

Jason Lee had the supreme satisfaction of seeing his dream for Oregon coming true. America was on the march westward and nothing could stop her. Streams of settlers were flowing in every year. With the heavy immigration of 1843, the population of Oregon was estimated at about 1200. Eventually, Hudson's Bay Company would be forced to "fold its tents and steal away," for the fur era would soon be forever at an end.

The Branch Missions

THE YEAR 1840 WAS A MOMENTOUS one in missionary history. It was the year Jason Lee returned to Oregon with the "grand" reinforcement, and it was the year his expanded plans were to go into operation. Whether or not it was wholly pleasing to them, the new recruits went off to the posts assigned to Christianize the Indians and, incidentally, to hold Oregon for the United States.

The Reverend John P. Richmond was to have the honor of being the first missionary in the Puget Sound country, and the first settler with a family. He was not going into a wilderness where no white man's foot had ever trodden. It had been explored by both the English and Spanish, and British fur traders were already established at Nisqually House, which they had built in 1833. Besides, Jason Lee had come here in 1838 and located a site for his mission near the fort. On June 3, 1840, shortly after their arrival on the *Lausanne,* the Richmond family with the mission supplies embarked in canoes that glided easily down the Columbia to the mouth of the Cowlitz River. Ascending the Cowlitz was more of a problem. As the stream narrowed, it began to exhibit a rollicking disposition that challenged the strength and ingenuity of the oarsmen. Navigation ended at the Hudson's Bay farms. The Richmonds stayed overnight here, then proceeded on horseback to Nisqually House. Here, the clerk, William Kittson, gave them a welcome and provided temporary living quarters.

Within three weeks the cabin was finished and the family moved in. Dr. Richmond began his duties by holding regular religious services for the natives, starting a school and, accompanied by an Indian interpreter, visiting some of the Indians in their dwellings. At the zenith of its short life, the school had an attendance of about fifty pupils.

One day in the summer of 1841 the missionaries were surprised by the appearance in the Sound of two American vessels, the *Vincennes* and the *Porpoise,* under the command of Lieutenant Charles Wilkes of the United States Navy. He headed a government expedition of a scientific nature that took him first to the South Seas and, now, to Oregon to make a survey of the coastline, the topography, the climate and the inhabitants.

To Lieutenant Wilkes and Dr. Richmond is due the credit of promoting the first Fourth of July celebration in Old Oregon west of the Rocky Mountains. To give his crew a treat, Wilkes bought an ox from the Hudson's Bay Company and barbecued it for the occasion. After the feast came the patriotic observance of American independence, when about 500 persons, including missionaries, company employees, a hundred Marines and some 400 Indians gathered on a sunny prairie not far from American Lake. As the uniformed men from the ships paraded, the two howitzers that had been hauled out from the fort boomed a salute, answered by prolonged cheers from the crowd. Prayer was offered by Reverend Richmond, followed by the singing of the National Anthem and the reading of the Declaration of Independence by the Sergeant of Marines.

The oration of the day, the first of its kind ever heard on the Pacific Coast, was delivered by Dr. Richmond. In his address, the missionary made a special point of saying that they were eagerly looking forward to the day when the whole of the wonderful Oregon country would be a part of the American Republic, when all the hills and valleys would be peopled by "our enterprising countrymen." He predicted the rapid growth of cities and manufacturing establishments. "In this new world," he said, "there is sure to arise one of the greatest nations of the earth." Referring to the objectives of the Methodist group he said forthrightly, "Our mission to these children of the forest is to teach them the truth of the Gospel that they shall be fitted for responsible and intelligent Christian citizenship. . . . We are here also to assist in laying the foundation stones of a great American commonwealth on these Pacific shores." [10]

Although his work had a successful beginning, Dr. J. P. Richmond was dissatisfied with his assignment. First of all, he resented being "pushed off into the wilderness" without having had an opportunity to visit the parent mission in the beautiful Willamette. Richmond disapproved so strongly of some of Jason Lee's methods that he filed complaints with the mission board in New York. Further, he was convinced that all his work with the Indians would prove futile, since the natives were immune to Christian teaching. Since the situation—from his point of view—was hopeless he resolved to remove himself from it as soon as possible. He aspired to something higher than being a simple farmer in the backwoods among Indians who resisted all teaching.

Dr. Richmond had presided over the Nisqually mission for only about a year and a half when he asked for a release, giving as his reason the condition of his health and that of his family. His request was granted and he left Fort Vancouver on the *Chenamus* in September 1842. There is no record of anything he accomplished at Nisqually, except possibly to strengthen the claim of the United States to the Puget Sound area. No one was sent in his place, and the Catholics, who did believe that the red men could be salvaged, led hundreds of Indians into their fold.

The Reverend Alvin Waller was appointed to take charge of the branch mission at the strategic cataracts a short distance from the mouth of the Willamette River. This was believed to be an ideal spot for a mission because of the many Indians who frequented it to fish and to trade at the Hudson's Bay Company station. The place, further, had attracted French-Canadians as well as an increasing number of Americans who were looking for a desirable location.

Waller was a man of promptness and inexhaustible energy, so it was not long until he had things moving. George Abernethy, treasurer of the entire mission, came as Alvin Waller's assistant, and the two soon had a small town in the making. Each built a frame residence. In addition, the village boasted a storehouse, a flour mill, two sawmills and twenty-one other buildings. Missionary Waller was a "jack of all trades." By his own testimony, he was a joiner, carpenter, receiver and forwarder of goods, boatmaker, salmon salter, farmer, blacksmith, nurse and physician—to say nothing of being an evangelist to the natives. On the Sabbath, he held as many meetings as the length of the day would permit. He went three miles to the Clackamas village to teach those Indians, returned at eleven to preach to the whites at his home and in the afternoon crossed the river to meet with the Indians of another village. In addition to these activities, Mr. Waller expended much energy entertaining and serving strangers traveling to and from the main mission at Salem. Each year brought a steadily increasing number of settlers stopping for necessities—this one for a boat, that one to obtain Indian rowers and another for a little grist or salmon.

By the time he had been at Willamette Falls a year Mr. Waller was thoroughly sold on Oregon. His thoughts as reflected in his letters to friends in the East were concerned far less with the Indians than with the profits to be made in this abundant land. He pointed out the need for "many wholesome settlers, embracing some capitalists, to open up trade with China and the Sandwich Islands." He complained about the monopolistic practices of the Hudson's Bay Company and argued that the first need was for the government of the United States to extend its jurisdiction and protection over the country.

In the fall of 1842 Mr. Waller became involved in a land controversy with Dr. John McLoughlin when he laid a counterclaim to property which McLoughlin had preëmpted in 1829, long before the Methodists had ever dreamed of coming to Oregon. The doctor appealed to Jason Lee but Lee maintained that it was outside his jurisdiction to interfere in the private business affairs of his associates. The legal contest was long drawn out. McLoughlin, who later became a United States citizen, lost his property, due to political maneuverings and the connivance of some American settlers. Many people thought that he had suffered a gross injustice. After his death, however, an adjustment was made and the property returned to his heirs. The whole affair reflected unfavorably upon the Methodists at the Falls.

That same autumn, 1842, Mr. Waller decided that the time was ripe for the erection of a church for whites. With his usual energy he made a canvass of the community, securing twenty-seven subscribers to the project. In a few weeks, an immigrant party of more than a hundred reached the Falls. Alvin Waller was elated. His hopes were being realized sooner than he had anticipated. The inevitable was coming to pass—the domination of Oregon by a progressive race of palefaces who would take the place of the "disappearing, tawny sons of the forest."

Alvin Waller's success in the conversion of the Indians was negligible, partly because he became too engrossed with trade, the interests of white settlers and Oregon's future. Visitors to the mission at the Falls were more impressed by the worldly side of the picture than by the spiritual. Lieutenant Charles Wilkes on his tour of Oregon reported that "it is quite unsuited to the life of a missionary to be entering trade of any kind" and that "missionaries should not engage in business that would detract from their main object." Catholic priests who were moving into the mission field with some success made like comments. A Methodist preacher of the old school, visiting Waller's mission on his tour of Oregon, left this remark:

> Brother Waller and Brother Wilson [mechanic] are very much enthralled in working and trading, and have but little time to do anything for the Indians. Perhaps times will soon alter.[11]

But Waller had energy and zeal for the cause he was promoting. Under his direction was built the first Methodist church on the long Pacific Coast from Bering Sea to Cape Horn. It was opened for worship in 1844. The church was not built for the natives, but for the edification of the whites; nevertheless the religious advocates of "Oregon for the Americans" argued that, back of every like institution, the red man's welfare was considered. Indians, it was assumed, could not profit by instruction—example was the only means whereby they could learn. There was no hope for the savage unless white people, by their upright, godly lives showed him the true way.

Joseph H. Frost with his wife and small son, Emory, arrived on the *Lausanne* in June 1840. His assignment was to convert the Clatsop Indians living at the mouth of the Columbia River on the Oregon side. During most of the first year in Oregon, he assisted Daniel Lee at The Dalles. The family went by Hudson's Bay barge to Fort George (formerly Astoria) where they were were welcomed by the caretaker, James Birnie, who offered the hospitality of the post until a site had been located and a mission house built. While her husband explored Young's Bay and environs Mrs. Frost spent her time profitably, teaching her son and the seven children of the Birnies.

This mission, known as Clatsop by the Sea, did not have an auspicious beginning. Shortly after the arrival of the Frost family at Fort George two Canadians came hurrying in with a report that an employee named McKay and an Indian boy had been murdered by savages at the company's salmon-fishing station a few miles up the river. Soon after the word was received at Vancouver a commission appeared to make an investigation. The two murderers were captured. One was accidentally shot in the skirmish that attended his seizure. The other was given a hearing, found guilty and hanged. Dr. McLoughlin was present to make sure that no injustice was done to anyone, even a savage. This was an example of the way the Hudson's Bay Company controlled crime—not brutally but with fairness and speed. The Indians knew that no major crime would go unpunished, and they respected the great fur corporation for keeping order and administering justice to all.

Mr. Frost wondered if this incident was a bad omen. How

could he establish a mission in a place where danger lurked everywhere? But after a few days comparative calm settled over the lower Columbia. Old Chief Chenamus, who had assisted the British traders in apprehending the criminals, stood ready to protect the whites and preserve the honor of his nation.

After considerable exploration Frost finally selected a building site on Clatsop Plain about five miles from Point Adams. But now the problem was to get the cabin built before the rains came, and there was no help. "Hire Solomon Smith," said Jason Lee, when apprised of this lack. However, Smith, an American settler, was having the same problem of finishing his own cabin before winter. He promised to assist the missionary as soon as possible. In the meantime Frost, somewhat irritated at Jason Lee's response to his request, decided to go to the Willamette mission where he felt sure help could be obtained. This took valuable time and when he arrived at Chemeketa he learned that illness had put a good many men to bed; the others were all employed at mission tasks. The only available man was the Reverend W. H. Kone, who was originally assigned to the Umpquas. Those Indians having demonstrated hostility, Kone remained at the parent mission. Frost's only alternative was to accept Mr. Kone, though he had little ability as a carpenter, and his pregnant wife, who was in very poor health and hardly able to travel.

The party, with extra supplies, left in two canoes, manned by a white called Paddy, three Indians and one Hawaiian. Bad luck awaited them at Willamette Falls. Here the larger canoe slipped out of control, was drawn into the rapids and went to pieces with a crash. In the space of a few minutes, barrels, bundles and Indians were all tumbling about in utter confusion. Frost, in the rear canoe, could do little but reach out frantically for the floating pieces of merchandise, while the Indians and the Owyhee righted themselves and began towing bundles to shore. It was near dusk and Mrs. Kone's clothing and a valuable watch were lost. At Vancouver Dr. McLoughlin provided another boat and the missionary party went safely on to Fort George, though in the face of wind-driven rain.

Leaving their families at Fort George, Frost and Kone took supplies and tools in their canoes and proceeded to the Skapanowin River. They paddled up this stream as far as possible, then carried their things overland about a mile to the mission site. With the help of a half dozen Indians secured by Solomon Smith, the missionaries soon had one cabin constructed, but not completely finished. The women came, however, and all joined in the task of putting the many finishing touches on—ceiling it with rush mats, caulking it with moss and laying a puncheon floor. In December the adequacy of their shelter was put to a stern test when the steadily howling southwest winds brought torrential and continuous rains. Part of the roof leaked, and had to be repaired in a downpour. "But," said Frost, "we trusted in God, and hoped for better things."

It took Joseph Frost only a few weeks to realize that he had chosen the wrong spot for his station. The accumulation of water in the upper reaches of the little Skapanowin River practically isolated the settlement. The new location was due north a distance of between two or three miles, and easier of access to Fort Vancouver. Assisted by Solomon Smith and another settler, Calvin Tibbitts, the two missionaries soon had another rude two-room cabin built. By the time the two families were established the salmon run had started, bringing many Indians into the area.

The winter passed without much actual missionary work having been done. In April, the two families repaired to the Willamette to attend a general missionary meeting called by Jason Lee. Both Joseph Frost and his wife were in poor health. He was exhausted by manual labor and suffering from a throat ailment he had contracted shortly after his arrival on the Columbia. Sara had been completely miserable because of an intermittent fever the Indians called "cole sick-waum sick"—chills and fever. It was a rest as well as a change to be in the delightful Willamette for those few days, renewing associations and listening to the plans for the expanded educational program.

The Kones were soon to say farewell to Oregon. Mrs. Kone was far from robust in health and her husband seemed to have been poorly adapted both physically and spiritually for the role of missionary. He secured a release with comparative ease and within a few weeks he and his family took passage on the Hudson's Bay bark, *Columbia.*

Mr. and Mrs. Frost went back to their task, though almost converted to the belief that it was futile to spend their lives trying to salvage the red people of this area. The Indians were fewer in number than had been originally supposed. The many dialects spoken made hopeless the thought of reducing them to a form for which an alphabet might be devised. The prospect of trying to teach the natives in English was equally discouraging. Yet duty was duty and the Frosts made an attempt. The Reverend Frost soon learned to communicate with his charges in the Chinook jargon but this was so limiting that he found it altogether inadequate for impressing the meaning of the Gospel on their "dark minds." With the help of the head chief, however, Frost did succeed in bringing some of the natives together in his home for hymn singing and simple Scripture expositions. When the meeting was over, the Indians pronounced it "good" and promised to attend the next service. But when the appointed time arrived these Indians were widely scattered—fishing, shooting fowl or diverting themselves in other ways. The congregation consisted of the chief, his wives and a single slave.

This indifference to the call of Christianity did not mean that the missionaries were to be ignored socially. At the opening of the fishing season the Frosts were invited to a salmon feast at the lodge of one of the head men, Wasuksul. The guests sat on clean mats and ate the choicest pieces of roasted salmon. There was nothing lacking in Indian hospitality.

The natives here regarded as slavery any activity that bore the slightest resemblance to work. The Frosts attempted to hire Indian help, hoping in this way to teach them some of the arts of civilization, but it failed. At the first opportunity the Indian man or maid would run away to the old life of dignity and penury. Frost's nearest neighbor, Tawint, was the very epitome of indolence. One day he promised to carry in some wood but soon gave up and went to lie down by the fire. When called to task for not finishing the job, he replied, "Other people get horses and blankets for working. I get nothing but a little to eat. You make me a slave."

Mr. Frost scolded Tawint, recalling the number of times that Sara Frost had carried him food. "The whites are really the slaves," said the missionary. "You should be grateful to them for putting a roof over your head."

"Oh," replied the Indian languidly, "what of those boards? They simply lie there, don't they?"

Mr. Birnie was fond of telling about an old Chinook woman, ill with fever, who came to him for medicine. He complied and when she had recovered she came back to him, saying, "I took a great deal of your bad medicine. Perhaps you will now give me some tea and sugar and something else good."

Infant mortality was appalling among these Indians, and infanticide a common practice. The women had no hesitance in telling Mrs. Frost the number of children they had disposed of. One woman said she had destroyed all her offspring except the last, a son. Her husband had threatened to kill her if she took the life of this child. Sara Frost asked the reason for this nefarious custom and was told that the lot of women was nothing but unending drudgery.

Many children were afflicted with venereal diseases, which took a heavy toll. Tuberculosis was prevalent, as was the "cole sick-waum sick," to which even the natives did not seem to become immune. In addition to diseases, there were some vicious practices that were hard to combat. Frost had reasons to suspect that in a few instances victims were actually buried alive. When he attempted to do a little investigating, he received the vague answer, *"Cultus michemus"* (bad slave).

Though the rain of winter came down in steady streams, Frost went dutifully from lodge to lodge, trying to teach simple Bible truths. He found Indians hungry and unable to listen. From the mission stores he fed many during those lean months—a hopeless, degraded, diseased, improvident lot, he believed them to be.

Jason Lee made an effort to keep the branch missions alive, but by the late summer of 1843, many of his helpers, released from their obligations, were taking passage for the States. Joseph Frost's throat trouble had run into a bad case of bronchitis and he was forced to request a release. He and his family sailed on the bark *Diamond* in August. Other passengers were Daniel Lee and Dr. Ira Babcock and their families.

Some workers left the mission field glad to be free of an unpleasant assignment, others with a feeling of regret that they had been able to accomplish so little. Most believed that they had helped prepare the natives for the inevitable day when the Americans would be the masters of all of Oregon. The Frosts gave their best to the cause and frequently looked back with a feeling of pleasure to the days they spent at Clatsop by the Sea. After they had left Oregon Daniel Lee and Joseph Frost collaborated in the writing of their experiences under the title, *Ten Years in Oregon.*

The most successful of all the Methodist missions in Oregon was the branch at The Dalles, started by Daniel Lee and H. K. W. Perkins in the summer of 1838. The mission post, called Wascopam, was located about three miles below The Dalles on the south side of the Columbia River. Both men were dedicated to the cause. Immediately on arriving, they began the practice of calling the Indians together on the Sabbath for instruction. The natives, squatting on the ground, were a quiet, bewildered lot. Sometimes they knelt in prayer when the missionaries gave the signal; sometimes they just looked and wondered.

Building went on very slowly, occupying the entire winter. This was due in large part to the loss of time spent on the rivers, bringing in supplies. It was estimated that each man spent five months out of the first year traveling in a canoe. In addition, Daniel went overland and brought back horses from Walla Walla and cattle from the Willamette. The remaining time was spent in farming, fencing, making harness and repairing tools. By degrees the housing was completed and all supplies gotten under cover.

Meanwhile, Daniel studied the native language and attended to his ministerial duties. Morning and evening prayers were said, and a passage of the Scriptures read and explained to any Indians who happened to be present. The Sunday congregations increased in size when the fishing season ended. The Dalles was a wintering place for a considerable number of natives. With December came the season of Indian festivities when the singing, dancing, chanting and drumming could be heard for miles. First one medicine man and then another would open his lodge for the dancing, which continued sometimes for five successive nights. A bright fire always blazed in the center. All danced—old and young, men, women and children. Or they danced solo, as each sang the song of his dream faith.

When a person had an urge to perform he leaped into the small arena, which was an elkskin spread in front of the fire, and kept time to the long, measured knocking of a pole suspended horizontally and struck endwise against a wide cedar board. Through all kinds of steps, jumping, chanting and cavorting, the dancer appealed to his *tah-mah-na-wis,* or guardian spirit, until he fell as one dead, completely under the influence of his "familiar." At this juncture, the medicine man would step in, using all the skill at his command to bring the dancer out of his trance. Around and around the unconscious person the old mesmerizer would go, muttering low and peeping and hooting at the toes, ears and fingers. If the magic worked, the dancer would shudder slightly, turn over, groan in a sepulchral tone and—yes, live again.

Like most natives, the Wasco Indians were superstitious and naïvely credulous. Fire-eating was a feat that caused whole congregations to stare in openmouthed wonder. Daniel Lee had heard so much about a celebrated fire-eater that he made up his mind to put the fellow to the test. He sought out the miracle man and said rather shortly, "Let me see you eat fire." All the self-confidence the Indian had possessed suddenly left him, and he stood before the missionary sheepish and reluctant.

"Let me see you do it," Lee repeated. "You cannot do it. You dare not try."

Not daring to risk his reputation before those who had seen him devour the blazing torch many times, the magician suddenly stepped forward, crying, "*Al-ta-nan-ich!* (See the doctor eat fire!)" Taking a bundle of small sticks, he lighted the ends, put them into his mouth, closed his lips and extinguished the flames.

A smile of triumph came to rest on every dark face. Meanwhile Daniel Lee took a bundle of sticks, lighted them and then proceeded to extinguish the flame by putting a kettle over them. "See," he said, "fire cannot live without air. Just like people." Turning to the conjurer, he said accusingly, "You deliberately deceive your people, don't you?"

"Oh, *nawitka* (certainly)," the Indian replied nonchalantly.

The medicine men were the most influential people among the Indians. According to popular belief, these great men held intercourse with spirits of another world and could command them at will. They could send a bad spirit into the body of an innocent person, causing his death unless counteracted by another, more powerful medicine. The services of the medicine men, much sought after, were paid for in advance. If the patient died the fee was returned; otherwise, the doctor might be charged with causing the death. There was not always good faith between the medicine men and their patients, or among the conjurers themselves. Sometimes the physician took all the worldly possessions of his patient, and instances were known in which medicine men contrived to have a rival killed for alleged malpractice.

Troubles among the Indians caused Lee and Perkins no little concern. Often there were disputes over property when a member of the tribe died. Lee became involved in one of these. The wife of Tah-lac-eow-it, a prominent Indian living near the mission, died of tuberculosis. Shortly after the burial a brother of the deceased came and demanded a division of the property. Finally the argument developed into fisticuffs and hair-pulling and the flourishing of knives. Lee happened along at what seemed to be the climax and succeeded in disarming both. Then, without ceremony, he took the aggressor by the hair and put him out of the lodge.

Before the Hudson's Bay Company established control, there was sporadic warfare among the tribes living along the Columbia River. They raided each other's salmon caches, fought for the possession of slaves and, in general, made river travel dangerous for everybody. Indians habitually lay in wait at the portages to demand tribute from passing brigades. But all this piracy had been stopped by the time the missionaries arrived.

During the illness of Cyrus Shepard in the fall of 1839, Daniel Lee was called to the Willamette to be with him for a few weeks. While he was away, the Reverend and Mrs. Perkins conducted a series of revival meetings that had brought about a miraculous change in the lives of many of the savages. Daniel was incredulous until he returned and found that what Perkins had told him was literally true. Public meetings were now held in the new Indian room but the Sunday congregations overflowed into the living room. Visiting Indians were showing signs of interest. One of the reclaimed Indians, called "Boston" by his people because his head was not flattened, attracted the attention of Mr. Perkins by his early rising in the mornings. When asked why he did this, Boston replied that the Gospel kept him awake. Whenever he slept he dreamed that he was at the revival meetings with his heart continually talking about what the preachers had said.

"All my life," he said, "my heart has been asleep. Now it is awake."

Many of the Indians learned to pray, both in their lodges and in public. One prayer, translated by Daniel Lee follows:

> O thou great God on high, we now pray to thee. Our fathers knew thee not, they died in darkness, but we have heard of thee, now we see a little. Truly we are wretched! Our hearts were blind—dark as night—always foolish; our ears closed. Our hearts were bad—all bad—full of evil—nothing good—not one. Thou knowest. Our hearts are hard like stone. Give us light. . . . Formerly, we stole, told lies, were full of anger. Now done. *Nash-ke-alka-ka-dow!* Never again so. Behold and bless.

One old Indian opposed the revival meetings because he said they lifted up the lower classes and made men of them. His conscience seemed to prick him but he continued to resist the spirit until Daniel Lee's persuasiveness finally won him. As they were going out to pray one day, Lee asked the Indian how he felt now.

"Oh," said the fellow, "my heart is very small and sorrowful. Yesterday I prayed almost all day behind that hill. But my heart is still bad."

After they had reached most of the Indians at Wascopam Lee and Perkins expanded the work from village to village down the river as far as the Cascades. At this latter place, as many as 1200 natives came to hear Lee. While he never knew the number converted, this was the most soul-satisfying experience he had ever known.

The great revival at Wascopam had a good effect on many,

many Indians but so far as some were concerned it was only temporary. It was too much to believe that savages could be so quickly transformed, and for all time to come. The "old Adam," Lee noted, was soon in evidence again. Tradition was often more compelling than the new "medicine" of the missionaries. Lee and Perkins were many times shocked at the application the savages occasionally made of Christian doctrine. One of the basic principles of Methodist teaching was reliance on prayer. The Indians expected material things, and when these did not come in answer to their petitions the red men were inclined to lose faith and reproach their teachers. A man approached Mr. Perkins one day and said, "I want a coat."

"Well, you must work for it then," the missionary replied.

"Oh," said the fellow, "I was told that if I took your medicine and prayed for what I needed I would get it. If I'm to work for a coat I can earn one any time from the Hudson's Bay Company."

Shortly after the close of the revival meetings at The Dalles, a Christian Indian was murdered in cold blood by one of the prominent men of the village. For a time it seemed that this tragedy might undo all the good that had been accomplished. It did have adverse results. More Indians lost faith in the power of the palefaces' religion. "What's the use of praying," some moaned. "Our brother prayed, but now he is dead. If prayer will not keep us from dying, why should we pray? And if we pray as your religion teaches us we cannot avenge the death of our relative."

It took patience, pleading and prayer, but Mr. Perkins managed to prevent the murdered man's family from requiring a life for a life, according to the first principle of Indian justice. It was a time of great stress for all concerned. On their own admission, the Indians' hearts were not very "full of pray." But the crisis passed and, though others followed, the missionaries had cause to feel they were accomplishing something toward winning the natives over to the ways of Christian civilization.

In the summer of 1840 Daniel Lee's lonely life was brightened when Maria Ware arrived to become his bride. While they were at Wascopam two sons were born to them. Maria's health soon became so feeble as to require most of her husband's attention. When this time came both thought it best to leave Oregon, Lee was given a release and in late August of 1843 he and his family boarded the bark *Diamond* to return home. Daniel had been in Oregon since 1834 and had given his all unstintingly to the mission cause. His was the only successful mission established by the Methodists. With the Lees on the *Diamond* were several other families who had had no heart for their work and who rejoiced in being released from thankless and irksome tasks.

As these Methodists followed the Columbia River out, they might have heard, if they had been listening, the sound of creaking wagon wheels breaking a deep and permanent trail to Oregon.

8 · *Curtain*

BY THE AUTUMN OF 1843 JASON Lee had decided to make another trip east, tedious and hazardous as it might be. For more than a year he had been painfully aware of a growing lack of confidence on the part of the Board of Missions. This, Lee believed, was the result of unfavorable reports made to the society by returning members of his own mission. He referred specifically to W. H. Kone, Dr. Richmond and Dr. Elijah White, whose barbed criticisms were not only hurtful to him personally but damaging to the mission cause as well.

For some time the Board had been expressing outright impatience because so little was being done for the Indians. Lee had been replying that quick returns could not be expected. Patiently he explained that he believed the redemption of the natives to be a long-time project in which material as well as spiritual forces must have a vital part. But the Board could not see eye to eye with the superintendent of the Oregon missions. With Lee unable to give tangible proof that the Indians were being benefited spiritually, the feeling was that time, effort and money were being squandered. Another criticism was that the missionaries seemed to be too much enthralled with worldly business. From the first some of Lee's assistants had argued that the work should be "purely spiritual." These had criticized their superintendent for spending so much time in the management of farms, mills, livestock and schools exclusively for the white population.

Although things in Oregon were going more smoothly after the dissatisfied members of the mission staff had left the field, Lee felt that soon he would be asked by the board for a financial accounting. His plans had not worked out one hundred per cent —of that he was fully aware. Because of Indian hostility, he had been forced to abandon the Umpqua project without ever sending a man there. By 1843 the Nisqually mission had been closed, and Clatsop by the Sea was accomplishing practically nothing. Some of his best helpers had been forced, for health reasons, to ask for releases. Jason Lee had a vision of the future of Oregon which few could comprehend. Those on the mission board who understood it, were not in sympathy. Why, they argued, should the Methodist Church finance colonizing schemes, even if they were nobly patriotic?

Lee wanted to go east. Perhaps he saw the handwriting on the wall. At any rate, the more he thought about it the more fervent became his desire. Yes, he would give an account of his stewardship and he would do it successfully, provided he could meet the board face to face. And regardless of how tongues might wag, Lee intended also to do some "must" things of a worldly nature. He intended to ask Congress for a title to the vast land claims of the Methodists. Further, he would request appropriations for his Indian Manual Labor School as well as for the Oregon Institute. The latter was the only one of its kind in Oregon, and would certainly be a godsend to the immigrant families that were filling up the Willamette Valley. The board, without question, should be made aware of the importance of the location of the various branch missions and with the value of the properties attached to them. The Congress of the United States as well should know all of this. These facts, the Lord being willing, Jason Lee would present when he went east.

He engaged passage on the English bark *Columbia,* which sailed for the Sandwich Islands February 3, 1844. A voyage of twenty-four days brought him to Honolulu. At the dock he was met by Dr. Ira Babcock, a mission associate who had been in the Islands since the previous September and who was preparing now to return to Oregon. He had shocking news for Lee, but this would be revealed after the two had gone to the doctor's residence. "You have been removed from your post." This, in effect, was the message that awaited Jason Lee. He had been recalled without a hearing before the board. The Reverend George Gary had been appointed as his successor and was already on his way to Oregon.

Lee maintained his composure, calmly announcing that he intended to carry out his original plan. Since no ship was leaving for the United States for several months, Lee seemed hopelessly stranded until he learned that a small vessel was about to sail for Mexico. He grasped the opportunity. The little schooner docked at Mazatlan and from there Lee made his way by difficult stages across Mexico to Vera Cruz. Thence he traveled in a mail packet to New Orleans where he boarded a river steamer whose destination was Pittsburgh. He arrived in New York City May 27, 1844.

Here he found the Methodist Conference in session and deeply absorbed in a case involving the slavery question. Lee at once applied to the Mission Board for a hearing but its time was so taken up that the Oregon business had to wait. The board advised Lee to go to Washington, D.C. and present the mission land claims to the President of the United States. President John Tyler assured him that an Oregon bill, then under consideration, would be passed in the near future. And the Methodist land claims, he was reasonably sure, would be respected.

On July 1, 1844 the Board of Managers of the Missionary Society called a special meeting for the purpose of giving Jason Lee the opportunity to present his case. The main charges against him were summed up as: failure to give a satisfactory report concerning mission property; wrong use of mission funds, especially for private speculation; failure to make the missions of benefit to the Indians for whom they had been created. Calmly and in a matter-of-fact way, Lee stood before the board and answered in detail all the charges that had been preferred against him. The hearing lasted ten days, and for hours each day Lee untiringly and forthrightly made his defense. He spared no item that would clarify his position, explain his every motive and, in general, give a vivid overall picture of the mission work in Oregon.

There was no question but that he made an admirable defense. After hearing everything he had to say, the Mission Board exonerated him from the charges made by disgruntled fellow-workers in Oregon. It is probable that he might have been permitted to continue as head of the Oregon mission if Dr. George Gary had not already been appointed. However, Lee was allowed to retain his title, "Missionary to Oregon."

When Lee had been freed from any suspicion of wrongdoing a load rolled off his heart. But, worn out physically by his strenuous trip across Mexico and by the strain of those ten days before the Board, he made up his mind to go home to Canada for a long rest. He remained in New York until the last week in July, then went to attend the New England Methodist Conference at Westfield, Massachusetts. Here, with eloquence and enthusiasm, he spoke out in favor of the land claims of the Oregon mission and for the school for whites which he had founded. At his own request, he was appointed "Agent for the Oregon Institute." It was his firm intention to return to Oregon where his heart lay, but he would first spend a year or two traveling around raising funds for the support of the institution. The vision of a new Oregon was still bright before his eyes.

In August Lee reached his old home in Stanstead, Canada, where he was joyfully received by his oldest sister, Mary Lee Morrill, who had been almost a second mother to him. Here, on her farm, he relaxed, hoping to be completely restored within a few weeks. But in late summer, much to his annoyance, he contracted a severe cold that he was unable to throw off. He lost weight steadily and his strength drained away. Although weak from the ravages of several weeks of illness, one Sunday in autumn he dragged himself out to preach in the little Stanstead church, a sermon which proved to be his last. The November wind sent a chill through his wasted body, but had no effect on his well sustained spirit. From the pulpit, he declared that he had never been "more alive to God, alive to the salvation of souls and alive to Oregon," than he was on that occasion.

As the winter months went by, Jason Lee began to realize that his work on earth was about done. Unless a change for the better appeared soon, he should never return to Oregon where in the sacred grove slept his two wives, equally beloved, and his infant son. He thought of his daughter much during those days when he coughed incessantly, rested little and suffered much. After he was too weak to write, he dictated a letter to the Reverend Gustavus Hines, the guardian of Lucy Anna. Referring to the child, he said, "Let her have, if possible, a first-rate education, but above all, do not neglect her religious education. Dear Brother and Sister Hines, I must hold you responsible under God, to train that child for heaven." [12]

When the physician pronounced his case hopeless, Lee made a request for Daniel to come to his bedside. It was none too soon, for the first missionary to Oregon had about reached the end of his journey. He died March 12, 1845, of tuberculosis and strictures in the intestines. He was buried in the little cemetery at Stanstead. As the cold earth of early spring closed over his grave, the mourners listened to the comforting words from the Book of Job: "I know that my Redeemer liveth."

Jason Lee had been exposed to the dangers of two sea voyages and three trips across the United States from ocean to ocean but Providence decreed that he should breathe his last in the arms of his family and at his birthplace. He died at the age of forty-two—his work completed in his early prime. Friends and relatives felt that Daniel Lee had voiced their sentiments when he said in the obituary notice: "His sun has gone down at noon."

The Oregon missions survived their founder a scant two years. When the new superintendent, Dr. George Gary, arrived in Oregon in June, 1844, he carried full power to do as he thought fit with the mission posts. He had the authority to write the last chapter in a project that had been ten years in the making. Dr.

Gary was soon convinced that the missions, with the exception of Wascopam at The Dalles, were not serving their intended purpose. Little by little he closed out the business of the Methodist Board of Missions in Oregon. He dismissed all the laymen connected with the various posts and sold the property, including livestock and mills. The Indian Manual Labor School, which had never served more than a small number of Indians, was sold to the trustees of the Oregon Institute for $4000. It had cost in the neighborhood of $10,000. Gary was criticized by some of the Methodists for selling it at such a financial loss when the Catholics had offered a much larger sum. Finally, Gary entered into negotiations with Dr. Marcus Whitman for the sale of The Dalles mission at a consideration of $600. Strong protests were again registered but to no avail. The transfer was made in August 1847, the year of the Whitman massacre, the year that closed all the Protestant missions in Oregon.

One by one, the remaining missionaries left the field. Those who chose to stay became settlers in the new Oregon that came into the possession of the United States through a treaty with England in 1846. Gustavus Hines was through in 1845. In September of that year he and his family and his ward, Lucy Anna Lee, left Oregon. It was his opinion that Jason Lee would never return, and that it was best for the child to be nearer her father. He could not know it, but at that time Jason Lee had been in his grave six months. When the Hines family arrived in the United States, they were fourteen months too late for Lucy Anna to see her father.

What results were achieved by the Methodists in Oregon? They arrived in 1834 and finished their work in ten years. Between seventy and eighty persons, including children, formed the corps of mission workers. The cost to the Board of Missions was approximately a quarter of a million dollars. Were the results worth the cost and the effort? Except at The Dalles, the missions exerted but little direct influence on the Indians. As colonists, however, the missionaries were a strong moral force wherever they set up their pioneer stations. They prevented violence among the natives and furnished examples of civilized living. Although they could not convert the red man they could prepare him for the day when the whites would dominate the land. The missionaries were the vanguard of thousands of American settlers. They started schools and industries and set up a civil government for themselves. At their head stood Jason Lee, the prophet of a new Oregon—missionary, colonizer, politician. Reverend Hines paid him high tribute when he said: "Jason Lee's work can never die; its influence will flow on through channels measureless by man forever. His place as first and most influential in determining the course of history in the Northwest can never be successfully contested."

PART TWO

MISSIONARIES OF THE AMERICAN BOARD

9 • *"Unheard-of Journey for Females"*

IT WAS FEBRUARY 18, 1836, AND the wedding night of Narcissa Prentiss. Friends and relatives had congregated in the little Presbyterian Church in Angelica, New York, to witness the ceremony. For days this event had been the subject of every conversation. News had traveled fast and it was soon common knowledge that Dr. Marcus Whitman had returned from his preliminary trip to the Rocky Mountains and was going to take a bride thither from their midst.

There had been other weddings in the village, to be sure, but this one was different. Narcissa, the beautiful accomplished daughter of an old respected family, was renouncing the world and marrying herself to a life of service among the Indians of Oregon. She would follow over prairie and mountain a trail which no white woman's foot had ever before trod. Just to look upon the face of a lady with such courage was an inspiration in itself. Surely this was an extraordinary occasion.

Every eye turned with well guarded curiosity as Judge Stephen Prentiss and his family entered and took their places in the pew. Narcissa and her sisters walked on to the choir and assumed their accustomed seats. Now the church was filled and the last tones of the bell died away in a prolonged echo. The choir members turned pages as the organist began the prelude. After a solemn hymn, the minister opened his Bible and read: "Go ye into all the world and teach all nations."

When the sermon was finished there were murmurs of expectancy as the scene shifted for the wedding ceremony. To the chancel rail came the bridal pair, the groom bearded and bronzed and wearing a plain dark suit; the bride, not in white satin but in black bombazine and with no veil to hide her shining hair. If not really beautiful, Narcissa Prentiss was striking in appearance. Somewhat above the medium height for women, she was well formed and the picture of health. Her skin was fair and her large eyes shone now blue, now gray from a frank pleasant face. But most conspicuous was her hair: long and fine and gleaming gold, it was a unique decoration that made her unforgettable, even to those who had seen her but once.

Narcissa stood at the altar, probably the calmest person in the crowded church. The future was clear before her. When she was a child of eleven, she had knelt at the "mourners' bench" and dedicated her life to God. Now the time had come for her to take an active part in the conversion of the heathen—and she was ready. Still, there would be the breaking of home ties. The large family had been a close-knit one. Her father, mother, four brothers and four sisters—she must leave them all, perhaps forever.

Beside Narcissa stood Marcus Whitman, with whom she was taking the sacred vows. While not a stranger, Marcus was certainly not a suitor of long standing. They had been engaged about a year, but the doctor had spent most of that time in his preliminary trip to the Rocky Mountains. Whitman was a medical doctor with a strong religious bent. At one time he had considered preparing for the ministry and he had been waiting for an opportunity to go into some mission field. In 1835, he was appointed by the American Board of Commissioners for Foreign Missions to accompany Dr. Samuel Parker on a tour of the West to find out what the prospects were for establishing a mission. This board consisted of representatives of several churches: the Dutch Reformed, the Congregational and the Presbyterian.

Dr. Whitman did not complete the journey to Oregon. Fully convinced by the attitude of the Nez Perce Indians met at the mountain rendezvous that the time was ripe for missions, Whitman let Parker explore the situation in Oregon while he returned home to urge the American Board to act at once. He told the board he was willing to serve in any capacity, as far as he was able—not only as physician, but as farmer, teacher, preacher or common laborer. He was promptly made manager of the small missionary group to be sent early in 1836.

The board believed that the superintendent of the Oregon mission should be married. This set Marcus Whitman to thinking. Up to that time he had found no one who he thought would be the perfect wife so at the age of thirty-three he was still a bachelor. It happened that Narcissa Prentiss was looking around for a more effective way of serving God. She applied to the American Board for an appointment but was informed that "unmarried females" were not being accepted for foreign fields. When Marcus, through the medium of the mission board, found out about this young lady he decided to renew his slight acquaintance with Judge Prentiss' family and perhaps persuade Miss Narcissa to go with him to Oregon. They seemed suited to each other and when, after a brief courtship, he asked her to be his wife she replied, "It is God's course. I will go."

Narcissa did not know whether she loved this tall strong man with the brown hair, the sparkling blue eyes and the determined chin. There had been too little time. Anyway, love was only secondary; her marriage was a matter of duty—her only door to mission work. In her diary she wrote, *We must do our courtship now that we are married.*

Narcissa Prentiss was not a schoolgirl. She was nearly twenty-eight—an "old maid" in the thinking of that day. But she was not a hothouse plant, pining away because no man had come to pluck her from the parent stem. Educated, intelligent and self-reliant, she had built a career in the "school for infants" which she and her sister, Jane Abigail, had successfully conducted. But now had come the opportunity to fulfill her obligations to God, and—love or not—her course was clear.

Visions of the past and the future flashed through the bride's mind in minutes. Almost before she was aware of it the ceremony was over and she found herself joining in the parting hymn, "Yes, my native land, I love thee." The words might tear at her heartstrings but Narcissa sang on through the second and third stanzas with unfaltering voice and tones rich and true. By this time different members of the choir were singing haltingly and suppressed sobs could be heard throughout the congregation. Still

Narcissa's sweet soprano voice rang out like bells from a wayside chapel. The last stanza was assigned to the bride as a solo. All the Prentiss family were musical but Narcissa's ability was outstanding. Now, to the amazement of all who knew her best, she carried the verse through without wavering:

In the desert let me labor,
On the mountains let me tell
How He died, the blessed Savior
To redeem the world from hell.
Let me hasten far in heathen lands to dwell.

Suddenly it was all over. The song was finished; the benediction said. Candles were snuffed out and the congregation dispersed.

The next day saw the bride and groom putting finishing touches to their packing. All too soon the sleigh was at the gate with the horses pawing the snow in their impatience to be off. Muffled in their overcoats, John and Richard, the Nez Perce Indian boys whom Dr. Whitman had brought back from the mountains, sat in the rear with the baggage. Narcissa was helped into the seat beside her husband and they were away on the first lap of the adventure that Narcissa described as "an unheard-of journey for females." The runners creaked frostily and there was a musical squeak in the harness as the loaded sleigh broke track and slid out into the lane made white with winter. At the last turn Narcissa lifted a mittened hand and waved a final farewell to Angelica, friends and home.

The trip across Pennsylvania was made step by step. Sleighs were hired by the day from one place to the next. Jerking along in the bright sunlight of midday or in the gloom of a March twilight, Narcissa found much to occupy her thoughts. Marcus—as his wife soon found out—was often silent, as if he had a heavy weight on his mind. The doctor, indeed, had many problems, for this was more than a honeymoon journey. It was a missionary enterprise of which he was the responsible manager. The whole physical setup of the man indicated ability to cope with all reasonable situations. Intelligence was written in the high forehead, determination in the prominent chin and firm-set mouth. He was

whose course they were to follow to the Rocky Mountains. The missionaries quickly adjusted themselves to the regulations of travel, rising when the call was given, doing guard duty and joining the hunters in the chase. Eliza Spalding was miserable, but once the routine was established Narcissa enjoyed the novelty of it all. She spoke to her diary daily, and wrote numerous letters. To the home folks, she said enthusiastically, "I wish all of you were going with us to the dear Indians."

Into the hollows and over the hills, hour after hour and day after day, the caravan crawled. Sometimes a shower burst upon the train with deafening thunderclaps, blinding flashes of lightning and sheets of falling water. But mostly the weather was kind, for it was springtime. Came the buffalo country, when fresh meat was a treat to the missionaries. It suited Narcissa's taste to perfection and she wrote, "We have meat and tea in the morn and tea and meat at noon—all our variety consists in the different ways of cooking. . . . So long as I have buffalo meat, I do not care for anything else." But the time came when even she was "cloyed with it" and wrote, "I do not know how I shall endure this part of the journey." Eliza could not eat buffalo meat, no matter how it was cooked. It nauseated her, so she had to depend for sustenance entirely upon cow's milk. Miraculously, it seemed, she recovered from one weak spell after another and the cavalcade, which slackened its speed for no one, pressed on to its first goal, Fort Laramie, where a rest of a few days was enjoyed.

Then they were at the mountain rendezvous, which this year was held on a little tributary of the Green River. It was the same riotous place that had greeted Jason Lee two years before. The women naturally aroused a good deal of curiosity. The mountain men held frail Mrs. Spalding in high regard. They considered her talented and refined, though not so handsome as Mrs. Whitman. They noted that her gentle, winning manners attracted the Indian women, who liked to linger around the pale, dark-haired lady of the wagon. Narcissa's company was more generally sought by the men. She was vivacious and fond of humor and always had a friendly word for everybody. Bashful trappers contented themselves with parading before her tent, hoping to get an approving glance from her. If she rewarded them they would touch their beaverskin caps and go away happy. Joe Meek, a mountain man not afflicted with bashfulness, boldly presented himself to Mrs. Whitman, walked with her, rode with her and entertained her with tall tales of encounters with grizzlies and skirmishes with Blackfeet.

The time at the rendezvous passed quickly. Since the caravan went no farther Whitman made arrangements to travel the remainder of the distance under the escort of Thomas McKay of the Hudson's Bay Company as Jason Lee had done two years before. Here they were faced with the problem of the wagon—Spalding's light one with the yellow wheels trimmed with blue. The heavy vehicle had been left behind at Fort Laramie. Even the small wagon—some argued—would be a decided handicap in crossing the mountains, and Narcissa secretly hoped it would come to a bad end. It had already caused her husband untold toil and trouble in crossing rivers. But Marcus Whitman was stubborn, and in the end his will prevailed. The wagon went. On July 18 the missionary party struck their tents and set out on the last 900 miles of the journey.

There was nothing but toil, fatigue and anxiety crossing the rugged country to Fort Hall, where they stopped to rest. The women especially came to look forward to these "houses of entertainment" where they could once again enjoy a few of the comforts of civilized life. One of the most trying parts of the journey was crossing the arid, sunbaked Snake River Plains. The hot southwest wind blew continuously. There were lengthy marches without drinking water and many camping places where mosquitoes almost drove the animals mad. It became necessary to discard more of their belongings. Months before, Spalding had reluctantly abandoned his prized theological books. But the load now had to be further lightened at almost any cost because the Snake River was strong, swift and treacherous. The wagon was taken apart and made into a two-wheeled cart, but even with this operation it became doubtful in all but the mind of Marcus Whitman that the vehicle could go much farther. Narcissa had to part with a little trunk in which she kept her treasured mementoes. It did not have to rot by the wayside, however, for Thomas McKay got permission to take it. "And thus we scatter as we go along," Narcissa wrote philosophically. At Island Ford the cart tipped over and the mules lost their footing. It was a dangerous and an exhausting task to untangle the animals and rescue the battered cart from what threatened to be a watery grave.

On August 19 the begrimed travelers drew up to another "house of entertainment"—the Snake Fort, later to be known as Fort Boise. Here the women were given time to do their washing, while the men made ever-needed repairs on saddles, bridles and harness. At long last Dr. Whitman was persuaded to leave what remained of the wagon and not attempt to take it over the Blue Mountains.

The Snake River had to be crossed once more. Luckily the missionaries were able to bargain with the Indians for a boat—a queer-looking contraption just large enough for the women and their saddles. Narcissa described it as a bunch of rushes tied together and attached to a willow frame. (It was probably a bullboat of a sort.) When the women were seated in this glorified sewing basket, two Indians on horseback, each with a rope attached to the boat, towed the queer craft across the river. Thrilled by the experience, Narcissa wrote in her diary that evening:

> Oh, if father and mother, and the girls could have seen us in our snug little canoe floating on the water! We were favorites of the company. No one else was privileged with a ride in it.[13]

As the journey drew to an end Marcus Whitman became eager to press on ahead. He wanted to consult with Dr. Samuel Parker and Dr. John McLoughlin on the location of the mission and get things operating as soon as possible. It was decided that William Gray and a company man would accompany the Whitmans on the rapid forward advance; the Spaldings, with the hired men, the Indian boys, the stock and the baggage, would follow more slowly under the guidance of Chief Rotten Belly. On the first day of September, 1836, the first white woman to cross the continent to Oregon rode up to the gates of Fort Walla Walla. Pierre Pambrun, officer in charge, welcomed another missionary party to the West and extended a hospitable hand in the name of

Hudson's Bay Company. The Spalding party arrived September 3, and by that time Whitman had made arrangements to go to Fort Vancouver by barge. A few days later, on a midafternoon, the party—with the exception of the two Indian boys, who had gone to their homes—embarked in a large bateau manned by six French-Canadians. After a horseback ride of more than a thousand miles, it was restful to glide along so easily on the current of the mighty Columbia. "It's waters are as clear as crystal," Narcissa wrote, "and smooth as a sea of glass, exceeding the beauty of the Ohio."

At Fort Vancouver Whitman was disappointed to learn that Dr. Samuel Parker, having made his survey of Oregon, had taken passage on a ship bound for the States, leaving the superintendent of the mission-to-be to his own devices. Whitman and Spalding did not delay, but set out at once to select sites for the missions. By this time they were both certain that there would have to be two missions instead of one. The overland journey had convinced both that they could not work together harmoniously in the same station. As finally decided, Henry Spalding would go as teacher to the Nez Perces and Dr. Whitman would minister to the Cayuses and neighboring tribes near Walla Walla.

It was thought advisable for the women to remain at Vancouver for a few weeks until sites had been chosen and shelters built. Before she left, Narcissa visited the store and bought several articles for John and Richard. She had a sincere attachment for the Indian boys and declared, "We shall treat them as our own as long as they deserve it."

As guests of the fort, Eliza and Narcissa were treated so graciously that time did not drag. They visited the dairy, the large farms and the orchard. Once a week they rode horseback, sometimes with the Indian wife of Dr. McLoughlin. They visited the village where lived the employees of the company, and the school attended by some fifty half-breed children. Narcissa enjoyed singing with the children for a half hour each day. One Indian woman and her daughter came for miles just to hear the palefaced lady sing.

On October 18 the Montreal Express arrived, and with it came Henry Spalding to conduct the women to their new mission homes. It was a cheerless day in November when the party, clad in raincoats, assembled at the dock where two thirty-two-foot bateaux loaded to capacity were waiting. The women settled down in their seats, the Canadian boatmen seized the oars and soon the giant canoes were plowing the dull gray waters of the Columbia. How different, thought Narcissa, from a few weeks previous! The chilling rain came down in a steady drizzle. Below, murky waters swashed restlessly against the boats. Above, the fog staged its own freakish pantomime. Appearing from nowhere, it rolled along the hills in frothy billows, then fell headlong in one soundless gigantic mass, swallowing up river, valley, and moving canoes, playing havoc with visibility. And through it all, the rain came down in a steady drizzle.

10 • *The Whitman Mission—Waiilatpu*

After ten wretched days of river travel and as many nights spent in chill encampment on the sodden shore, the party disembarked at Fort Walla Walla. Marcus Whitman was on hand to meet his wife and to confer with Spalding on mission business before the two families went their separate ways. Whitman had arranged for Narcissa to stay at the fort until their house was in somewhat better condition. She was several months' pregnant, and although her health was good the doctor did not want to expose her to any more hardships than necessary.

The Spaldings planned to go at once to their location. William H. Gray, who had done most of the work on the Whitman house, would accompany them. They expected to live in skin lodges until their habitation was ready. Now came the job of unloading the bateaux and of dividing the five tons of supplies.

More than a hundred mounted Nez Perces were waiting to escort their teachers into the Idaho hills. Twenty horses carried Spalding's share of the equipment and provisions. It was a sad day when Narcissa and Eliza had to part. On the long trip they had become warm friends—and now who knew when they would meet again?

One day in December Marcus came to Fort Walla Walla to take his wife to the mission house at Waiilatpu. "It is an agreeable thought," she said to her diary, "to be so near a fixed location after journeying so long."

It was night when she first saw her bare cabin home with no furniture and with blankets hung over the window and door openings. Soon a bright fire was burning in the wide hearth. The dampness disappeared and the room was cozy. Having come at last to the end of that "unheard-of journey for females," she sat down and wrote thankfully, "Where are we, and who are we, that we should be thus blessed of the Lord?" The next morning Narcissa hurried out to take a look at her surroundings. The house, she noted, stood near the bank of a small stream that came winding down through a pleasant valley. Rye grass—bleached now—covered the ridges that bordered the valley, and not far to the northeast rose a bald dome-shaped hill standing like a sentinel above the plain. This was Waiilatpu, the "place where the rye grass grows," said the Indians. The cabin would open its doors to Cayuse Indians and their neighbors and some time in the future it might be a house by the side of the road for trail-worn immigrants. For the immediate present it was just a little half-finished adobe shack which Narcissa called home. Writing to her mother about her surroundings, she said, "It is, indeed, a lovely situation."

The cabin had changed greatly in appearance within a few months. Doors and windows were in place, crude furniture acquired, two other rooms added. Mr. Pambrun donated a small heating stove and his wife gave Narcissa a washing machine—a barrel in which to pound the clothes.

Personalities played a part, too. Before long, Whitman was compelled to expel Richard for misbehavior. John was with the

Spaldings and doing well. Both boys had given excellent service but now Richard had become a disappointment to both the doctor and Narcissa. Another problem was the conduct of William Gray. He had done his part in building the two mission houses but was no longer content to serve in the humble capacity of carpenter and handy man. He wanted a mission station of his own and began scheming to get one. He selected Spokane as his field but Dr. Whitman rejected his proposal. Gray then left for Spokane and it was here that his two-fold purpose was conceived. With Indians to help, he would drive horses east and exchange them for cattle. He would convince the American Board of the need for more missionaries and perhaps lead the reinforcement party to Oregon. Being a man of decision, he lost no time in getting his horses and his Indian drivers and starting toward the Rocky Mountains.

Dr. Whitman early began establishing good relations with the Indians. Friendly chiefs allowed him the use of land for his buildings and farms. The Cayuses were haughty people who had never asked for white teachers. They were a small tribe, numbering only from two to three hundred, but with considerable collective wealth in horses. They and their neighbors, the Umatillas and the Walla Wallas, were typical plateau Indians, nomadic and averse to learning a "settled" way of life.

March 1837 found Whitman and his Indians breaking the sod for spring planting. Many seeds he had started out with had been discarded on the trail as excess baggage but what remained were put carefully into the ground. The natives were curious and some of them were really interested.

March brought to Marcus and Narcissa one of the greatest events in their lives. The fire in the mission house burned brightly all afternoon and evening of that windy day in early spring. The Indian woman, Mrs. Pambrun, moved silently around on moccasined feet, occasionally stopping to attend to the wants of her two small children. The doctor sat by Narcissa's bed and waited. The day became evening, and evening dragged on into the night. And then a child was born. Of this occasion, Narcissa later wrote the details in a letter beginning: "On the evening of my birthday, March 14, we received the gift of a little daughter—a treasure invaluable."

The days following were hectic ones for both Narcissa and the doctor. The place was thronged with Indian visitors for an entire week, all curious to see the little paleface. Her white skin, her large size and her strange clothes called forth endless comments. The white Cayuse was not bound to a cradle board! Unheard-of! She was not even going to have her head flattened but was to live forever a "turnip-head"!

Alice Clarissa—named for her two grandmothers—was the first white child born of American parents west of the Rocky Mountains. The day after her birth, Chief Tiloukaikt came in all his trappings and made an impressive demonstration. He was a great Indian. He gave permission to the missionaries to build on Cayuse land and now he insisted that the paleface child be called Cayuse *te-mi* (Cayuse girl) because she had been born on Cayuse land.

The Spaldings were expecting their child in November and Dr. Whitman planned to be in attendance. When the time approached, an Indian messenger arrived from Lapwai, bringing a leather lodge for the doctor's accommodation on the way. Though winter was coming on, Whitman decided to take his family with him. It would do the women good to visit with each other again. There was, indeed, a joyful reunion at Lapwai. For the time being old animosities were forgotten. The Whitmans were pleased to see John I-tes again and to learn that he was still contributing a worthy bit to the mission cause. On the morning of November 15, little Eliza arrived—the first white child of American parentage born in what later became the State of Idaho. The Whitmans prolonged their stay for three weeks. On the Sabbath before the families parted again Henry Spalding held baptismal services for the two infants.

Mrs. Whitman had a parent's natural pride in her child and her letters contained numerous examples of Alice Clarissa's precocity. However, she expressed concern about rearing her daughter among Indians. Alice early began to imitate their speech and it pleased them that the Cayuse *te-mi* was learning their language so readily. They appeared to have a real affection for the child and old Chief Cut-lip, who did not expect to live much longer, said he intended to give his land to the little pale Cayuse.

The Whitmans, regrettably, had but a short time in which to enjoy their "treasure invaluable." On a Sunday afternoon, June 23, 1839, she slipped away with her cup to get a drink of water from the river and was drowned. Although overwhelmed with grief, Narcissa could bravely say: "Lord, it must be right. She is not mine but Thine; she has been left to me for a brief season, and now, dearest Savior, Thou hast the best right to her. Thy will be done, not mine."

Narcissa did not let her sorrow embitter her life or interfere with her work at the mission. The child had been in her grave two years before condolences came from relatives in the States. In her frequent letters, Narcissa always made some reference to Alice Clarissa. Once she said: "Though her grave is in sight every time I step out of doors, yet my thoughts seldom wander there to find her. I seem to feel that she is not there, but in that bright world where joys are perfect."

Dr. Whitman had his hands and mind so full of mission problems that he had little time to brood. Settling the heathen, trying to convert them, healing their bodies and instructing their minds were enough to put him constantly to the stretch. By the fall of 1837 the school was started. Being a novelty, it was well attended at first. But trying to teach without a knowledge of the language or the aid of an interpreter was uphill business. Chief Lawyer of the Nez Perces lent considerable assistance, as did Umtippe before he became arrogant and mercenary and began demanding payment for the smallest service.

As to religious instruction, the doctor's purpose was to present a few plain truths from the Bible, beginning with the Ten Commandments. During the first year there was a gratifying show of interest, although some Indians always objected to hearing about sin and repentance. These clung to the customs of their forefathers. It was good to know nothing but to eat and drink, sleep and hunt, as in the olden days. Indians—whether young or old—were all children and had to be treated as such. They were sensitive to imagined slights, jealous of each other and frequently suspicious of the motives of their teachers. Toil was something all males were taught to avoid. Women and slaves were created to do the necessary drudgery. Some families refused to send their children to school for fear they might be compelled to work.

For the first year the natives showed respect for mission property. Narcissa could leave her clothes on the line all night without having them disturbed. But time brought an unhappy change. Some Indians grew envious of their teachers—envious of the house they lived in, of the food they ate and of the clothes they wore. Dr. Whitman ignored what he called petty annoyances and went courageously ahead with his program. He enlarged his house, built an Indian room and put $200 of his own money into farm implements to lend to the Indians.

As early as the spring of 1837 Dr. Whitman had some unpleasant experiences, which he tried to minimize. With the breakup of winter a sickness diagnosed as "inflamation of the lungs" became prevalent. The Indians—their suspicions aroused—began to complain that the medicine was "bad" and that the doctor was no good. The most serious case was that of the wife of old Umtippe. When Dr. Whitman said he had slight hopes for her recovery, the chief flew into a rage and said threateningly, "If woman die, you die." Knowing that Indians sometimes killed the *te-wat* who failed to cure, Whitman realized what might happen to him if this patient died. It was a relief when Umtippe dispensed with his services and sent to Walla Walla for a noted medicine man. The *te-wat* went through the usual conjurations, pronounced the evil spirit driven out, took his pay and left. The following morning the woman was ill as ever and again Umtippe swore death to all *te-wats*. Whitman refused to take the case again. Fortunately for everyone, the woman recovered without further medical help. In a few weeks, Umtippe himself came to the doctor for treatment. He was a very sick Indian for a while but eventually recovered. Again, a kind providence was on the side of Dr. Whitman.

The sickness ran its course at last, thus relieving the anxiety of the Whitmans. It was camas time in the grasslands and the whole tribe picked up lodges and set out for the hills.

Stickus, whom Narcissa called an "excellent Indian," returned ill and came to the mission for treatment. The medicine had a good effect but the poor fellow was restless and worried. There was a conflict in his mind. Reason told him that the practices of the *te-wats* were fraudulent, yet he could not give up tradition without a struggle. Narcissa and Marcus took turns sitting up at nights to give Stickus his medicine. He recovered and lived to be their staunchest Indian friend. Umtippe, however, was of a different mold. Narcissa's opinion of "that savage creature" was expressed thus:

> His heart is still the same; full of all manner of hypocracy, deceit, guilt. He is a mortal beggar, as all Indians are. If you ask a favor of him, sometimes it is granted, or not, just as he feels. If granted, it must be well paid for. A few days ago he took it into his head to require pay for teaching us the language and forbade his people coming and talking with us for fear we should learn a few words from them.

Some time after this—possibly three months—Mrs. Whitman had a different story to tell about Umtippe. One Saturday he came to the mission and announced he would spend the Sabbath there. He was concerned about his health—he had fainting spells and he would die soon, he declared. He was disturbed, too, about the welfare of his soul. He did not know where his soul would go when it quit his body, for he had been a wicked man. A sermon preached by Jason Lee, who happened to be a visitor at the mission, seemed to affect the chief deeply. He declared that he had seen the light as never before. This time he had really heard and understood the word of God. The Whitmans were thankful, and hopeful that this change in Umtippe's heart would be permanent. Now Narcissa could write with feeling:

> Never can a person manifest a greater change. This selfish, wicked, troublesome old chief now so still and attentive to the truth, so grateful for favors given.

On August 21, 1838, just as the last meeting in the revival series conducted by the Reverend Henry Spalding was closing, a messenger announced the approach of an overland party. There were all kinds of speculations till the leader of the group galloped up and was found to be none other than William H. Gray. He had been successful in his undertaking and was now bringing more missionaries. This was an agreeable surprise for Whitman in view of the fact that Secretary David Greene's last letter had not given any encouragement as to help for the near future.

In this small reinforcement party came Cornelius Rogers, a young single man, and four married couples: Gray, Cushing Eells, Elkanah Walker and Asa B. Smith and their wives. All were married just before starting west, so it was a honeymoon journey for the entire party, with the exception of Cornelius Rogers. Several meetings were held to discuss plans for broadening the scope of the work. Since the Spokane Indians had shown an eagerness for teachers, Walker and Eells were sent to that field. Eventually, A. B. Smith went to Kamiah on the Clearwater River above Lapwai; the others had to be content with being assistants wherever they were needed.

A man of less courage and determination than Dr. Whitman might have become discouraged; instead of improving, the Cayuses were becoming more and more of a problem. Whitman was forced to go to a great amount of work fencing his fields to keep the Indians' stock from ruining his grain. "Fences are also needed," declared Narcissa in not a very good humor, "to keep the Indians from making a highway of every part of the house and breaking our windows."

Some Indians were attending devotions pretty regularly but others resented the application of Bible teachings to their lives. They called it "bad talk" and ordered Dr. Whitman to stop. They rather enjoyed the Bible stories as such but they did not want their own actions called sin. One spring when the Indians returned from their wintering grounds Dr. Whitman suggested that they throw some of their lodges together and make a long house for public worship. They refused, saying that they wanted to worship in the doctor's new house. "Are there not houses in heaven in which to worship?" they asked.

The Cayuses thought Whitman was a fool for treating his wife with consideration. One day when he and Narcissa were getting ready to start to the Spokane mission, Chief Tiloukaikt asked the doctor, "Why do you take your woman with you? You see I'm here without my wife. Why do you pay so much attention to a woman?"

Marcus Whitman tried to explain that a wife was meant to be a companion but the chief failed to comprehend.

In the autumn and winter of 1839–1840, neither Narcissa nor her husband was well. It was fortunate that William Gray was there to shoulder most of the work of the mission. The long trips were exhausting to Marcus and irritated the pain in his side. (He is believed to have had appendicitis.) He became so completely spent that he prescribed for himself a two weeks' stay in bed. When he was up again he received an urgent call to attend some Indians at Walla Walla. In crossing the river, his horse stumbled and fell, throwing the doctor into the icy water. He suffered a relapse that confined him to his room for several more weeks. He never expected to recover fully but seemingly he did.

It was a hard winter for Narcissa. In spite of her own poor health she carried her share of the responsibilities of the mission. She became depressed. The Indians annoyed her with their constant hanging around—coming in without invitation and taking liberties everywhere. Sensing that she held aloof from them, they harbored resentment. Most of them were never drawn by her personality. She wanted to help the red people but did not have the power to bridge the gulf between herself and them. In her despondent state she began to feel that she was not really fitted for the place she occupied "on heathen ground" and wondered why she was ever permitted to come.

In the fall of 1841, the Cayuses became decidedly troublesome. They believed that the missionaries were getting rich at the red man's expense and as proof cited all the material things that had been accumulating: buildings, cattle, pigs, implements, clothing. The chiefs began making demands for payment—not only for the land, but for wood and water, as well. One day a group of Indians led by I-a-tin came up to Gray, who was working on his house, and told him not to cut any more timber on Cayuse land.

And there was old Tiloukaikt again, who let his horses feed on Whitman's green corn. "If you put horses out," he told the doctor, "I'll take one of yours. I will ride him far off and leave him there."

Whitman tried to reason with the chief but Tiloukaikt struck him on the chest, saying insolently, "Stop talking. How many time you talk, anyway?"

The doctor calmly said that he had been talking since childhood and expected to keep on talking as long as he lived.

Dr. Whitman built a large Indian room so that the missionaries could have some privacy in their own quarters. The Indians resented this curtailment of their liberties. To some of the mischief-makers, Whitman said positively, "If you come into Mr. Gray's house or mine, and do not behave, it is right for us to put you out." At this, one of the ruffians took hold of the doctor's ear and tweaked it, then struck him on the chest saying, "You hear? You hear?"—meaning that the Indians intended to have their own way. Following the teaching of the Scriptures, Whitman literally turned the other ear. The savage pulled first one ear and then the other. Not stopping with this, he snatched the doctor's hat and threw it into the mud. A friendly Cayuse put the hat back but the scamp repeated the performance several more times, after which Whitman said, "Perhaps you are just playing."

Marcus Whitman's policy was to take no notice of such insults. The Hudson's Bay Company, however, viewed these antics in a different light. It was in the best interests of all concerned to keep the natives in check. When rumors of what had happened filtered through to the proper officials, something was done. The agent at Fort Walla Walla sent word to the Cayuses that any insult to the missionaries would be regarded as an insult to the company and that those who conducted themselves as dogs would be treated like dogs.

This warning did not immediately put an end to the annoyances. By a ruse, a few Indians pushed into the kitchen and dining room and demanded the run of the entire house. Old Pa-la-is-ti-wat stood at the window and threatened Mrs. Whitman with a hammer, while Sa-ki-aph, already inside, tried to unlock another door and throw the whole house open. Dr. Whitman pushed one invader out and bolted the door. Then the enraged Sa-ki-aph, with the help of other savages, broke the door open, admitting the lawless group to take possession. The doctor was able to disarm those with weapons, but not without a struggle. During the scuffle, Sa-ki-aph managed to seize a gun which he drew on the doctor, saying, "*Now,* are you afraid to die?"

At this point the hired men arrived and the situation was quickly brought into control. The Indians still insisted that the doctor promise that none of his doors would ever be shut against them. He refused, telling them that if they wanted peace they would have to respect the rights and property of others. Then they demanded an outright gift but this he also refused.

Defeated, the Indians went away sullen and Whitman feared this would not be the end of the trouble. The Cayuses stayed away from Sunday services, troubled the stock and broke a window in the mission house. The missionaries had about decided to go to the fort and stay until the danger was past when word came from the Hudson's Bay Company. The agent at Fort Walla Walla had been busy with the problem and soon sent the assuring report that the Cayuses had promised to cease their unfriendly acts. Some of the troublemakers came to the mission and made as complete an apology as was possible for savages to make. The flurry of hostility over, peace and progress were resumed at Waiilatpu.

11 • The Man with the "Book"

At last the Nez Perces were to have a teacher. They had composed the majority of the delegation to St. Louis in 1831 seeking the white man's "Book of Heaven." They did not carry away the coveted book but they inadvertently started the missionary movement to the West. This, in turn, was the forerunner of a tide of immigration that in a few years flooded Oregon.

Henry Spalding had had an unfortunate start in life. An illegitimate child, he had been deserted by his mother and given into the care of others. At seventeen he was shifting for himself; at twenty-one he could read but poorly. It was about this time, however, that he began to see the glimmer of something better ahead. When he was converted, life took on a different meaning. He graduated from the academy and was soon teaching school. Finally he entered Lane Theological Seminary at Cincinnati and he was ordained as a Presbyterian minister in 1835. He married Eliza Hart, who became the mainstay of his life.

Probably because of the unhappy beginnings of his life, Spalding developed an extreme sensitiveness, almost a feeling of inferiority. To compensate for this, he often indulged in outbursts of bitterness and sharp criticisms, which won him the reputation of being a fault-finder. While it did not change him completely, his conversion modified his outlook considerably. As he delved wholeheartedly into the work of the Lord, life became filled with a new purpose. He could forget the unhappy past, for the most part, in the satisfactions of the present. Henry Spalding was known to be strictly honest and kindly intentioned, though overzealous and extremely erratic. What he felt, he felt to the depth of his being and he had little tolerance for all who were lukewarm in any cause.

Not long after his ordination Spalding received an appointment as missionary to the Osage Indians on the Missouri River. He and Eliza were in the throes of preparation when suddenly came Dr. Whitman's call, "We want you for Oregon." The American Board was willing to make the change in assignment but Spalding left the decision up to his wife. Yes, she was willing to go to Oregon. Her husband reminded her of her frail health and the hardships of such a journey, but she answered, "Duty is mine," and those words were final.

The Whitmans and the Spaldings parted at Fort Walla Walla in November 1836. On the twenty-ninth of that month the twenty-horse train pulled to a halt at Lapwai, about three miles from where Lapwai Creek joins the Clearwater River and some twelve miles from the present city of Lewiston, Idaho. It was a narrow valley crowded on either side by a range of crinkled ridges whose bleached dun-gray surface was relieved by patches of evergreens. Under the shadow of the highest bluff, which the Indians called Thunder Hill, Spalding located his mission, Lapwai, meaning "the place of butterflies." Eliza spoke of this chosen site as "a delightful spot where we expect to dwell for the remainder of our earthly pilgrimage."

The Spaldings lived in a skin lodge until their house was built by the combined efforts of himself, William Gray and willing Indians. When the house was finished and Spalding began calling the Indians together for devotional services the Lapwai mission was considered started. Gray stayed for a while, then went to Spokane to carry out his projected scheme of driving horses east to exchange for cattle, which were in short supply in Oregon.

Henry Spalding was a versatile as well as an energetic man. Every hour of those short winter days was turned to good purpose in finishing the interior of the house, making furniture, building fences and putting tools in order for the planting. With spring came his first experience in breaking raw land and in giving the Nez Perces their beginning lessons in agriculture. To the end of his days, he firmly believed that the natives had to be "settled" before their Christianity could really take root. As soon as the weather was favorable Spalding hauled out his plow and hitched up the horses. But soon came disappointment. The horses were willing but too weak for the task of breaking sod. Spalding was defeated before he had plowed a single furrow. He unhitched the sweating animals, wondering what the next step would be. He did not have long to wonder, for some of the Nez Perces, who had been silent observers, said to their teacher, "Don't let your heart cry. Give us hoes and we will cut up the land for you."

The missionary saw a ray of hope. At least they could try. Out came thirty hoes and out reached as many pairs of hands. "Now," said Spalding, "you work one week for me and two weeks for yourselves, and I'll furnish the seed." The Indians worked faithfully but even so Spalding's grandiose dreams for breaking a hundred acres of land the first year began to fade away. A few acres were made ready and on them Spalding planted some grain and a variety of vegetables. He also set out an apple orchard. The Indians put in fifteen acres for themselves.

The "man with the Book" also became the man with the primer and the medicine kit; and beside him worked his constant companion, the frail but efficient Eliza. The Indians came to adore her, whereas the commanding manner and high standards of Narcissa Whitman tended to antagonize the Cayuses. It should be pointed out, however, that the Nez Perces were more intelligent, more teachable and more appreciative of what was done for them than were the Cayuses.

On January 27, 1837 Eliza Spalding began teaching the first school in what became the State of Idaho. On that day old Thunder Hill looked down and saw a sight it had never before witnessed—pupils going to school! And what a strange lot! Old gray grandfathers and grandmothers, half-grown youths, mothers with babes on their backs! All came silently into the Indian room and sat down on the crude benches. School—they must have thought—what is school, and what do Indians do in school? For many weeks Eliza Spalding had been asking herself that very question: What do we do in an Indian school? But Eliza happened to be an ingenious teacher. Having no books, she taught without them. Simple lessons were printed in ink and illustrated by drawings. The blackboard was in constant use.

The school was popular. In a short time more than 100 pupils were enrolled, but the attendance—as could be expected—was irregular. The Indian room, which was always open, was occupied from morning till night by interested redskins, talking about what they had learned and instructing others. Twice a week Eliza taught sewing to a class of girls. She taught housework by taking a few girls at a time into her home. There was singing, too, for the Indians were fond of it and Spalding liked working with them. At first English words were used but as he gained command of the language, he began translating into Nez Perce. Chief Rotten Belly (Tack-en-su-a-tis) was a great favorite of the Spaldings. He had met them at the rendezvous and had been their guide through the Blue Mountains. It pleased him to see so many of his people sitting before teachers whom they had long wanted. When he first heard them singing a hymn in their own language tears came into his eyes.

Henry Spalding knew less about medicine than Marcus Whitman knew about theology, yet he was forced to practice it. He kept a few simple and safe remedies upon which he relied. Many of the ills that afflicted the Indians were caused—he thought—by bad food or senseless gorging. For ailments so caused, Spalding prescribed large doses of physic, often without seeing the patient. Pills were in such demand that he could hardly keep a supply on hand. In that day, bloodletting as a treatment for all diseases was popular, and Spalding made use of it. The Indians were fond of being bled and often came and demanded it. In such cases, he would go by, opening up the veins of the whole waiting group, then return to his business, leaving the patients to stop the bleeding when they pleased. If Spalding refused to bleed them, his patients would sometimes take an arrowhead and dig away until they had found a vein or an artery. This often caused swelling of the arms and legs and—Spalding believed—even death.

In the spring of 1838 it seemed advisable for Spalding to move the mission to the south bank of the Clearwater River, not far from the mouth of Lapwai Creek. The spot is now known as the "Old Mission site." Dr. Whitman concurred and came up to help in the construction of the first building. From this time on construction was a continuing activity at the Spalding station. Logs were plentiful and Indian help could always be obtained. Soon there grew up a veritable village on the bank of the Clearwater: the long mission house; a small one for the native children who were living with the Spaldings; one for the hired man; a blacksmith and other shops; and a sizeable schoolhouse which was also used as a place of worship. In time came a grist mill and a sawmill and extensive fencing.

After the buildings were finished and reinforcements arrived Spalding had more time to devote to his preaching and the holding of revival meetings. He found the two greatest vices to be gambling and polygamy, and at these he struck relentlessly. His first converts were Timothy and Old Joseph, father of the famous

Nez Perce chief. The first to receive baptism were Mary and Martha, girls who had helped in the Spalding home. Spalding has the honor of founding the first Presbyterian Church in Oregon.

The tireless and ingenious Spalding could find a solution for nearly every problem, even that of getting books for his red children. He wrote to the mission in the Hawaiian Islands asking for a printing press, and got one. The church there consented to lend a missionary, Edwin O. Hall, along with the printing press, to the new Oregon mission. In April 1839, the first printing press in the Pacific Northwest reached Fort Vancouver. The Hudson's Bay Company sent the Reverend and Mrs. Hall and their precious baggage to Walla Walla in a large bateau. Here the eager Spalding was waiting to receive all with open arms. The press was taken the remainder of the distance by pack horse. The Halls followed in a canoe. On May 13 the party and the press arrived at Lapwai in good condition. Spalding, beside himself with joy, wrote in his journal:

> Arrive home before sundown, and canoe soon after. All well—everything safe. Thank the Lord, O my soul, for His goodness during the journey, for His watch over everything during my absence.

Then he recorded the arrival of a new colt, some little pigs and the old white cow's calf. Continuing, he said:

> Mrs. S. health much improved, also that of Eliza. She has now eight teeth. Bless the Lord for goodness to this dear girl.

Spalding could hardly wait until he could set up the press and strike off a proof sheet. The first book printed in Oregon came off the press at the Clearwater station. It was a primer of eight pages, of which 400 copies were made. The next project was a twenty-page book, also intended for school use. In two weeks' time, Spalding and E. O. Hall had struck off 500 copies. In all, during the next several years, eight books were printed in the Nez Perce language. Spalding was the author or translator of seven of these.

In the meantime the other work of the mission went on at a steady pace. Eliza's influence was deep and far-reaching. The con-

Jason Lee (1803-1845), first missionary to Old Oregon (Ore. Historical Society)

Jason Lee's "First Oregon Mission," at edge of French Prairie in the Willamette Valley (Ore. Historical Society)

Cushing Eells (1810-1893), Tshimakain Mission near Spokane (Ore. Historical Society)

Dr. Marcus Whitman (1802-1847) (Ore. Historical Society)

Narcissa Prentiss Whitman (1808-1847) - likeness drawn on basis of various descriptions (Ore. Historical Society)

Waiilatpu, the Whitman mission near Walla Walla – drawing by N. A. Osborn (Ore. Historical Society)

Tshimakain, the American Board's Spokane Mission – drawing by Charles A. Geyer (Ore. Historical Society)

Left to right: Rev. Magloire Blanchet, Bishop of Nisqually; Most Rev. F. Norbert Blanchet, Archbishop of Oregon City; Rev. Modest Demers, Bishop of Vancouver Island (Ore. Historical Society)

Jake and Martin Spedis, Eastern Oregon Indians in full regalia (Ore. Historical Society)

Father De Smet, Henry Harmon Spalding, Elkanah Walker

Father Pierre Jean De Smet with hostile chiefs of the Upper Columbia (Ore. Historical Society)

Fort Astoria, from a sketch in G. Franchere's *Narrative of a Voyage to the Northwest Coast of America* (B. Driessen)

No-Horns-On-His-Head – from the painting by George Catlin, in Paris: *Winning the Oregon Country* (B. Driessen)

Rabbit-Skin-Leggings — from Catlin's painting in *Winning the Oregon Country* (B. Driessen)

Chinook mother and infant of Lower Columbia, showing head-flattening device—Smithsonian Institution (B. Driessen)

Fort Vancouver, drawn from an early sketch (B. Driessen)

"Old Mission," the Sacred Heart of the Coeur d'Alenes, near Cataldo — drawn from a photograph (B. Driessen)

version of Timothy was due, in a large measure, to her. She gave him a picture of blind Bartimeus being healed by Jesus. This cheap print hung on the wall of his lodge as long as he lived. Her memory was precious to the faithful Indian. When he asked a blessing over his meals, he always ended with the words, "In the name of Jesus Christ and Mrs. Spalding."

The Spalding mission had no idle corners. Many of the girls became fascinated with the art of knitting. Some made stockings, others mittens and leggings. Spalding constructed a spinning wheel, which the girls under Eliza's patient direction learned to use. Machinery for weaving was also set up. Off this loom came several yards of carpet, besides material for clothing. Wool was becoming plentiful because Spalding's sheep were increasing with the years.

The Spalding home life was happy. Memories the children had of their father bore out the fact that he was devoted to his family. Four children were born to Henry and Eliza at the mission: Eliza, Henry Hart, Martha Jane and Amelia Lorene.

12 • *The Spokane Mission—Tshimakain —"The Place of Springs"*

In faraway Maine a young minister, recently ordained, was pondering over a serious problem. He had been appointed by the American Board to go as missionary to the Indians of the West. He had looked forward to such a service but now he found that it brought complications. The trouble was that he was a bachelor—always too busy or too bashful to seek a wife. And before him lay a letter from the secretary of the board in which he read, "You should have a wife, a good, patient, healthy, intelligent, pious wife." The writer even went so far as to recommend a young lady who might be considered a likely prospect. Mary Richardson of Baldwin, Maine, had the missionary urge but had been refused because it was not the policy of the board to send "unmarried females" into foreign fields. If Miss Richardson wanted to be a missionary she must meet the requirements and find herself a missionary husband.

No wonder Elkanah Walker was troubled. He was thirty-two —moody, introverted and too conscious of his weak points. His opportunities for schooling having been limited, he was older than most of the students in his graduating class. William H. Gray, who made critical analyses of all his co-workers, gave the following opinion of Elkanah Walker:

> Rev. E. Walker was a tall, rather spare, stoop-shouldered black-haired, brown-eyed, rather light-complectioned man, diffident and unassuming, always afraid to say "Amen" at the end of his prayers, and requiring a considerable effort to speak with confidence or decision upon any subject. . . . He had no positive traits of mind, yet he was studious, and kind as a friend and neighbor; faithful as a Christian, inefficient as a preacher. His efforts among the Indians were of a negative cast. The Indians respected him for his kindness and feared him for his commanding appearance. Not at all adapted to fill the position he undertook as an Indian missionary in Oregon—yet as a citizen and settler, one of the best.[14]

Reared in hardship, Elkanah Walker was prepared to face the austere life of a missionary but at the thought of meeting and wooing a strange woman he quailed. "Mary Richardson," he repeated to himself. "Who is this young lady who wants to be a missionary?" William H. Thayer was the man who knew. An old friend and classmate of Walker, Thayer was glad to help matters along. He was as forward as Walker was shy, with a proper sense of humor and an appreciation of the fitness of things. He was well qualified to be the intermediary between his friend and Mary Richardson.

Writing to Walker, Thayer spoke flatteringly of Mary Richardson, her charms, her capabilities and her piety. To Mary, he represented Elkanah Walker as being, not brilliant, but of good character, worthy and kind, though afflicted with bashfulness.

Walker was, he admitted, somewhat raw and uncultivated and had to be known to be appreciated.

With the co-operation of Walker, Thayer managed cleverly to bring the two together. Walker was sent to preach in Mary's home town. He was invited to her father's house, entertained at dinner and subjected to the closest inspection by the many members of the Richardson family. Mary was not taken into the confidence of the two conspirators. Her frank admission to her diary revealed the fact that she was impressed neither by Walker's appearance nor by his sermon.

In addition to the letter of introduction William Thayer wrote a proposal of marriage, just in case Walker should need it—and he did. After an acquaintance of only two days Elkanah Walker handed Mary the letter without warning one morning before breakfast. She was so stunned by the suddenness of it that she asked for time to think it over. After a few hours of consideration Mary capitulated, although the conflict within her continued and was severe. She had another suitor of longer acquaintance who was wealthy but after weighing the two in the balance, she came to the conclusion that it was better to marry a poor, godly man than a rich "infidel." Besides, it was her religious duty to do mission work. All through the brief period of their courtship and during the first years of their marriage there were times when Mary wondered if she had been too hasty. Eventually, though, she came back to her original conclusion: "The path of duty must prove the path of peace."

Mary Richardson was twenty-six years of age—not handsome but with a high degree of intelligence. Educated in a young ladies' seminary, she possessed a keen, original, independent mind. As critical of herself as of others, she often felt that she was not a good Christian—that she lacked the spirit. From first to last, her well-known diary brings out the fact that when she condemned others she did not spare herself; if faults were to be found in others, her own life contained more.

Elkanah and Mary were married March 5, 1838 and that same afternoon started on the long journey to Oregon. After stopping for a short visit with his people they went on to New

York, where they were to meet other members of the reinforcement party. Here Walker met the man who was to be a close associate in mission work for over ten years. Cushing Eells was, in many ways, Walker's opposite, yet they had enough in common to enable them to get along in harmony during the years when bickering almost wrecked the enterprise. Eells was an unassuming man, short and slight, with brown hair and kind eyes. He was educated for the ministry and had had some experience in teaching school. Myra Eells was thirty-three years old, five years her husband's senior. She, too, had dreamed of a missionary career, and when Cushing proposed marriage, she said, "I doubt whether you could have asked anyone who would have been more willing."

When Mary Walker and Myra Eells made each other's acquaintance they learned that their lives had flowed along in similar channels. Both were well educated for women of that day, both had been reared in large families and both had been married on March 5, 1838. The two kept diaries of this momentous journey into the West, and these journals were as different as the dispositions of the two women. Myra's was a brief, matter-of-fact recital of events, with a careful avoidance of anything personal; Mary's, on the other hand, was original, intensely human and shockingly frank. Its pages were alive with personalities and her reactions to them.

The third member of the missionary party, Asa B. Smith, had also taken a bride on short notice. Sara Gilbert was a frail, mild young woman, whom Mary Walker called "a little dear." Smith's health was not good; this might explain his irritability and his inability to work in harmony with his fellow men. Gray, who had more than one disagreement with Smith, said this about him:

> Rev. A.B. Smith, a man whose prejudices were so strong that he could not be reasonable with himself. He attempted to make himself useful as a missionary, but failed for want of Christian forbearance and confidence in his associates. As to literary ability, he was superior to his associates, and probably excited their jealousy.[15]

The three couples set out over the same route taken by the Whitmans and the Spaldings two years before. At Cincinnati they met Cornelius Rogers, twenty-two years of age and eager for service among the "heathen" of the West. When the party embarked on the river boat he was a member. Later, he was given an official appointment by the American Board. After days of travel on overcrowded boats the missionaries reached Independence, Missouri, at the edge of the great frontier. Here the organizer and guide, William H. Gray, was waiting with his bride. Undoubtedly, Augusta Dix Gray was the handsomest female in the quartet bound for Oregon. Gray had achieved one of his ambitions; he had convinced the American Board of the need for reinforcements and of his personal fitness to lead such a party.

On April 22, 1838 the recruits, who constituted a honeymoon party as well, were off to the great plains under the protection of a fur caravan bound for the mountain rendezvous. The rigorous demands of the trail—the long hours, the monotony of the meals, too little time for rest—had their effects upon everyone. Both Mr. and Mrs. Eells suffered from sickness but made no complaints, as did Augusta Dix Gray. Mary Walker soon found herself in "feeble health" and was so miserable that she felt like crying most of the time. Mary's diary told of the numerous times her feelings were hurt by her husband, who seemed totally unaware that he had said anything amiss. This journal reveals, too, that there were frayed nerves and bickerings that were a discredit to a group of Christian people. One day Mary wrote, "Mr. Smith short as pie crust." And again, "Mr. Smith very much out with Mr. Gray, in a fret all the time." She was glad that she could truthfully say about herself, "So far I have been able to keep my temper on all occasions, though my feelings have been tried exceedingly by some members of the party." Asa B. Smith seemed to be the chief irritant, although Gray's lordly ways and arbitrary decisions were resented by the entire party.

It was a trip which few—if any—of the wedding party enjoyed. At the last crossing of the Platte, the rain was coming down in torrents but the missionaries worked savagely with benumbed hands all forenoon in order to keep up with the caravan. The tent was wet and cold and Mary Walker's spirits were sadly depressed. Seeing her in tears, Mrs. Smith asked, "Why, Mrs. Walker, what's the matter?" Without raising her head, Mary replied dolefully, "I was thinking of how comfortable my father's hogs are."

There was no respite. It was up and on—in rain or shine, in warm weather or cold. There came a time, though, when the bedraggled travelers could gaze in admiration at the Rocky Mountains, capped with snow and chiseled in marble against the blue. When this time came, all began using spare moments in writing letters to be sent to the States with the returning fur caravan. Gray reported to secretary Greene about the progress of the party to date. And Asa B. Smith reported to the secretary about Gray. He objected to Gray as a leader and called him "injudicious," "rash" and "inconsiderate." Said Smith:

> He has assumed a great deal of authority over us, and talked to us in a very harsh & I may say abusive manner, regardless of the feelings of others, even of the ladies. . . . These things have been a severe trial to us.

In spite of discord and the discomforts of traveling there were no casualties, and the missionary group reached Waiilatpu on the last day of August 1838. Since Spalding had just closed a series of meetings the place was thronged with Indians, all eager to meet the new palefaces, especially the women. Mary Walker complained that she was obliged to stop eating in order to shake the filthy hands of forty or fifty Cayuses. It irritated her to have the Indians looking through the windows, watching every move. "They annoy me very much," she wrote, "and I will teach them better manners as soon as I acquire language enough."

A missionary meeting was held in order to discuss assignments for the new members and general plans for expansion. Mary's diary for that day contained the significant statement, "Had an interesting, and I think happy season, notwithstanding the harshness that has existed among us."

The Spaldings went back to the Clearwater. For the present, Gray and Smith were to remain and assist in the erection of new buildings at Waiilatpu. All of the overland group, apparently, made it clear that they would not work in any station with William Gray as superintendent. Cornelius Rogers would help where he was needed most. Walker and Eells were assigned to Spokane, and as soon as they could get ready they made a trip to the scene of their future activities to make the acquaintance of the leading chiefs and locate a building site.

When Elkanah Walker left for Spokane he asked two things of his wife: to study the Indian language earnestly, getting as much help as possible from Chief Lawyer; and secondly, to remember that she was not the mistress of the mission, and that she was obligated to the Whitmans for everything.

Mary complied. She made herself a dictionary of Indian words and sought every opportunity to hear the words spoken. Being an energetic person, she kept employed from morning till night with a variety of tasks. She gathered seeds, picked corn husks for the bed ticks, made soap, washed and ironed and took care of Alice Clarissa. The other women were not so helpful. The mission was crowded to capacity that winter. In all, there were fifteen to cook for including the five Sandwich Islander servants —fifteen persons to gather in the kitchen and huddle around the hearth when November days grew chilly. People got on each other's nerves; tempers were ruffled at little or nothing. Mary Walker often criticized Narcissa Whitman adversely, at the same time realizing that the mistress of the mission had a great deal to try her.

In October Walker and Eells returned from Spokane. They had selected a site and built the foundations of two mission houses but had decided against moving until spring. Myra Eells was disappointed, being unhappy at the very thought of wintering at Waiilatpu. Mrs. Smith was glad in a way for she feared her husband could not get along with Dr. Whitman when the harmonizing influence of Walker and Eells was removed. Mary Walker, satisfied to have a haven as the hour of her trial approached, declared to her diary "I am glad I am not one of the worrying sort."

As soon as Walker returned, he built a separate room for them to insure a little privacy. When the little room was finished, Mary scrubbed the floor, built a fire to dry it out thoroughly and hung curtains. The first week in December, when Elkanah Walker returned from a trip to Walla Walla for supplies, he found that a son had been born. The boy was named Cyrus Hamlin in honor of Walker's best friend, who was also engaged in missionary work. Myra Eells took care of Mary and the baby during the day and Elkanah did night duty. Mary appreciated more than words could express the thoughtfulness and kindness of her husband, who was often blunt and apparently insensitive to her feelings. She developed milk fever and was ill and miserable all through the month of January. But she improved gradually and when spring came to the valley she was back at her former level of health, and was eager to be off to her new home.

On March 5, 1839, the wedding anniversary of both couples, the two families started to Spokane. Milk had to be provided for Cyrus Hamlin, so a cow was driven along. Cushing Eells willingly became chief cow tender and bottle warmer. He would gallop ahead, stop at a desirable place and build a fire for heating the milk so the child would have meals on time. In the beginning the weather was fine and the party made from ten to fifteen miles a day. They crossed the Snake and followed up the west side of the Palouse River, where the scenery in places was frightening in its grandeur. Fed by spring rains, the swollen stream chafed within its narrow confines, tumbled over a precipice some 160 feet in height, then went charging on its way. High rocky cliffs rose up on either side but the Indian guides threaded their way over a winding trail—now close to the river's side, now back into the cliffs, finally emerging into the rolling Palouse Hills.

Before the journey was ended March storms of snow, rain and hail beat unmercifully upon them. On March 20, after fifteen days in the saddle, the first white women to live in the Spokane country alighted at Tshimakain, the "place of springs." They looked with gratitude upon what was to be their home for ten years: two partly built twin cabins—now only log "pens" waiting to be finished. The head chief, Big Head, whom the missionaries called Cornelius, welcomed them and gave all aid possible. He was not a stranger, having been among the welcoming committee at Waiilatpu the previous August. While Walker and Eells were

he was denied everything he asked for, he invariably became unpleasant. Walker anticipated trouble with Garry and was thankful that it never materialized.

Walker and Eells were devout, self-sacrificing missionaries but perhaps they lacked an understanding of Indian nature. The greatest loss to the Indians may have been their failure to win Spokane Garry and develop his unlimited potentialities for good.

Pioneer life was hard at its best. Toil, sacrifice, homely joys and disappointments filled the lives of the missionaries. Here at Tshimakain was isolation, to be sure, but in a way this was a blessing, for it removed these four people from the bickerings connected with the other missions. On a few occasions Mary Walker became vexed with Cushing Eells but molehills were never exaggerated to the magnitude of mountains. The women shared all the burdens with their husbands except the long business trips that required absence from home. Eells estimated that in the year 1841 he traveled 1200 miles in the interests of the mission. This took him from home fifty-seven days. In addition, he went more than 400 miles on preaching tours among the Indians. The men arranged things so that one of them would be at the mission all the time.

Food-getting was as essential to the missionaries as to the Indians. Since they were allowed only $300 a year for living expenses it was absolutely necessary to make the station almost self-supporting. They kept chickens and gradually increased their herd of cows. Staples like sugar and flour had to be brought from Colville or Walla Walla. The women tried to do a little teaching at first, but since Myra's health was poor and Mary soon became burdened with a large family both finally gave up the idea.

The Walker house gave no end of trouble. The roof leaked and the chimney was constantly in need of repair. Mary's complaint to her diary shows how annoyances could accumulate:

> Felt quite out of patience this morning on account of the miserable old door and the cats and the Indians; first one and then another would knock out a piece, and the wind came in without ceremony, so that I could not be comfortable in the

> room long enough to get breakfast. I was tempted to fret, but concluded I would go to work to see if I could fix it. I nailed it together as well as I could.[16]

A short time later a part of the wall fell, taking the chimney with it. It crushed Cyrus Hamlin's little chair and just barely missed Elkanah, who was in bed. This convinced Walker that a new house would have to be built so he made a trip to Walla Walla to get a carpenter. Gray grudgingly consented to do the job but he quit before the house was finished. Another workman was employed but it was two years before the dwelling was ready for occupancy. On August 2, 1843 Mary Walker at last moved into her new home. There was now no water trickling from the ceiling and no more lugging of heavy buckets from the spring, because of the new well close by. New furniture came and when Mary sat in a comfortable rocker once more she felt like a princess in a palace.

Elkanah Walker did not enjoy the best of health. He had frequent sick spells that caused his wife no little worry. He chewed tobacco and Mary believed that this was in part responsible for his indigestion. Walker, half convinced, made an unsuccessful attempt to break the habit. The first winter, when his supply of tobacco ran out, Elkanah became restive and moody. It was no use to struggle against odds. He decided to make the trip to Colville in the dead of winter for the sole purpose of laying in a supply. He was caught in a hailstorm before he had gone very far and would have turned back had it not been for the want of "that stuff" he "so much loved."

There were many children at Tshimakain in the course of a few years, most of them belonging to the Walkers. In 1840 their only daughter, Abigail, was born; after her followed a succession of sons. Dr. Whitman made a professional visit to the Walker home in March 1842. The sixteenth day of that month was one of the busiest days in Mary's life, as this bit from her diary reveals:

> Rose about five. Had early breakfast. Got my housework done about nine. Baked six more loaves of bread. Made a kettle of mush, and have now a suet pudding and beef boiling. My girl [an Indian] has ironed, and I have managed to put my clothes away and set my house in order. May the

> merciful God be with me through this unexpected scene. Nine o'clock P.M. I was delivered of another son.[17]

The new arrival was named Marcus Whitman. Although Elkanah and Mary were provoked with the doctor on many occasions they still held him in high regard. Walker's diary contains this item, written after a visit by Marcus and Narcissa:

> Was rather displeased with the doctor this morning and took little notice of his fixing off. . . . They left us today to return home and I must say I did not regret to see them depart.

The fourth Walker child arrived in February 1844 and was christened Joseph Elkanah. Dr. Whitman reached Tshimakain just twelve days too late to be of any assistance. With a hint of mischief, Mary wrote in her diary:

> Dr. Whitman arrived in the evening. I met him at the door with my babe in my arms.

Other sons born at Tshimakain were Jeremiah and John Richardson. These children were not perfect and on the pages of Mary's diary are found many references to problems of discipline, especially with the first-born, Cyrus Hamlin. Quite naturally, as the work piled up through her years of childbearing, Mary gave less and less time to writing.

Cyrus was provoking and stubborn and Mary earnestly hoped that if he were ever called upon to suffer at the stake he would be as "unrelenting" as he was on many occasions. When he was two years old he told a "deliberate lie," much to his mother's distress. Mary wanted to punish him but Elkanah insisted on leniency. She feared her husband was following a wrong course and wrote with concern, "When a child can contrive so wilful a lie he knows what it means to be punished for it."

When Cyrus was seven years old he was sent to the mission school at Waiilatpu. Mary was pained when she learned that her son was something of a trial to his teachers but it was more heartbreaking when Cushing Eells refused for a time to permit his two sons to play with the Walkers' "problem child." When the fall of 1846 came around Cyrus and Abigail were invited to attend school at Waiilatpu but the Walkers declined. Mary then took upon herself another task—that of giving regular instruction to her children.

In the fall of 1842 Walker went to Lapwai to print his Indian primer. He came back with 200 copies of a sixteen-page book which his Indians could read. That night Mary sat up late stitching, pressing and binding copies of "the first book in Flathead." With pride she wrote, "It is indeed a marvelous little book." Within another year, Walker—with a little help from Spokane Garry—had finished the translation of the first ten chapters of the Gospel of Matthew. At the same time Spalding was making similar translations into the Nez Perce tongue.

To the surprise and pleasure of the isolated missionaries, visitors from faroff places found their way to Tshimakain Valley. In 1841 a contingent from Lieutenant Charles Wilkes' Exploring Expedition reached the Colville country to collect all manner of information for the United States government. Robert Johnson, the leader of the small group, later reported that the most pleasant sight he had seen in Oregon was "a lady milking her cows." That "lady" was Mary Walker, who was duly humiliated that she should be found at such a task.

In the autumn of 1843 the German botanist, Carl Andreas Geyer, came to Tshimakain and remained about six months. The scientist outstayed his welcome and Walker was finally obliged to tell Geyer that he could not entertain him any longer since the mission funds were not intended to support any except missionaries. When Geyer said good-by to Tshimakain he left as a memento a pen-and-ink sketch of the mission and a long letter of appreciation written in Mary's memory book. He left, also, a part of his deep interest in botany. Having a scientific turn of mind, Mary was inspired to begin a systematic study of both plants and animals. This led her to make a large collection of specimens. In the summer of 1847, much to Elkanah's displeasure, Mary turned her attention to taxidermy. Her diary for August of that year contains the following items:

Tues. 3—Purchased a bow and a trout and salmon skin and spent half the afternoon stuffing and fixing them.

Wed. 4—Bought a mocking bird.

Thurs. 5—Stuffed a sparrow skin and bought a rattlesnake ready stuffed, except it wanted fixing a little nicer.

Fri. 6—Purchased a duck skin and stuffed it, also a cross-bill. Mr. W. gets out of sorts not liking my new trade of stuffing birds etc.

Sat. 25—Spent the afternoon in skinning a crane; think I will not undertake another crane soon.

In the early autumn of 1847 the mission was honored by the visits of two noted artists. Paul Kane, a Canadian, came up from Walla Walla where he had spent several weeks painting portraits of noted Indian chiefs. Mary Walker thought Kane was a "clever artist" but an ungodly man of not much learning. However, he did give her a good deal of information about birds. John Mix Stanley came by way of Fort Okanogan and brought letters from the home folks in distant Maine. A heavy October rain forced him to stay longer than he had intended but during this time he painted portraits of Elkanah Walker and of seven-year-old Abigail.

The Jesuit missionary, Father Pierre De Smet, passed through the country in the spring of 1842 and camped in the Tshimakain Valley. He criticized the Protestants for holding aloof from the Indians—keeping a safe distance from the heathen whom they had come to convert. It is true that the missionaries—especially the women—felt that they were often imposed upon by the natives and that their privacy was forever being invaded. Mary was frequently in a state of irritation because of the prying curiosity of her Indian neighbors, some of whom were always around the house watching everything she did. If they had learned anything by observation, she declared, the case would have been different. They could watch her make bread every day but never show any desire to learn how.

One undesirable feature of mission life—as the women saw it—was the lack of suitable companionship for their children. Mary referred to this many times. She objected to having the Indians put their dirty hands on the babies. Getting efficient help was another problem. Indian boys and girls were hard to teach and furthermore they could not be trusted. Mary once caught a girl stealing and after that she was suspicious of the whole tribe.

Her next girl chose to sleep outside one cold night in October, thus causing Mary a great deal of anxiety. Every day she found more and more in Indian character to perplex and annoy her. William Three Mountains, however, proved to be a shining exception. He learned readily and was trustworthy and likable. He did faithful work at the mission for about two years. For some unexplained reason Chief Big Head was jealous of the boy and schemed until he finally got William away from the mission. Three Mountains grew up to be a credit to his tribe and to the Christian church. He was one of the many baptized by Henry Spalding some years later.

And so the years passed at Tshimakain—years filled with toil, hardships, anxieties and disappointments. Yet they were happy years. If the missionaries lived in isolation, they also lived in an atmosphere of peace. Though they were not able to go out into the wide world of people, a small part of that world came knocking at their doors.

13 • *Discord and Growing Indian Hostility*

FROM THE BEGINNING THERE HAD been a lack of complete harmony among the missionaries. For the most part they were good, sincere people, interested in converting the heathen. At the same time, they were individualists with decided opinions about everything. Henry Spalding was the focus of most of the criticism although some of the others received a fair share. William H. Gray, after repeated disagreements with Spalding, began sending letters of complaint to Reverend Greene, secretary of the American Board. At the same time, no one could work easily with Gray himself. Asa B. Smith and Gray agreed on only one point—opposition to Spalding.

In many ways Smith was not suited to the role of missionary. His outlook for the conversion of the Nez Perces was dark. "Every day," he wrote, "shows me more of their selfishness and the awful depravity of their hearts." He was unfitted to be a pioneer of any sort. His health was poor and his disposition irritable. He could not adjust himself to any situation and by the beginning of 1842 was ready to leave even if the board had not called him home.

Gray was erratic, ambitious and overbearing. In the spring of 1840 he had a moody spell during which he gave little assistance of any kind. When he came out of his depression, he announced to Spalding that he would take over the secular affairs of the Clearwater station and that Spalding could be responsible for the teaching. Spalding deferred to him but after two weeks Gray gave up the management of the mission and left for the Willamette. Spalding then went to his spring planting with a joyful heart.

When the Reverend Edwin O. Hall arrived with the printing press in the spring of 1839 he was shocked at the lack of harmony that prevailed. In his letter to Secretary Greene dated March 16, 1840, he wrote:

> The state of things is truly lamentable, and I have been exceedingly grieved to find such a want of confidence and brotherly love (in fact, common politeness) among those who bear the name of missionaries.

The relations between Narcissa Whitman and Spalding were at times most unhappy. In her diary and letters Mrs. Whitman hinted at unpleasant meetings and hard feelings but never gave a full explanation. In a letter to her father bearing the date October 10, 1840 she gave her most direct criticism of Henry Spalding. In part, she said:

> The man who came with us never ought to have come. My dear husband has suffered more from him in consequence of his wickedness and jealousy, and his great pique toward me, than can be known in this world. But he suffers not alone—the whole mission suffers, which is more to be deplored. He has nearly broken up the mission. . . . The pretended settlement with father before we started was only an excuse. . . . The same bitter feeling exists.

The source of these bad feelings seems to have been a remark made by Spalding some time previous to the overland trip. He admitted saying that he would never go into the same mission with Narcissa because he questioned her judgment. What prompted the statement is not known but from this seemingly trivial thing sprang years of bitterness.

Complaints against Spalding continued to find their way to Secretary Greene's desk. When eleven such letters had been received and duly considered the American Board felt impelled to act. The fatal order, issued February 25, 1842, struck like a thunderbolt in Oregon six months later. Whitman was greatly disturbed over the drastic changes the board demanded and immediately called a missionary meeting. By this time several of the workers were not affected by the recall order: the Smiths, the Grays and Cornelius Rogers had left the field. Briefly, the order recalled Spalding and directed him to return to the States as soon as possible—overland, preferably. Whitman was to close the stations at Waiilatpu and Lapwai and move to the northern post. The missionary meeting at this time was brief and resulted in Whitman's decision to go east to plead for the retention of Spalding and the mission organization as it existed. With one companion, A. L. Lovejoy, who had come to Oregon with an immigrant train during the summer, Whitman set out on horseback in the face of approaching winter.

Mrs. Whitman had decided to stay and supervise the mission, but an incident which happened the first night after the doctor left caused her quickly to change her mind. An Indian entered her room, giving her such a fright that she decided to go to the Methodist mission at The Dalles till her husband's return. She left an able man, William Geiger, in charge but even so the mission was like a plantation without a master, and the Indians like "sheep without a shepherd," as Narcissa expressed it. Shortly after Mrs. Whitman left, the grist mill was burned to the ground with the resultant destruction of some 200 bushels of wheat and corn as well as a quantity of flour and a part of the waterwheel. Indian Agent Dr. Elijah White came up from the Willamette to put things to rights. There was no organized hostility, however, and the Cayuses soon subsided and gave no further trouble that year.

Meanwhile, back east, the American Board had had a change of heart. On April 28, 1842 Secretary Greene rescinded his former order and instructed Whitman and Spalding to carry on the work as usual. Since some of the main complainants had voluntarily left the field the remaining difficulties between Whitman and Spalding—Greene probably thought—could be resolved. When Whitman reached his destination after his stupendous effort, the problem was nonexistent. Apparently the board received him rather coolly and intimated that he should be in Oregon tending to mission affairs.

In October, 1843—just a year after he left—Dr. Whitman returned leading the largest train of immigrants that had yet traveled in one group along the Oregon Trail. He had not gone back with that purpose in mind but when he was asked to be the pilot he did not refuse. Nor did he go back to "save Oregon" for the United States from the domination of the British—as earlier legends declared. He rode to save Spalding; he rode to save his own mission which he would convert into a "house by the side of the road" for wayworn immigrants. And he was returning full of enthusiasm for the future even though he would have some reconstructing to do at his mission.

There was promise of brighter days ahead for Narcissa, as well, and both were thankful for every encouraging sign. After the school was reopened and devotional services started again, the Indians seemed to experience a revival of their interest. Narcissa expressed their joint sentiments in one paragraph:

> Our united choice would be to live and die here, to spend our lives for the salvation of this people. We have been contented and happy, notwithstanding all our trials, and let come what will, we had rather die in battle than retreat, if the Lord will only appear for us, and remove all that is in the way of his salvation. Our ardent prayer is "Lord, let not this mission fail."

In a letter of 1842, Narcissa commented, "The Lord has taken our own dear child away so we may care for the poor outcasts of the country and suffering children." That year she was mothering two little halfbreed girls who were a great comfort to her. They were Helen Mar Meek and Mary Ann Bridger— about five and six years of age—daughters of the mountain men Joseph Meek and Jim Bridger. She had also taken under her wing David Malin, a half-Indian, half-Spanish waif. When Dr. Whitman returned from the East in 1843 he brought his thirteen-year-old nephew, Perrin Whitman, who became a valuable assistant.

The year 1843 was a turning point in Dr. Whitman's career as a missionary. From that time he became less the Christian teacher of Indians and more the servant of the American settlers, who would eventually take complete possession of Oregon. He had come to believe that the Indians' day was about at an end and that his greatest work in the future would be to aid the white colonists in founding their religious institutions. Whitman eagerly looked forward to that new day. To Narcissa the prospects of another avalanche of immigrants in the summer of 1844 were little less than overwhelming. In a letter she wrote:

> We are all of us, I suppose, on the eve of another scene as last fall—the passing of the emigrants—and as it falls heavier on my friends at The Dalles, I hope they have laid up a good stock of strength, patience, and every needed grace for the siege.[18]

It was October first before the delayed trains began arriving —and high time, too, for the Blue Mountains were already capped with snow and the nights were getting chilly. In one of the trains was a family of children made orphans on the trail. The captain, William Shaw, rode ahead to find out if the Whitmans could care for the children, at least temporarily. Seven more! Narcissa and Marcus looked at each other, then nodded consent. When Narcissa saw the unkempt, woebegone flock her heart was touched. There were John Sager, thirteen; Francis, eleven; Catherine, nine; Elizabeth, seven; Matilda Jane, five; Hannah Louise, three; and a girl baby of five months.

The children were soon assisted out of the wagon and started toward the house. "Have you no children of your own?" asked Captain Shaw, who was walking beside Mrs. Whitman. Narcissa pointed to the fenced grave and answered softly, "The only child I ever had sleeps yonder."

The Whitmans later adopted the children and Narcissa treated them as she would had they been her own. She put them in school and taught them to work. They found her stern but neither unkind nor unreasonable. Hers was the Puritan discipline that hewed straight to the line. In later years one of the Sager girls gave this clue to Mrs. Whitman's manner of control:

> There was no danger of any of us being spoiled. She would point to one of us, and then to the dishes or the broom, and we instantly got busy with our assigned tasks. She didn't scold much, but we dreaded that accusing finger pointing at us.[19]

But life was not all labor for the children. There were picnics and holidays and time for play. Narcissa tried to develop in them a love of the beautiful. Her hobby was flowers and she gave each child a little garden to care for in his own individual way.

Narcissa had heavy responsibilities but she also had many to share her burdens. William Geiger taught school during the winter. Andrew Rogers, a young theological student who came with the immigration of 1845, became the music teacher. Narcissa's health being much improved, she wrote again in a cheerful, optimistic vein. Following is a description of her household in November, 1846—just ten years after her arrival at Waiilatpu:

> We set the table for more than twenty three times a day, and it is a pleasant sight. Mr. Geiger serves the children. Mr. Rogers, the young man who taught last winter, is still with us, studying for the ministry. He is a good man, and his Christian society affords me much comfort. He is an excellent singer and has taught the children to sing admirably. When they came here not one of them could make a noise toward singing; now they constitute quite a heavy choir. None of them could read, except the three eldest very poorly; now they are quite good scholars and are making good progress.[20]

Ten years brought great changes to the place where the rye grass grows. The Whitmans now had a large establishment with a grist mill, a sawmill in the Blue Mountains, many acres of land under cultivation, irrigation begun, lands fenced and a school attended mostly by whites. The mission had ceased to be an important factor in the lives of the Indians; it was now serving principally as a life-saving hostel to thousands of westward-bound immigrants.

After his reinstatement Spalding resumed his duties with a thankful heart. The year 1843 proved the happiest and most successful up to date. The Indians were interested in everything pertaining to their own advancement. School attendance reached its peak and as many as 2000 came to the Sunday services. Farming was being carried on seriously and many of the Nez Perces were eager to acquire sheep and hogs, in addition to cattle.

Spalding's chief concern now was for his wife, who was occasionally so ill that her life was despaired of. One day when she was sick a certain chief came and sat by her bedside. He talked about the good work she had done and declared that he would gladly die in her stead if only she could be spared to teach his people.

Although the majority of the Nez Perces were friendly toward their teachers, Spalding began to have difficulties similar to those experienced by Whitman among the Cayuses. Troubles increased in proportion to the settlers that arrived. The Indians could not help being suspicious when they saw the steady stream of whites. This flame of suspicion was fanned into a blaze by Tom Hill, a Delaware Indian who had drifted into the Clearwater country. By 1846, some of the villages had recognized Hill's leadership and had made him their chief. Tom Hill was an atheist who repeatedly condemned the Christian religion. He warned the Nez Perces that the whites were conniving to take all the Indian lands. Following the example of the Cayuses, some of them began to demand payment for water and land.

Spalding charged William Craig, the mountain man who had settled in the valley not far from the mission, with stirring up trouble. From the time Craig moved in, the cordial relations between the missionary and his red people began to deteriorate. Allegedly, Craig told the Indians they were being treated like dogs and hogs. Spalding had a talk with the mountain man but got little satisfaction. Upon the heels of this conversation, some Indians—supposedly under the influence of the white man—destroyed Spalding's mill dam. In the Sunday service following this act old James, whose daughter was married to Craig, rose in meeting and boldly stated that Spalding was making the people miserable and bringing them to ruin.

Sick at heart, Spalding said no more but rebuilt his dam, this time using rock to make it more substantial. In the meantime, Craig and the other mountain man who had come to the Clearwater with him went away. But within a year the troublemaker was back and Spalding returned good for evil by sawing the logs for Craig's new cabin. After this Craig worked for Spalding for a while, seemingly with a change of heart.

After a temporary lull, the troublemaking Indians were again up to their old tricks—gambling in defiance of Christian teachings and stealing fence rails to make their fires. Again Spalding charged that the evil influence of the mountain man was back of it all. He called Craig's cabin a "resort for gamblers." From 1845 on Spalding looked with sorrow upon the decay of what he had hoped would be a creditable piece of work pleasing to the Lord. The worst element—though a minority—occasionally broke windows, disturbed the Sabbath services, threatened those who tried to do right and even offered insults to Eliza and the children.

Perhaps the deepest disappointment was the deterioration of the school. Where 234 pupils once came to learn, only a few now appeared—some merely to disturb. For two winters, it was this way, with no prospect of better things to come.

Even nature—it seemed—conspired against the missionaries. The winter of 1846–1847 was the worst within the memory of the oldest inhabitants. Food was scarce. The wild game died. The Nez Perces lost about half their stock. The Indians themselves suffered in their skin lodges. All of this discomfort tended to increase the discontent.

In August, 1847 matters seemed to be approaching a crisis. Hoodlums seized Spalding's mill and he would not fight to recover it. There was no grist ground and the malcontents blamed their teacher because they had no meal. Despite the fact that he considered his position precarious Spalding did his duty by accompanying the Indians out to the root ground to preach to large gatherings of natives. His intention was to spend a week with them before they "went to buffalo." But something happened to cause him suddenly to change his mind. The threat came in a most dramatic way one night after the fires had burned low and the Indians, wrapped in their robes, were all asleep—or pretending to be. Spalding was lying near, motionless but wide-eyed. Presently, an Indian crawled out from his blanket and began to deliver a speech. According to Nez Perce custom, if anyone had an important message to communicate, he would wait till all had gone to bed, then rise and deliver it in flowery oratory.

The brave's harangue was an attack on Spalding for his refusal to grind grain—and it was a threat of violence to be carried out against him the following day. This was enough for Spalding; he arose at dawn and set out with all possible speed. He did not believe that the Indians really intended to kill him but he was taking no chances.

Things looked dark indeed. Evil forces were at work and Spalding could not foresee what the outcome would be. But he refused to desert his beloved Indians. He continued at his post without fear, trusting that in God's good time they would see the errors of their ways and turn back to the path of right and reason.

14 • Night Falls on the Mission Field

THE YEAR 1847 DAWNED OMINOUSLY for the American Board missions. The Indians were uneasy. The missionaries were uneasy, too, yet there did not seem to be anything tangible to warrant a feeling of panic. Spring of that year brought word of the coming of the largest body of immigrants that had ever headed westward. When summer arrived, bringing between four and five thousand settlers over the Oregon Trail, the Indians were fully aroused and began to vent their anger in various ways. They stole goods and even attacked some wagons in one train, compelling Dr. Whitman to use stern measures to prevent a repetition of such acts.

The time for improving conditions was fast passing. Whitman had lost the confidence of many of the Cayuses, who were thoroughly convinced that their teacher was more interested in the palefaces than in them. He took their side in disputes. He sheltered them, fed them, cured their ills, cared for their orphans and kept a school especially for them—and they firmly believed that he was giving Oregon away to the white settlers.

Malcontents worked to poison the hearts of the natives against the missionaries. Joe Lewis, a halfbreed troublemaker, arrived with the summer immigration of 1847 and began preaching to the Cayuses that they would surely lose their lands if they did not act. Chief Tiloukaikt was not friendly any more and Tamsucky, whom Narcissa called "a villain of an Indian," was working against the whites in an underhanded way. The atmosphere was charged with danger, yet Dr. Whitman—on the surface, at least—remained indifferent. If he saw signs, he obstinately refused to read or heed them. Hudson's Bay Company suggested that he go away for a while until the threat blew over. Whitman did not go, although he talked about the time when the missions might possibly have to be given up.

Paul Kane, the artist, saw a demonstration at Fort Walla Walla that convinced him the Indians were definitely planning to take the life of Dr. Whitman, as an act of revenge for the death of Elijah Hedding. Hedding—named by Jason Lee after a Methodist bishop—was the son of a Walla Walla chief, Peu-peu-mox-mox, or "Yellow Serpent." Young Hedding had been killed by white renegades while he and some companions were driving a herd of cattle from California. When the outrage became generally known, all the Indians in the area were inflamed and began threatening revenge on some well known white man.

It was one of these demonstrations which Paul Kane witnessed. Alarmed, Kane mounted his horse and set out to warn Dr. Whitman. Reaching Waiilatpu about nine o'clock at night, he related everything that happened at Walla Walla. Even this failed to rouse the doctor. He thanked Kane for his concern but said he did not fear a general uprising. There had been critical times before; they had passed, however, as this too would pass. For Whitman life would go on as usual—planning, building, riding near and far to attend the sick. He had no intention of deserting his post.

In the later summer a virulent form of measles broke out, striking down white and Indian alike. Death followed death, in spite of Whitman's efforts to cope with the epidemic. All of this was magnified by Joe Lewis and Tamsucky. Whitman, finally convinced that Joe was the key troublemaker, contrived to get rid of him. It happened that an immigrant wagon needed a driver. Joe was persuaded to take the job. However, he was soon back in company with another halfbreed, Nicholas Finley, and continued his subversive work. He told the Indians that the missionaries were scattering poison through the air that the red men breathed.

Fear and suspicion of the whites had been accumulating for years in the minds of the Indians. As far back as 1811, when Fort Astoria was being built, the natives were held in check by a threat to spread smallpox among them. It was believed that Americans had used smallpox to try to exterminate the Blackfeet, the most warlike of the mountain tribes. It was remembered, too, that back in 1841 Whitman had put a drug in the watermelons to keep the Indians from stealing them. What he had used, really, was a strong cathartic—not poison. It was true that the missionaries had put out poison for wolves. Indian dogs had died of it and some of the Indians had been made deathly sick by eating the poison bait. Fear of being poisoned was persistent, as was suspicion of the white man's medicine. The Indians sometimes killed their *te-wats* if they failed to cure. The Whitmans were well aware of this; they knew also that the doctor had been blamed for the deaths of two prominent Indians.

The Indians had cause for their deep despondency that terrible fall of 1847, when so many of them died. William Craig declared that deaths among the Cayuses numbered 197. If true, this must have been about half of the entire tribe. In the warped opinion of the natives, Dr. Whitman had become not only the betrayer of their interests but a dangerous medicine man, as well. Nor could they forget an incident that happened in August of the same year. An immigrant had been murdered at The Dalles and suspicion rested on a certain Cayuse. When the doctor met the accused, he refused to shake the Indian's hand. That same night the young Cayuse choked to death on a piece of dried buffalo meat. The Indians at once blamed Dr. Whitman for casting an evil spell on the man. Feelings rose to such a dangerous pitch that Mrs. Whitman felt impelled to give a feast in honor of the young brave who had died.

The year wore away to November. On the twenty-second of the month Henry Spalding arrived at Waiilatpu with a pack train of seventeen horses loaded with grain. His own grist mill was not in operation—thanks to unfriendly Nez Perces—so he had brought his grain to Whitman's station to have it ground. He also brought his daughter Eliza, now ten years old, to be placed in the mission school. Spalding found the station crowded to capacity with immigrants occupying every available space, including the blacksmith shop. All told, there were seventy-two persons, not including Joe Lewis and Nicholas Finley.

The measles had been rampant at the mission. Most of Whitman's family were on the mend, except Helen Mar Meek and Louise Sager, who were at death's door. Two children of the Osborn family had died. Three to five Indians in the community died each day, which did not speak well for Dr. Whitman's skill in medicine from the Cayuse point of view.

Dr. Whitman was preparing to make a call on certain Indian patients in the lodge of Five Crows, some distance from the mission, and asked Spalding to accompany him. During the trip Spalding's horse fell and bruised him rather badly but in spite of the accident they arrived just before dawn at the lodge of friendly Stickus, near the present site of Pendleton, Oregon. While Spalding recuperated here, Whitman paid his professional calls at the camps of Five Crows and Young Chief. Afterward, he visited the two Catholic missionaries at Umatilla and had tea with them. Father J. B. Brouillet later testified that Whitman had expressed a willingness to sell his station at Waiilatpu whenever a majority of the Cayuses desired it.

About sunset, the doctor returned to the lodge of Stickus. Although almost exhausted, he felt that he had to hurry back to his patients at the mission. Spalding was too stiff to undertake the trip that night so Whitman prepared to go back alone. Before the doctor left, Stickus warned him again against Joe Lewis and the evil reports he was spreading. "I do not believe him," said the old Indian, "but some do, and I fear they intend to harm you. You had better go away for a while till my people have better hearts."

On Monday, November 29, 1847, the occupants of the mission went about their usual business. The shops were busy, the mill was grinding grist and the school bell was ringing for a new pupil, Eliza Spalding. The tailor was fashioning a suit for Dr. Whitman and the music teacher, Andrew Rogers, was working in the garden. Fifteen miles away in the Blue Mountains several men were turning out lumber at the rate of about 2000 feet per day. Several people were sick in bed, and most of the other men were helping to butcher an ox while some blanketed Indians looked on.

It had been a cloudy, dismal day and at midafternoon fog still clung to the hills. Two Indians emerged from the mist around the mill pond and made their way toward the mission house. The first was Chief Tiloukaikt, who claimed ownership of the mission land. Following him came Tomahas, known variously as Red Cloak, Feather Cap and "The Murderer." Several of the Whitman family were in the living room and the doctor was sitting by the fire reading. Mrs. Whitman answered a knock at the door and found two Indians wanting medicine. The doctor went into the kitchen to get the drugs from the cabinet and asked Narcissa to lock the door behind him. In a few minutes a shot was heard in the kitchen, and Narcissa cried out in terror, "The Indians will murder us all!" At that moment, Mary Ann Bridger burst in, crying, "They've killed Father!"

It seems that Mary Ann, who was about thirteen, and John Sager, seventeen, were busy in the kitchen when the doctor entered with the two Indians. While Chief Tiloukaikt held Whitman in conversation Tomahas stepped up behind and struck him with a tomahawk. There was a struggle, then a shot. John Sager jumped for a gun but was shot dead before he could pull the trigger. Terrified, Mary Ann climbed through the window and ran to the main door of the living room.

The shot was a signal for a general attack. The robed Indians who had been spectators at the butchering now whipped out weapons and began their frightful work. The facts of the massacre will never be completely known because the survivors, being in different places, told varying versions of the story. Mrs. Whitman, assisted by two other women, managed to lift the doctor onto the sofa. When Narcissa saw that he was dead she cried out, "That Joe! That Joe! He has done it all!"

The blows fell fast and there were cries of horror as one victim after another was felled. Mrs. Whitman, who was looking through the glass door, received a shot under her left arm and fell screaming. Staggering to her feet, she began praying aloud, "Lord, save these little ones." Then came a hammering on the locked door. At Mrs. Whitman's command, all the members of the mission house—about twelve—took refuge in the room above. Hardly had they got up the stairs when a shattering of glass announced the entrance of the savages. After gashing the face of their teacher and hacking the body of John Sager, the murderers went on in search of other victims. When they started up the stairs, they were met by the point of an old matchlock which Narcissa had hastily handed to Andrew Rogers.

Tamsucky, nevertheless, came on cautiously, all the time trying to persuade Mrs. Whitman and the others to go to a place of greater safety—to Finley's lodge, where they would be protected. Although she had called Tamsucky "a villain of an Indian," Narcissa, deceived by his false assurances, led the way downstairs, murmuring, "God has raised up a friend." While they were en route to Finley's lodge several shots were fired at them. One struck Narcissa, who was already weak from loss of blood. Her body was thrown into the mud and Tamsucky hurried the children away to the promised safety.

When night closed in, Dr. Whitman and his wife, Andrew Rogers and six other men lay dead. Peter D. Hall, carpenter, W.D. Canfield and the Osborn family escaped. Hall reported the massacre at Fort Walla Walla, then started for the Willamette. He was never heard of again and it is believed that he was drowned while trying to cross the Columbia River. Canfield hid in a corner of the blacksmith shop and when darkness fell set out on foot for Lapwai to warn the Spaldings.

In two days the savages took the lives of fourteen people, Mrs. Whitman being the only woman. John and Francis Sager were among the victims. Louise Sager and Helen Mar Meek died of disease within a few days. The forty-seven survivors were held captive at the mission. Father Brouillet, who was on his way to visit Chief Tiloukaikt, was stunned by the frightful news. He hurried to Waiilatpu where he looked upon the wreckage of what had so recently been a prosperous mission. Mutilated bodies were lying where they had fallen. It was the priest's sad task to direct the burial of the slain. Joe Stanfield, an undesirable French-Canadian who had been hanging around the mission for some time, dug the trench. Marcus and Narcissa, who had given their all for Oregon, were put into this long, shallow grave.

Meanwhile, at Lapwai, another scene was being acted out. On Saturday morning, December fourth, a stranger suddenly appeared at the door of the Spalding mission house. Upon being invited he came in and, leaning against the mantel as if for needed support, asked, "Has Mr. Spalding come yet?" Without waiting for a reply, he continued huskily, "I have heavy tidings; they are all murdered at the doctor's."

The messenger was W. D. Canfield, who had escaped from the scene of the carnage. Eliza stood pale but in perfect control while he related what had happened. He warned that the Cayuses would soon be on the Clearwater and that it would be necessary to take immediate steps for the protection of the mission. Mrs. Spalding insisted that their only safety lay in the friendly Nez Perces. Canfield was dubious but she said firmly, "The quicker we throw ourselves on them the better." Immediately, she summoned two chiefs and sent them with a message to William Craig, who had caused Spalding so much trouble in the past. At the same time, she dispatched Timothy and Eagle to Waiilatpu to rescue little Eliza, if she were still alive.

Following consultation it was decided that the whites should move to Craig's house, where strong protection could be set up. In the midst of the moving Henry Spalding himself appeared, to the complete joy of the family. He had been riding at night and hiding by day, tortured by the fear that he would find nothing at the mission but corpses and smoking ruins.

Some of the hostile Nez Perce warriors had hoped for a chance to wipe out the settlement but were thwarted by the firm stand taken by Craig and the few immigrants on the premises. Smarting under the defeat of their purpose, they fell to looting the mission buildings. A few of old Chief Joseph's followers took part in the dishonorable act. When Spalding learned of Joseph's "treason" he was sick at heart, for he had believed the chief's conversion to be permanent. "Joseph turned back to Egypt," the devoted teacher said regretfully, "but Timothy was faithful, not only to God, but to his white friends."

Timothy and Eagle arrived at Waiilatpu on the very day that the savages finished murdering the last two victims, whose bodies were still lying out in front of the door. They found little Eliza alive but so weak she could hardly get up without help. She greeted Timothy with a glad cry but when she learned that her captors would not let her go she broke down and sobbed bitterly. Old Timothy took up her apron, wiped her tears and said brokenly, "Poor Eliza, don't cry. You shall see your mother."

Word of the massacre reached Vancouver December sixth, and at once Chief Factor Peter Skene Ogden and several men made their way up the river to ransom the captives. The news had spread into the Willamette Valley where the Americans, aroused to fury by the bloody deed, were soon organizing an armed force to move against the murderers. Ogden was bent on rescuing the prisoners before word of the military plans reached the Cayuses. He feared that such knowledge would result in violence against the women and children still at the mercy of the savages.

Ogden arrived at Fort Walla Walla December 19 and at once called a council of the chiefs. Expecting punishment, the Indians were hesitant and skeptical. After some haggling, though, they agreed to accept the ransom consisting of thirty-seven pounds of tobacco, sixty-two blankets (twelve of these and some smaller articles to go to certain Nez Perces), sixty-three cotton shirts, twelve guns and 600 loads of ammunition. As soon as the agreement had been made, word was taken to Waiilatpu to release the prisoners and send them all to Fort Walla Walla. Oxen were hitched to wagons and in due time the captives, fifty-two in number, were on the road to the fort and freedom.

When the order came for the Spaldings to leave the Clearwater without delay they lost no time in complying. Gathering up necessities, they placed themselves in the care of an escort of fifty mounted Nez Perces and struck the Walla Walla trail for the last time. At the time of their departure, a Christian Indian—thought to be old Timothy—paid his respects to Mrs. Spalding in this simple eulogy:

> Now my beloved teacher you are passing over my country for the last time. You are leaving us forever and my people, O my people will see no more light. We shall meet no more in the schoolroom & my children, O my children, will live only in a night that will have no morning. When we reach Walla Walla I shall look upon your face for the last time in this world. But this book [holding it in his hand] in which your hands have written and caused me to write the words of God I shall carry in my bosom till I lie down in the grave.[21]

The Spaldings reached Fort Walla Walla on January the first, 1848, where they were reunited with their daughter, Eliza, who, as Spalding said, was "a mere skeleton, and too weak to stand." He feared that her mind might be as much impaired as her body.

On January second, a fleet of boats manned by skillful oarsmen nosed into position at the wharf, and on the shore stood Peter Skene Ogden, directing the embarkation of fifty-seven men, women and children. David Malin, the little halfbreed Spanish boy, now a ward of Hudson's Bay Company, was not permitted to go. As the bateaux launched out into the current the Sager girls looked toward the shore and saw the boy crying as if his heart would break.

At Tshimakain the news of the massacre left all the missionaries stone cold. There followed days of uncertainty and anxious waiting. To stay might mean death if the Cayuses were able to turn the Spokane Indians against their teachers; to go in the dead of winter, with Mary Walker in poor health, a houseful of children and another expected soon, was impossible. It seemed best to await developments, especially since the Indians did not want their teachers to leave.

On the last day of December, John Richardson was born to the Walkers. Come what may, this event forced the family—for the immediate present, at least—to put themselves in the care of their Indian friends, who vowed they would die in defense of their teachers. Chief Big Head—or Old Chief as he was sometimes called now—was eager to do the right thing by the missionaries. He co-operated in every way with Walker and Eells in combating the rumors and propaganda that filtered into the community. Since the times were so uncertain and the mission work nearly at a standstill anyway, the men thought best to take their families to Fort Colville for a while. The men then returned to Tshimakain to take care of the property and keep in touch with the Indians.

Word came that an Indian council was to be held. John Lee Lewes, in charge at Colville, thought it inadvisable to attend a meeting which drew together such a large number of savages; it was hard to predict what might happen. But the missionaries felt that it was in their interests to keep informed on every development. One of them should be present and the man better fitted for the job was Cushing Eells. Walker, it was pointed out, "was five years older, considerably more infirm and much heavier." This might prove a handicap if he should be hard pressed and forced to flee. (Walker had then reached the ripe old age of thirty-eight.)

Eells attended the council and from that time was almost constantly on the move in the interests of peace. He opened up communications with Fort Waters near Waiilatpu and with the help of old Solomon sent messages back and forth. He was in the saddle most of the time and, according to his own story, spent only ten nights at Fort Colville during the ten weeks that his family were there. Since he was a counselor of peace he never went armed. He rode a fast horse and led a pack mule, which seemed to have the uncanny power of scenting an Indian thief a mile away. In camping, he hobbled his horse and staked out the mule. He said that when Indians came within smelling distance the long-eared sentinel would "snort and tear, and make such a fuss that the master would be awake in no time." Cushing Eells deserves great credit for his self-sacrificing, courageous work at that critical time. Besides traveling 1400 miles to help keep the Indians at peace, he managed to give Walker some assistance at the mission farm.

Mary Walker was convinced that their services among the Spokane Indians were concluded forever and was resigned to the change. At the end of more than nine years she had small hope for the salvation of these people. She believed that they were a doomed race. There were none who were pious, although there were some who talked and prayed and pretended to be religious. There were none who were honest, none who would not lie if it were an advantage to do so. She thought that "mean" was the most appropriate word for describing Indian character.

The last of May 1848, word came to Colville that a body of sixty American volunteers was on its way to Tshimakain to escort the two missionary families to the Willamette Valley. John Lee Lewes took over most of the cattle, trading horses for cows. He arranged to send by boat such household goods as could not be carried on pack horses. Since the farm implements were given to the Indians there were few things to go on the bateaux.

Leaving the place they had called home was not easy. There were hundreds of associations built around Tshimakain that were heartwarming and unforgettable. In memory of their life here Mary Walker composed a poem for her six children. In part, it reads:

Tshimakain! Oh, how fine,
Fruits and flowers abounding;
And the breeze through the trees
Life and health conferring.

And the Sabbath was so quiet,
And the log-house chapel,
Where the Indians used to gather
In their robes and blankets.

Now it stands, alas! forsaken.
No one with the Bible
Comes to teach the tawny Skailu (*people*)
Of Kai-ko-len-so-tin (*God*).

Other spots on earth may be
To other hearts as dear;
But not to me; the reason why
It was the place that bore me.

On June 25, 1848 the missionaries were in the Willamette Valley, attending Sunday services among white people exclusively. This was their introduction to the future that was opening before them—a new world of new people, new activities, new problems.

The American expeditionary force under the command of Cornelius Gilliam left The Dalles for Umatilla on February 24, 1848. After a short skirmish with hostiles the troops made camp near the Whitman mission, which now lay in ruins. The buildings had been looted of everything that could be carried away, and then burned. Scattered about the grounds were the bones of some of the victims of the massacre, disinterred by wolves. Perrin Whitman was able to identify his uncle's skull with the two hatchet marks in the back of it. Mingled with the grime and dried blood were strands of Narcissa Whitman's golden hair. The soldiers gathered up the scattered remains and, using a wagon box for a coffin, buried them again.

After some light skirmishes with the volunteers, the Cayuses fled to the mountains where they were safe from pursuit, and there for two years, guilty and innocent alike—homesick for their valleys—led a miserable existence. For their general welfare, they decided to deliver up five of their number to pay the price of the Whitman massacre. These were Chief Tiloukaikt and Tomahas, the ringleaders, and three others known as Klokamas, Isaiachalakis and Kiamasumpkin. They were given a trial at Oregon City and all five were sentenced to be hanged June 3, 1850, although Kiamasumpkin is believed to have been innocent. When Tilaukaikt was asked why he gave himself up he is reported to have said, "Did not you missionaries teach us that Christ died to save his people?—So we die to save our people." Henry Spalding offered his services as spiritual adviser but all five preferred to receive the last ministrations from the hands of a Roman Catholic priest. Joe Meek—then United States marshal—played the role of executioner.

It would be a solace to Marcus and Narcissa Whitman if—in that "Beyond Land"—they could know that only a small group of Cayuses actually participated in the massacre. Most of the Indians regretted the tragedy that robbed them of their teachers and brought woe to the tribe. Many kept up the daily devotions as taught them by the Whitmans, and held to the strict observance of the Sabbath for many years after Waiilatpu had been blotted out. And Marcus Whitman lived on in the memory of loyal old Stickus, who could never keep back the tears when he spoke of the tragic death of his teacher.

PART THREE

THE CATHOLICS ENTER THE FIELD

15 • *Two Priests from Canada*

For years the Canadian settlers on French Prairie had lived like sheep without a shepherd. Former employees of the Hudson's Bay Company, they had settled down on their little farms, married Indian wives and were rearing their children without benefit of clergy. They were all Catholics, yet no priest had ever been among them. After the coming of the Methodists—with whom they lived on friendly terms—they began to ponder the question of getting a pastor of their own faith. They took the matter up with Dr. McLoughlin, who offered to send their request to the Bishop of Quebec.

This seemed easy. Hudson's Bay Company would provide the transportation for the priests and the settlers would build a church and contribute toward the support. But the Bishop disappointed the people, saying that he had no one to send at present, although as soon as a priest was available he would be sent. Well, they would wait—Joseph Gervais, Etienne Lucier, Louis La Bonte and all the rest. And while they waited they would build a chapel against that future day.

Meanwhile, Dr. McLoughlin was wondering whether the Catholics should work in the same field as the Protestants. The two denominations were usually in disagreement and this might confuse the Indians and cause trouble all around. He did give his consent, but took no responsibility in the matter.

After three years, hope flamed anew in the hearts on French Prairie. The Bishop had not forgotten; he was sending not one but two missionary priests. The one chosen to bear the responsibility under the title of Vicar General of Oregon was Francis Norbert Blanchet, born of a good family in the parish of Saint Pierre, Lower Canada, on September 3, 1795. As long as Francis Blanchet could remember, he had had a brother, Magloire—younger by two years—a playmate at home and a companion at school. The brothers were both destined for Oregon but neither was aware of this when he entered St. Joseph's, the parish school at St. Pierre.

Francis was ordained in the old cathedral at Quebec. From now on, he would be out of the little family circle, doing service for God and the church. When he was twenty-five, he was sent to the isolated parish of St. Antoine in New Brunswick, and he could have found no better school in which to train for the career of missionary. It was a primitive spot. There were no roads or bridges; all the traveling that was done took place in the summer, and by means of canoes up and down the small streams and along the broken coast.

After seven years, Father Blanchet was transferred to The Cedars, a parish near Montreal on the St. Lawrence River. Montreal was the fur capital of North America and Abbe Blanchet was located where he could see and feel the current of life moving endlessly toward the West or returning with news and furs from the faroff region. But as pastor Father Blanchet had other duties than watching the bateaux splashing by on the shimmering waters of the great river. He had a flock to guard and instruct. In 1832 the cholera broke out and it became his duty to minister to all, of whatever race or creed. It was a heartbreaking experience. In Montreal whole families were wiped out. The dead wagons rumbled by incessantly and there were barely enough well persons to care for the sick and dying. When the plague finally loosened its grip, the parishioners—Catholic and Protestant—presented Father Blanchet with a silver cup in appreciation of his heroic self-sacrifices during the epidemic.

Father Blanchet's summons to Oregon came in April 1838, along with orders to leave as soon as possible. Appointed as the Vicar General's assistant was Modeste Demers of Red River, who had been ordained the previous year. He had been serving St.

Boniface, a frontier parish where he was introduced to Indians as well as to some of the problems connected with teaching them.

Since Father Blanchet had no worldly goods to think about it did not take long to make preparations. Following a short visit with Magloire, he joined the Montreal Express, westward bound. After several weeks of canoe travel he arrived at Red River where Modeste Demers was waiting for him. Here, they talked over the instructions given by the Bishop of Quebec. Their first duty was to convert the scattered Indians of Oregon. Their second object was to minister to the "wretched Christians who have adopted the vices of the Indians and live in licentiousness and forgetfulness of their duties."

In July 1838 the Vicar General and Father Demers set out on the tedious journey to the Rocky Mountains, which they reached in a little less than three months. On a high mountain in what is now the province of Alberta, at three o'clock in the morning of a crisp autumn day, Father Blanchet held mass as a praise service to the Almighty. When the next Sabbath fell upon them, they were at the big bend of the Columbia River, at a place called Boat Encampment, where Abbe Demers said the first mass ever celebrated in Old Oregon.

Traveling on, they reached the House of the Lakes in ten hours. Here a happy company—chiefly employees of Hudson's Bay—waited with their wives to leave on the barge bound for Fort Vancouver. At daylight the two priests embarked in the first of two large canoes launched on the Columbia. The water roughened as the cascades were approached. Here the river, crowded between two high basaltic walls, was treacherous. The first boat rode the riffles with no damaging results. The second barge was overcrowded but would have been safe enough had the passengers obeyed the order to sit still. The first stretch of rapids was safely passed but when the second was entered and the boat began to take water panic ensued. Wallace, an English botanist, jumped up, took off his coat and, with his wife, plunged into the foaming rapids. This unsteadied the craft. It careened, spun around crazily and overturned, spilling the occupants into the surging waters. When the survivors struggled to the shore, they sadly counted their losses. The rapids, which from this time forward would be known as "The Dalles of the Dead," had claimed the lives of twelve out of twenty-six. "Sad, long, and excruciating was the night," wrote Father Blanchet in his narrative of the tragedy. The two priests had the task of saying requiem mass and of erecting twelve crosses.

When the canoe had been repaired, the remainder of the passengers embarked for the long downriver trip. There were no more accidents and the priests gave thanks for a safe arrival at Fort Vancouver November 24, 1838. Father Blanchet's journey from Montreal had occupied six months. Here at the fort they were welcomed by Sir James Douglas, who was acting as Chief Factor in the absence of Dr. John McLoughlin, enjoying a year's leave from his duties. Douglas was more reserved than the genial, white-haired "Father of Oregon" but his hospitality was genuine. Welcoming their priests, also, was a delegation of Canadians, including Joseph Gervais, Etienne Lucier and Pierre Belique.

On the first Lord's Day mass was said in the schoolhouse at the fort. It was attended by French-Canadians, many of whom had not been a part of any religious service for as long as fifteen years. They were all eager to renew their connections with the church. "If only our task were to reclaim these simple earnest folk, how easy it would be!" said the priests. But they had the halfbreed children to instruct and the Indian wives to convert. Then there was the language to learn. This last was a harder problem than the priests had anticipated for, instead of one language to master, there were numerous dialects complicated still further by the Chinook jargon, a commercial medium used both by white traders and the natives. The wives did not speak French, but a mixture of their own language and the Chinook jargon. The Vicar General was baffled. He looked again at his instructions. They still said, "Learn the language, so that teaching may be done as soon as possible without the aid of an interpreter."

Since the Chinook jargon had such a widespread use on the coast the priests decided to concentrate on the learning of it. Father Demers, a linguist with some experience in Indian dialects, went to work and was soon able to teach some prayers in that hodgepodge of words. In time he composed some simple hymns which the Indians enjoyed singing. Meanwhile Father Blanchet was spending his time with the French-Canadians and their families. He instructed them in both English and French and began preparing the ablest of them to hold the flock together in the absence of a priest. A census taken at the fort showed seventy-six Catholics, including a number of Iroquois Indians in the company's service.

With so many diverse and scattered people to reach, the priests decided—in the beginning, at least—to adopt the practice of "holding" or "giving" missions of a few weeks in length in different areas of Oregon. They made the Indians' acquaintance, taught catechisms, prayers and songs, and gave as much in the way of instruction as the Indians were able to understand. When they moved on, they left in charge an official of the company or the most capable Indian, who would call the village together regularly for simple devotions. In a few weeks again the priests would return for another period of teaching.

Having received permission from Dr. McLoughlin to build a mission in the Willamette Valley, Father Blanchet made his way by canoe to French Prairie where the residents proudly showed him the crude little chapel they had built in 1836. On January 6, the feast of the Epiphany, mass was said for the first time in what later became the State of Oregon. At this time Father Blanchet blessed the first church built in the Pacific Northwest and dedicated it to the Apostle Paul. The parish was to be known as St. Paul's.

The Vicar General spent four weeks teaching, baptizing some and preparing others for the sacrament at a later time. During this period even the most ignorant learned to make the sign of the cross and to repeat the Lord's Prayer, the Hail Mary and the Apostles' Creed. Father Blanchet also blessed marriages and performed rites for other couples who had been united in marriage by Indian custom not recognized by the church.

Soon after the arrival of Father Blanchet in the Willamette some friction developed with the Methodists who had come in 1834. The Reverend Mr. David Leslie, acting superintendent of the mission in the absence of Jason Lee, resented the Catholic policy of re-marrying couples already married under the Methodist discipline. Further, the Methodists objected to Catholic encroachment on what they considered their sphere of missionary activity. They charged the Catholics with baptizing Indians wholesale, without proof of conversion. On their part the Catholics found the Methodists spending too much time on themselves and neglecting the Indians; they also accused the Protestants of deliberately circulating false reports that were derogatory of the Catholics and their beliefs. Despite differences, the two denominations continued as neighbors for several years to come.

16 • *Planting the Cross at Cowlitz*

ON DECEMBER 12, 1838 FATHER Blanchet took Augustine Rochon, the only personal servant that had been allowed him, and set out in a canoe with four Indian paddlers. They floated down the Columbia to the mouth of the swift Cowlitz River, then went up this stream until they reached Cowlitz Prairie. Here were located Hudson's Bay Company's extensive farms, managed by Simon Plomondon, assisted by five farmers.

Before he did anything at all Father Blanchet celebrated mass, the first to be held in the Cowlitz area. Here was a suitable spot for a mission—convenient to Fort Vancouver, flat land with timber on the borders, fertile soil and a river for a roadway. There was lush grass, green even in December. There was fish for food and game not too far distant. What better place could one ask? The scenery, too, was pleasing to the eye. St. Helen's loomed in the distance; nearer rose majestic, elusive Mt. Rainier, reflecting the first bright flush of morning and catching the last gleam of the setting sun.

Father Blanchet selected 640 acres of land and set Augustine

Rochon to work splitting rails. Soon religious services were held regularly for the natives and the company men. One day in the spring there arrived a delegation of strange Indians led by their chief, Tslalakun. They were hungry and tired and their lacerated feet were showing through makeshift sandals. They had come by canoe from Whidbey Island. Having heard that a "blackrobe" was living here, they had come to verify the report. Now that they had found him they could do little at first but stare in wonder.

It was while laboring here with the Indians that Father Blanchet invented a teaching device known as the "Catholic Ladder." It was a chart, showing by horizontal bars, dots and religious drawings the history of the Universal Church from the time of Adam. It represented the Catholic Church as the straight road, the right road to Heaven; all other, newer teachings were wrong. The Spaldings devised what became called the "Protestant Ladder," which showed graphically another point of view. Blanchet's pupils believed that some kind of magic lived in the "ladder." They called it *sahale,* meaning "stick from above."

The winter was unusually mild, permitting plowing and fall planting and work in the woods. Rochon made 600 rails for fencing and squared timbers for a house and barn. The timbers would be hauled in as soon as he could get the loan of a yoke of oxen from Simon Plomondon. In a few weeks a mission house was built. A barn also took shape and was ready for the first harvest—six bushels of wheat and nine of peas. Before time for the next planting, Rochon had fenced twenty-four additional acres and put fifteen more under the plow. A small chapel under the patronage of St. Francis Xavier was soon on the way to completion.

An unpleasant incident occurred which for some time gave Father Blanchet considerable worry. An Indian sold Rochon a horse, then in a few days came and demanded it back. The Frenchman refused; the Indian became insistent. A fight started in which Rochon was stabbed, though not seriously. At the critical moment a halfbreed employee of the company came running to the scene and the savage fled. The priest had little peace of mind for a long time. The incident—small as it was—might lose him all the prestige he had won for the church on Cowlitz Prairie. The Indian, however, gave no further trouble. The Vicar General learned that the Hudson's Bay Company was a strong factor in keeping the peace in Oregon. Its officials were always on the alert for any occurrence which might endanger good relationships between the whites and the red men.

In 1840, the two priests changed places for a while. Father Demers, who had started the mission work at Nisqually on Puget Sound, now came to Cowlitz while the Vicar General went to Nisqually.

Father Demers arrived in the Cowlitz in a canoe with his halfbreed assistant, J.B. Boucher, and three oarsmen. He carried a stock of provisions and, what was dearer to his heart, a fifty-pound bell for the chapel of St. Xavier. It was hard work installing the bell in the crude belfry, but the reward was worth the effort. To hear the sweet tones pealing out the Angelus gave comfort to the priest and inspiration to the newly converted Indians.

Demers spent the winter here with the forty-six residents of the community. He was not overoptimistic about the quick transformation of the natives from savagery to civilization. He had learned by experience not to rely altogether on the first demonstration made by the Indians at their conversion. The Cowlitz people, however, gave better promise than some others he had taught.

Many obstacles lay in the way of a quick change: their wandering life, suspicion of the white man's customs, belief in polygamy and magic, inability to understand fully what the priests were trying to teach them. The magic by which the sick were treated was a fraud, yet the Indians clung to it. No matter what was asked in the way of fees they would gladly give it, lest a worse evil spirit come to torment them.

When a person died, his corpse was laid out in the best garments obtainable and wrapped in blankets or mats. His eyes were covered with a bandage of *higua*—rare shells—and his nostrils filled with the same. The casket was an open canoe set upon four stakes driven into the ground. In the canoe, the body was placed face downward, with the head pointing toward the mouth of the river, and finally covered with a thick layer of mats. Necessities for the journey into Spiritland, such as kettles, skins and shell money, were then placed upon the coffin canoe. As the final act came the demonstrations of grief in the form of weeping, wailing and shrieking. Father Demers witnessed a funeral of this kind conducted for an unbaptized child. He tried to persuade the parents to take the body out of the canoe and give it Christian burial but the forces of tradition were too strong. The mortality among these Indians, the priest said, was "frightful."

Both priests believed that progress toward civilization would be very, very slow and that it would be unwise to try to push the Indians. They observed caution in baptizing adults without careful preparation. They encouraged farming and gardening among their charges, and did everything in their power to show the advantages of a "settled" way of life. Said Father Demers, "The peas and the potatoes may make them forget the berries and the camas."

17 • The Mission on Puget Sound

THE VICAR GENERAL WENT TO Fort Nisqually in the spring of 1840. William Kittson was the commandant and there were five families at the post, including his own. Mr. Kittson spoke the Indian tongue as well as English and French, and his services as an interpreter were in demand. The Methodist missionary, Dr. Richmond, had just arrived with his family and assistants.

Father Blanchet began by devoting the afternoons to teaching. The first day, only a handful of Indians put in an appearance, but each succeeding day brought larger and larger congregations until the number reached about three hundred. Prominent among the chiefs was Tslalakun, who had visited the blackrobe at Cowlitz. At first, the meetings were held in a tent, but the swelling numbers soon forced a move out into the open. Here the priest used his ladder with the same success. It was hung on a tree where all could see it. After listening to one of the illustrated Bible stories Chief Tslalakun said, "That man Noah had more children than the first man, Adam." Although the Indians flocked around to hear Father Blanchet's stories and shake his hand they presented only two children for baptism. They were afraid of the "new medicine."

Chief Sahiwamish headed a band of Indians who had come a long distance to hear the teachings. Among these was a man sick of tuberculosis, whom Father Blanchet began preparing for baptism. One day the ill man mysteriously disappeared. It took Blanchet's messengers two days to locate him and bring him back to the mission. Some of the invalid's friends, suddenly stricken with a superstitious fear, had decided to remove him from the strange "medicine" of the blackrobe. However, the man finally received baptism, after which he gave evidence of having found peace in God and resigned himself to death which was his lot.

On May 26, 1840 Father Blanchet was just making ready to take a trip to Cowlitz when his attention was attracted to a canoe rounding the point. The occupants, Chief Tslalakun's wife and six of his tribesmen, carried a message from the chief, who was sick and begged the blackrobe to visit him. As proof of good faith, the wife presented to Father Blanchet the *sahale* stick which the chief had received on that first visit to the Cowlitz in April, 1838.

The Vicar General now changed his mind, thanking God that a way had been opened to the doors of other tribes. On May 27, with his own canoe and oarsmen, he set out for the island home of Chief Tslalakun. At many places along the coast he stopped just long to address a few friendly words to curious, silent natives. The following day as he was skirting the west side of Whidbey Island he was arrested by a great commotion along the shore. Indians were running back and forth shouting at each other and crying out excitedly to the approaching canoe, "Who comes here? Who are you? What do you want?"

Father Blanchet had no real fear, yet it was a relief when his paddlers beached the canoe at the village of Tslalakun. Here he learned that a battle had just taken place between the chief's warriors and a band of Klallams from Port Townsend. The enemy had made the attack and had suffered the loss of two braves because, as Tslalakun explained, "these men do not know God nor pray to Him." He maintained that he had tried to prevent the fight but had failed. He felt his own life had been spared only because of the cross that hung around his neck.

The priest was surprised to find that Tslalakun was not ill as represented but he readily forgave the chief for the ruse he had used to bring the blackrobe to his village. It was soon noised around that the blackrobe was going to talk to all who would listen. A crowd gathered. The short service, ending with the Great Prayer, was hardly closed when a band of Klallams—this time in peace—set foot on Chief Tslalakun's shore. The head man paved the way for better feelings all around when he gave what was, in effect, an apology. Some of Tslalakun's old men performed a commendable act of friendship when they assisted in the burial of the two fallen Klallam warriors. Young men were barred by tradition from doing such a thing because it was believed that the handling of a corpse would shorten their lives.

Father Blanchet accepted an invitation to visit the village of

Burial canoe used by many Coast Indians, from an etching in J. C. Swan: The Northwest Coast *(B. Driessen)*

Chief Netlam on the northern extremity of the island, where he found fifteen lodges of Indians who had never before seen a blackrobe. In awed silence they lined up 150 strong to make the sign of the cross and to offer dark grimy hands to the Father.

The next day the priest found himself in the midst of a band of Skagits with their inferior chief Witskalatche, popularly called "Le Francais" (the Frenchman). Le Francais cut a unique figure in his "full French costume—trousers, vest, overcoat garnished with porcupine quills." Gathered here also were Indians of Chief Tslalakun's village, raising the total to about 400. All had come in response to a general invitation to attend holy mass.

After the service was over all sat down to a dinner of smoked venison and salmon, served on mats. The climax came in the smoking of the calumet of peace. The quiet was broken by a joyful shouting as Indians bearing a cross twenty-four feet in length moved toward the place that had been prepared for this huge symbol of their faith. While hundreds looked on Father Blanchet blessed the cross, after which it was lifted into position. When the cross had been erected, the Indians—following the example of the priest—prostrated themselves before it. Then followed the ceremoney of baptism. Requirements for this were a profession of faith and a renouncing of sins. Their responses were given in loud confident tones:

> Yes, we believe in Jesus Christ who came to redeem us. Yes, we believe he made seven medicines to make us good. Yes, we believe he has made but one road to go to Heaven. Yes, we promise to keep and follow the road of the Blackgown, which is the only one Jesus Christ has made. Yes, we reject all other roads lately made by man. Yes, we desire to know, love and serve the Great Master of all things.[22]

When the ceremonies were finally over, Father Blanchet prepared to go on his way. He gave his large ladder to Chief Netlam, who begged the blackrobe to go back with him and talk peace to the tribe. Blanchet could not refuse. His canoe was taken over to Netlam's village while he rode in the chief's war craft, which skimmed over the water like a sea bird even though it carried twenty-three passengers.

Father Blanchet counted this a rewarding visit. He prayed with, sang to and gave instruction to more than a thousand Indians. He was also permitted to baptize ninety-six children. Further, he spent four hours in a peace council where, after continuous haggling, a satisfactory agreement was made between this tribe and its neighbors. Chief Witskalatche was glad when he could start the peace pipe around the now harmonious circle.

18 • *The Sisters of Notre Dame de Namur*

WINNING THE WILLAMETTE INdians was not an easy task for any missionary but the priests felt that they were somewhat more successful than the Methodists, especially among the friendly Clackamas people. St. Paul's was gradually attracting the attention of Indians from farther away. Chief Harkley from Yakima, with his family and some of his tribesmen, came and received instruction for three weeks. At the end of that time, they returned to their homes, carrying a cross, a string of beads and a sacred picture. The chief said he understood well how to explain the mysteries of the new religion to his tribe. Lateh, a chief from Okanogan, came; and after him the head man from Priest Rapids brought his wife, three children and a brother-in-law, and stayed all winter at St. Paul's.

One of the greatest triumphs of the year 1842 was the conversion of Dr. John McLoughlin. He made his profession of faith under the guidance of the Vicar General in November of that year and took his first communion at midnight mass on Christmas Eve with a large number of company employees.

Physical improvements came slowly but steadily to St. Paul's on French Prairie. The community took on a more settled appearance when its cemetery was reclaimed from the jungle and the church was renovated and adorned with a belfry and a bell. The prairie in general and the missionary work specifically were given a spiritual uplift by the visit of Father Pierre De Smet, the tireless Jesuit who had just established the first mission among the Flatheads in the Rocky Mountains. He was eager to set up a mission in the Willamette and was then on his way to Europe to recruit helpers and solicit funds to carry on the expanding missionary program. He had come down the Columbia from Spokane, intending to take passage on a Hudson's Bay ship.

Not long after De Smet left, two more assistants for the Catholic mission arrived by way of the Columbia. These were Fathers J. B. Bolduc and A. Langlois. After their lone struggle for four years the Vicar General and Demers welcomed this addition to their slim force. Assisted by the Canadian settlers, the priests built a school for boys which they named St. Joseph's. Entering as boarding pupils were thirty boys, the sons of farmers, and one Indian, the son of a chief. Father Langlois was appointed director and Father Bolduc became assistant and instructor in French. A little later the school was fortunate in securing a transient, a Mr. King, as an English teacher.

When the year 1844 came to Oregon it found the Catholics anticipating a glorious future. The Methodists, who had been in the field ten years, were closing their missions, one by one. Some of them were leaving for the States; others were settling down as laymen in the beautiful and fertile Willamette Valley.

In the meantime Father De Smet, the devoted "Apostle of the Indians," was crossing the ocean to plead the cause of the red man. Assured by the enthusiastic Jesuit that teachers could be obtained from abroad, Father Blanchet began the construction of a school for girls, which he hoped to have ready when the promised women instructors arrived. It was not an easy matter, however, for the church in Canada could give only the most meager support.

On a hot day in July the ship *Indefatigable* was coasting easily along the shore of Oregon toward her destination, the Columbia River. The principal character on deck was Father De

Smet, leader of the missionary recruits. He had gone back to his native land, Belgium, certain of getting helpers and he had not been disappointed. On the ship with him were four Jesuit fathers and several lay brothers. There were also six Sisters of Notre Dame de Namur, coming to take charge of the new school. They were devout women, trained for the various tasks required to build a school from its foundations. Sister Mary Aloysia was the leader and spokesman for the group. The others were Sisters Mary Catherine, Albine, Norbertine, Mary Loyola and Mary Cornelia.

The passengers had been on their way six months. They had experienced seasickness and a few bad storms and now were rejoicing that the end was in sight. But a chill cut through all when it was learned that before them lay the most formidable danger of the entire voyage—the sandbar lying across the mouth of the Columbia River, an obstacle that had been the terror of sea captains since the day of its discovery. The captain, who had not been able to get a chart of the river mouth, trusted to caution and his own ability to cope with the situation. Toward evening of July 28 the vessel approached the north channel, giving the skipper an opportunity to survey the scene. He could see Cape Disappointment rising above the north entrance like a sentinel. Opposite was Point Adams, and between these guards dashed the mighty volume of the waters of the Columbia. It was a relief to Father De Smet when he heard the captain's decision to stand out to sea until morning. As dusk came on the passengers lingered on the deck gazing toward the lonely shore, the shadowy forests and the waters rolling endlessly over the bar.

The next morning dawned gray and gloomy but about ten o'clock the sky cleared and the ship cautiously approached the river mouth. The breakers looked ferocious as they lashed against the shore. "We can never get through," complained some of the passengers, as they entreated Father De Smet to order the captain not to try it. "Tell him," they said, "to take us back to the Sandwich Islands." De Smet, however, believed this to be outside his province. The problem was the captain's and no doubt he was capable of solving it. At any rate the missionaries decided they had better let him grapple with it. A small boat was sent out to make soundings but the water was so rough and the wind so high that nothing could be accomplished.

Another day passed and still the ship stood out to sea, not daring to risk entering the channel. On St. Ignatius Day, July 31, five masses were said. Sister Mary Aloysia, reporting to her Mother Superior, wrote:

> Assisted at Mass said to render Heaven propitious to our prayers; the first in honor of the Most Blessed Trinity; the second in honor of the Blessed Virgin, Star of the Sea; the third in honor of the Holy angels, the guides of man in his exile here below; the fourth in honor of St. Joseph who had helped us in a wonderful manner during the voyage; and the fifth in honor of Saint Francis Xavier who had braved the perils of land and sea in seeking the salvation of souls.[23]

The night passed and about eleven o'clock the next morning the jolly boat came alongside. The foreman gave out the information that a channel had been sounded with five fathoms of water and no obstacles that could be observed. The order was promptly given, and the *Indefatigable,* with the aid of a light breeze, moved into the channel. All nature now seemed to be in a co-operative mood. The wind was just right, the water comparatively smooth and the sky without a cloud. Yet it was best not to be overoptimistic.

The sisters went below to recite a chaplet and when they returned the craft was all but on the bar. The soundings were enough to cause alarm—five fathoms . . . four and a half . . . three fathoms. When this shallow depth was reached the passengers stood tense. Any moment now the anchor would be cast—and then a mad scramble for the boats. The captain made no comment but kept his eyes on the course. Three fathoms! A tight squeeze, but his vessel could scrape over the bar if the water got no shallower. After a long, agonizing wait, the skipper's voice at last rang out, "The *Indefatigable* can pass! Go ahead!" The next sounding was four fathoms, and each succeeding one showed a marked increase in depth. Soon the channel seemed to be bottomless and the ship picked up speed.

The danger was passed, the *Indefatigable* had cleared the bar and was moving up the broad estuary toward Fort Vancouver. The passengers were at their ease now, gliding along on the glassy surface of the river where no dangers lurked. They were fascinated by the rich beauty of the scene—wooded coves, timbered fingers feeling out into the stream, small enchanted islands and evergreen forests stretching back into the never-ending hills.

Fort Vancouver was a complete surprise, with its broad cultivated fields, its diversity of activities and its hosts of employees. It seemed a veritable medieval manor in an untamed wilderness. Although they were comfortably located at the fort and well entertained, the sisters were eager to go to work in their new harvest field. A smallpox epidemic had broken out in the vicinity of the fort and had taken a toll of twenty lives in six days. This was another reason for the urge to leave as soon as possible.

Father Blanchet arrived from the Willamette August 12. Without undue delay the sisters, along with their baggage, were placed on a Hudson's Bay barge for the trip to St. Paul's. This was a new adventure and they were almost gay, laughing softly from the depth of their somber garments and making witty observations. It was restful, sailing along under summer skies, camping at night, cooking their meals in the open and, before bedtime, taking walks by moonlight or starlight. Cares of the past and fears of the future did not intrude. Misgivings concerning the wilderness and nostalgic thoughts of the old sheltered life in Belgium were for the immediate present forgotten. This was peace. At Champoeg, on the edge of French Prairie, they disembarked. The sisters, chuckling at the prospect of another experience, clambered into the rough carts drawn by oxen. Soon they were jolting over the dusty, deeply rutted roads to the mission. It had been a good season in the valley. The hay had been cut and the abundant grain harvest about gathered in. The little world of the Willamette looked peaceful and prosperous.

If the six nuns had been accustomed to comforts, they quickly resigned themselves to discomforts; if they had formerly been surrounded by beauty, they now patiently settled down to raw ugliness. The house was far from being completed, but they would presently be living in it, even if the cracks were wide enough for a cat to crawl through. Withal, on August 15, they celebrated the feast of the Assumption by kneeling in the little chapel which Sister Aloysia declared to be "as lowly as the stable of Bethlehem."

To unpack their things was a real pleasure and they gave thanks for a glorious freedom of movement after those cramped months on shipboard. Getting ready for the Sabbath service and the feast of the Immaculate Heart they regarded as a Heaven-sent privilege. When the day came it found the crude little chapel dressed up for the occasion. At nine o'clock the bell rang out the invitation, and the eager congregation filed in, the men taking their seats on one side of the room and the women on the other. Practically all the inhabitants of the prairie were present. Those who lived some distance away had started the previous day in order to be on time.

It was a soul-satisfying service. After mass, Father Blanchet gave an exhortation to the flock and asked them to pray for the sisters who had come among them. "You will, also, pray for the Bishop," he said in closing. Under a new organization the western territory had been created into a separate vicarate apostolic and Father Blanchet had been raised to the rank of Bishop. It was to help him bear the new responsibilities that the Father was now asking prayers.

The new missionaries had hardly arrived at St. Paul's when one after another of the group was stricken with the intermittent fever. Sisters Aloysia, Norbertine and Mary Albine were incapacitated for several weeks. Father Michael Accolti became ill and unable to do any work. Before he could leave the captain of the *Indefatigable* fell a victim to the fever and became alarmed lest he never see his wife and children again. Father De Smet recognized the captain as a worthy man and a skilled navigator but he was never able to excuse the shipmaster for not repressing the "horrible swearing" on shipboard from the beginning of the voyage to the end. De Smet himself was in bed on a rigid diet for fifteen days. Even the Indians, who should have been immune, fell under the grip of the fever. Those unable to travel with their families were abandoned; it was a pathetic sight to see them stretched out on the sands, dying from lack of attention.

As their health was restored the sisters fell into the routine and completed the organization of their household. Each had the assignments for which she was particularly fitted. Sister Catherine got out the piles of soiled clothing that had accumulated during the voyage and cheerfully went down to the river to wash. One nun played the role of nurse. Sister Norbertine found her sphere in the garden. Another laughingly called herself a *bouche-trou,* or jack of all trades. Sister Mary Albine's fingers had been trained to ply the needle but now, instead of doing Belgian embroidery, they would be shaping coarse materials into garments to cover some child's nakedness. All of the sisters were able to see the humor in many situations and their pens never failed to record it. Said one, "Sister Mary Cornelia and several Canadian women have been trying to find the floor of the church for the dirt that covers it."

Religious instruction began almost immediately even though the sisters had to meet their pupils out under the open sky. The lessons were given in the form of catechisms to women and children in preparation for their first communion. Ages ranged all the way from sixteen to sixty. The task of teaching belonged to Sisters Mary Catherine and Mary Cornelia and they were devoting six hours a day trying to teach novices how to make the sign of the cross and to say "Our Father." Many of the pupils showed great eagerness. Some camped in the nearby woods rather than waste time going back and forth to their homes. One elderly woman had been without food for two days before the sisters found it out: a dog had carried off her provisions and she had refused to miss her lessons by going home for more. Sister Mary Cornelia devoted her time to preparing a woman of eighty for her first communion. It was a pathetic sight to see the aged woman trying to learn what her feeble brain could neither comprehend nor retain. "Father," said the ancient forest-dweller to the priest who was encouraging her, "look at my wrinkled forehead. How can anything get into it?" The pupils often showed their appreciation by bringing the sisters gifts of melons, potatoes, butter and eggs.

Late summer came and found the dwelling house still unfinished. Labor was almost impossible to obtain, although the highest wages of from ten to twelve francs a day were offered. The sisters finally decided that if their place were to be livable before winter they would have to turn workmen. When the doors were at last hung and the windows put in, two nuns did the painting. Fearing that there would be no plastering done before the rains came, they went to the woods and gathered moss to chink the cracks.

Thirty boarding pupils—all halfbreeds—were enrolled in the school. The tuition, paid in farm produce, would help feed the orphans of the prairie but finding clothing was a more difficult problem.

Father De Smet recovered, but slowly. While the Sisters were busy getting their school into operation, he was employed with Jesuit duties. He selected a site for St. Francis Xavier's mission at a bend of the river where there were several springs. When the two-story building was finished he left for the Rocky Mountains the first week in October.

Toward the middle of the month the nuns finally moved into their house. The first prolonged rain proved that the roof was indeed "loosely joined" but the Sisters good-naturedly declared that the constant dripping of water did not keep them awake.

When the sisters saw thirty women take their first communion they felt well paid for all their intensive efforts. After the impressive ceremony one of the nuns remarked, "Their faith makes Jesus Christ almost visible to them."

St. Paul's looked forward with no pleasure to the months ahead without the guidance of Father Blanchet. He had been honored with a bishopric, and was expected to go to Canada for consecration. On his way back to Oregon he intended to make a detour to Europe to recruit more sisters to aid in the expansion of the mission work. There was an opportunity to open a school at Willamette Falls, which had been abandoned by the Methodists. If he could enlist recruits in Canada, all well and good; if not, he would be compelled to go to Europe. The sisters considered Blanchet a godly, self-sacrificing priest. Once he stopped at their house, tired and thirsty, and asked for a drink of water. The sister who responded wanted to add a little sugar to make it more appetizing but he refused gently, saying, "Oh no. Our Lord had only gall and vinegar on the cross." His humility and devotion were a constant wonder to them.

There was an appalling number of orphans in the community. Food could be obtained but the sisters were constantly bemoaning the scarcity of cloth. Since there was no money in circulation the barter system prevailed. Leather was scarce and even if it had been plentiful there were no shoemakers. A strip of cloth wound from the foot to the knee often had to do the duty of both shoe and stocking for some girls. To eke out clothing for her orphans Sister Aloysia drew to the fullest extent upon her ingenuity. From materials brought from Belgium she cut and made eighty dresses. Some of the older girls aided in finishing the garments.

When the children first came to school they were awed and quiet for a few days but after that their true dispositions were frequently on exhibition. Being untaught at home, many were disobedient and had to learn to conform. When a school command contrary to their wills was given these obstreperous ones would protest without any inhibitions, *"Wake, wake, wake!"* (meaning no). But the sisters with patience unlimited looked forward to the day when the undisciplined halfbreeds would change their negative attitudes and answer, *"Ah-ha"* (yes), or *"Flanch, flanch"* (That is good).

The Indian mother had nothing to say about her child. Its welfare was the sole responsibility of its French-Canadian father, who did all the talking, the telling and the inquiring about his offspring. When he brought the girl to school for the first time, he would say, "Sister, my daughter is very fortunate to be thus enabled to learn of the good God. We are great sinners only because we are ignorant." One day Sister Albine noticed a father looking blankly and wistfully at his child's report. He was completely illiterate. When the daughter spelled out some of the words he almost cried for joy. "O, my child," he said, "you will soon be able to read the beautiful stories about God! You will soon be able to teach your brothers and sisters!"

The children were taught the alphabet and simple hymns which they enjoyed. At the Bishop's request much attention was given to the teaching of the domestic arts—cooking, washing, milking and gardening. The Indian mothers knew nothing at all about housekeeping; consequently, their families lived almost as primitively as the wigwam-dwellers. At stated periods, the sisters gave out "awards of premiums" in the form of small religious pictures which were the delight of every halfbreed's heart. In time evening singing was started, and a Sunday School for the women. Both were well attended until the rains came, flooding the valley for miles around.

The celebration of the Epiphany was a novel event for the girls. They drew lots for roles in "The Three Kings" and were costumed in all the finery that the sisters could resurrect from the boxes and chests that had been brought from Belgium. After the play all went to the dining room for a special supper.

Then there was the wedding—a strange one, the sisters thought, and a stranger union. Yet it was typical of what took place on French Prairie. In a particular church service an Indian girl was baptized by the priest in charge and immediately afterward was married to old Baptiste, a servant on the mission farm —the baker, the meat curer, the fruit picker. His young wife could speak neither English nor French.

There was always a need for a great deal of soap. The housekeeping nuns made their own. It was not white and pretty, they admitted, but it did have "good cleaning properties." Something more potent was required for fighting vermin. Invariably, when the month's vacation was over the girls returned completely infested. Many of the pupils had scrofula, which took the form of sores on the face and neck. It was Sister Albine's duty to dress the lesions on as many as eighteen patients in one session. Some of the girls also had venereal diseases, caught from their parents.

The sisters felt rewarded a hundredfold when they learned that the non-Catholics in the valley looked favorably upon their school. This gave them new courage. But the longer they were in the work the less optimistic they were about the girls' future. They were finally brought to admit that these pupils had scarcely any aptitude for the intellectual. Reading had some appeal to the limited few. All were fairly successful in handwork and in this activity they found happiness. Even the younger ones learned to spin and knit, after a fashion.

The children responded warmly to the religious instruction and looked forward to the awarding of premiums. At her first confession one child said solemnly, "My heart is white now. Our Lord is in it. It will never be bad again. When you take me to be a sister, I will love our Lord. I love him a little now."

A new chapel eventually came to take the place of the old one but apparently it was not well built either. One of the nuns, in writing to her mother superior, said, "The wind enters in unrestrained freedom through the cracks which are wide enough to give a good view of the outside." In spite of its glaring defects, the sisters gladly decorated it for the day of its consecration. They tacked on all the white muslin they had, put bright paper in front of the altar and draped over the tabernacle two curtains that had done duty in a classroom somewhere in Belgium. They made a canopy for the Blessed Mother and brought wild flowers in great quantities. The chapel was blest on Palm Sunday, 1846.

The year 1846 was an important one in the history of Old Oregon. The civil government for which Jason Lee had striven had been in operation for three years. The *Oregon Spectator,* the first newspaper in the Northwest, had begun to publish semimonthly issues. In that year, the United States and England settled the "Oregon Question" by dividing the territory on the forty-ninth parallel. 1846 saw thousands of immigrants on the trail to Oregon—most of them to the Willamette Valley. In that year, the future of western Catholic missions seemed bright. Said Sister Aloysia to her Mother Superior, "The rapid progress of civilization contributes not a little to the extension of our institute."

19 • *The Ups and the Downs*

IN JULY 1845 BISHOP FRANCIS Blanchet arrived in Montreal for his consecration. When the elaborate ceremony was over he was surprised how quickly it slipped from his mind. His thoughts were woolgathering back on the Pacific shores where the sisters struggled without funds and where opportunities for service were allowed to pass because there were too few hands and no money. There was no money in Canada, nor any missionaries available for the West. "Go to Europe," he was told. Yes, that was where he would go, for he did not intend to return to Oregon emptyhanded. He would appeal to the Old World where men had been accumulating wealth for ages and Mother Church for about as long a time had been educating workers.

Bishop Blanchet went from one country to another, soliciting help but falling short of his goal. The Pope—he knew—was an ardent advocate of missions so to the Holy City he went to ask for a conference. He tarried in Rome for four months, waiting for an appointment. Finally it was granted but his hopes were suddenly blasted by the unexpected death of the Pontiff. Now he would have to wait till another Pope had been chosen and another interview arranged. It came in time and—happily—Pope Pius IX was of the same opinion as his predecessor. The interview brought quick and surprising changes to the church organization in Oregon and a personal honor that Bishop Blanchet never dreamed would come to him. He was advanced to the position of Archbishop of Oregon City and in a colorful ceremony invested with the pallium, the symbol of his high office. His brother, Magloire, would be called west to become Bishop of Walla Walla, while Father Demers was honored with the bishopric of Vancouver Island.

The future of the Oregon missions assured, Archbishop

Blanchet began to gather up his recruits for the return. After some delays the party at last sailed from France, arriving on the Columbia late in August 1847. Blanchet had been gone from Oregon two years and seven months and he could see—on the surface—many improvements. At Oregon City (Willamette Falls) a chapel with living quarters in the rear had been completed, while at St. Paul's several additions had been made.

There was unsuppressed excitement in the Willamette when the Archbishop returned with a reinforcement party of twenty-one. This included three Jesuit fathers and three brothers, five secular priests and seven Sisters of Notre Dame, among whom were Francesca, Aldegonde, Renilde and Odelia. The sisters would open a school in the coming metropolis, Oregon City. This was not all. Father Magloire Blanchet, coming overland from Canada, brought several more priests. It looked now as if Oregon would be well served.

The auspicious beginning—regrettably—was followed by a series of sharp blows. Archbishop Blanchet had just completed his reorganization when the Whitman massacre occurred in the last days of November. All of Oregon was soon tense with anxiety and fear. This in turn brought on the Cayuse War. It all happened in a comparatively short time. Came the defeat of the Indians, the closing of the interior to settlement and the consequent weakening of the Catholic efforts at Walla Walla.

While this crisis was cooling, a series of misfortunes for the Oregon church were in the making for 1849. This was the year of the gold rush to California, when men from all parts of the country hurried along the "golden road" by every imaginable mode of travel. They left the farm, the office, the school room and the forge to go in search of the glittering dust. And the gold fever—unfortunately—did not bypass the Canadians on French Prairie. Gathering up what poor equipment was at hand, many of them set out hopefully for San Francisco. Their homes? Oh, *oui-oui!* They would build many fine things with the gold that they found. Chiefly the women and the incompetents were left behind—the helpless, the indolent, the ill, the aged.

St. Joseph's School for boys, founded in 1844, closed its doors for lack of pupils and never opened them again. Since his charges had gone, Father Langlois himself followed the trail to California. Perhaps he could minister in some small corner to white men moiling for gold down there.

Farming and industry lagged. California sent out a call for more food for her increasing population but the people left in Oregon could not supply the demand. There were vessels to carry the produce but few sailors to man them. Even men of the sea were following hard upon the gold trail. The exodus of settlers forced the closing of the mission of St. Francis Xavier and, soon afterward, the withdrawal of all the Jesuits from Oregon.

The Sisters of Notre Dame clung as long as practicable to their responsibilities, but eventually had to abandon the school at St. Paul's, as well as the new one at Oregon City. Most of the nuns, too, found their way to California.

By the Oregon Donation Land Act of 1849, the church claims were set aside and the lands taken over by the State. Thus one blow after another laid low the Catholic educational institutions as if they had been nine-pins. The next near-disaster was an epidemic. Some of the fortune hunters returned home, bringing not gold but the germs of a fever which spread like a grass fire over the prairie. It was no respecter of persons. Graves by the score were dug and marked with the sign of the cross. It crept into the convent at Oregon City and when it left it took Sister Renilde and two of her pupils.

Other problems that plagued Archbishop Blanchet might be classed under the heading *Debts—no funds.* He learned that the new buildings at St. Paul's and Oregon City had been heavily mortgaged, due either to mismanagement on the part of Father Demers or to his taking too optimistic a chance on the future. To make bad matters worse, the debt was owed to bankers and not to the Catholic Church.

While the archbishop was trying to untangle the debt problem, a worse misfortune hit him amidships, as it were. The *Vancouver,* a company vessel, was wrecked at the mouth of the Columbia. It happened that she carried several thousand dollars' worth of goods for the Catholic missions. The loss could not be replaced and this greatly aggravated the missions' already deplorable financial plight.

The year 1855–1856 marked the nadir in Catholic mission fortunes in Oregon. The men and women of the religious orders had left. No one ministered to the Indians. Bigotry and prejudice were running unchecked. The number of the clergy dropped from nineteen to seven. Pastors still served small flocks of whites only in The Dalles, Oregon City, St. Paul, St. Louis on French Prairie and Portland.

In an effort to salvage the properties of the Oregon missions Archbishop Blanchet spent two years in South America raising funds with which to bolster Catholic power in Oregon. When he returned with a generous contribution the dawn of a new day was brightening (for the whites, principally) the once darkened horizon. The Indian wars north of the Columbia were at an end and the federal government was preparing to reopen the interior to white settlement.

1859! In that year, Oregon State was admitted to the Union. Peace prevailed in the Northwest and thousands of immigrants were plodding their weary way over the Oregon Trail. The future of the Catholic Church in the West was assured. There would be obstacles in places and slow growth in general but it was enough to know that the sun was on the eastern horizon.

1859! In that year, Archbishop Blanchet completed twenty-one years in Oregon. Had he been able to read his own horoscope he could have seen written for him almost a quarter of a century more.

20 • *Father De Smet, Apostle of the Indians*

LIVING AMONG THE FLATHEADS of the Rocky Mountains was Insula, known to the tribe as Little Chief and Great Warrior. In 1835, he heard by means of moccasin telegraph that certain white men representing the Great Spirit were on their way to the "Shining Mountains." Perhaps these were the long-looked-for blackrobes. Wishing to secure them for his people, Insula, accompanied by some of his tribesmen, set out to look for the great ones with the "Book."

Eluding the hostile Blackfeet, they made their way to the Green River rendezvous, only to be disappointed. The missionaries proved to be Dr. Samuel Parker and Marcus Whitman on their exploratory tour. These were not what Insula and his friends were seeking. He returned home, resolved to send a deputation to St. Louis.

Old Ignace was appointed leader of the delegation to St. Louis in search of blackrobes. He was an Iroquois Indian who, with others, had been brought by fur traders to the Rocky Mountains. These Iroquois lived with the Flatheads and liked them—marrying with them and teaching them a little about the Catholic faith. Old Ignace had become a man of influence in the mountains.

Ignace started east in the summer of 1835, taking with him his two sons about twelve and fourteen years of age. The details of the journey are not known but they arrived at the Jesuit college in St. Louis where the boys were baptized under the names of Charles and Francis. Old Ignace sought out Father Joseph Rosati and told him of the Flathead need for blackrobes. He was informed that missionaries would be sent to the mountains as soon as possible.

After eighteen months had passed and there was still no sign of the promised blackrobes, another deputation was appointed to start east in 1837. This party met with foul play at the hands of the Sioux, and all lost their lives. Undeterred, the Flatheads organized a fourth delegation. In midsummer of 1839 Young Ignace and Pierre Gaucher (Left-handed Peter) set out with a party of trappers, traveling by canoe down the Yellowstone and Missouri rivers. At Council Bluffs, Iowa they stopped at St. Joseph's Mission to see the Father there. Here they met the blackrobe who was to be the answer to their prayers, Father Pierre Jean de Smet. Although impressed by their sincerity the priest could not appoint himself. That must be left to someone higher up. The Indians were given letters of introduction to be presented to the Reverend Father Superior at St. Louis.

Bishop Rosati gave them a definite promise of a teacher for the following year. Having accomplished his part of the mission, Pierre Gaucher started home over the interminable miles he had just traveled. Young Ignace remained to accompany the teacher, whoever he might be. Undoubtedly Left-handed Peter had a difficult journey but he arrived in the Bitterroot Valley early in the spring of 1840 with the cheering message "A blackrobe is surely coming."

The red man never had a better friend than Father De Smet, the young Belgian priest who became a loyal citizen of the United States. No teacher was ever more enthusiastic, more lovable, more sympathetic, more long-suffering than he. And no missionary—in the interests of the cause—ever traveled more miles than Father De Smet. He saw Indians at their best and at their worst, in the glory of conversion and in the depths of heathen rites. He befriended them without condoning their filth, their cruelties and their backslidings. He always talked to them frankly, never with a "forked tongue."

Father De Smet was born January 30, 1801 in the village of Termonde, Belgium. He attended the seminary of Malines until he was twenty-one and then decided to embark on a missionary career among the Indians in America. Five others of the most promising men of the seminary were impelled to interpret literally the Biblical command, "Sell what thou hast and follow me." Since the families were not eager to have their sons go the young men sold their personal effects to obtain money for the ocean passage.

Young De Smet was endowed with intelligence, good health and a keen appreciation of life in all its fullness: nature, religion, travel, people. He liked sports and excelled in them, and for his superior physical prowess he was nicknamed "Samson."

In due time the young men were in the United States. The sight of the prosperous cities on the eastern seaboard gave De Smet something of a surprise. He had envisioned young America as a wilderness inhabited for the most part by wild Indians.

Pierre De Smet entered America's first novitiate at Whitemarsh, Maryland, to begin his training as a Jesuit under the motto, "For the greater glory of God." After two years he was transferred to the new novitiate near St. Louis. Here he spent several years of hard study and manual labor. In 1827 he successfully finished his novitiate and was ordained a Jesuit priest. At this time he was a man of unusual personal attractiveness. His full face beamed frankness and friendliness. He had a sense of humor that saved him the day in many tense situations on the Indian frontier. He also had a curiosity to see and learn new things and a benevolent attitude toward the poor and downtrodden. He was of medium height but of heavy build, weighing in his prime about 200 pounds. His presence was commanding, whether on horseback in a band of savages or holding solemn mass.

De Smet's health broke in 1837 and he was advised to go back to his home in Belgium. While he was recuperating he worked diligently in behalf of the St. Louis University, soliciting books, musical instruments and laboratory equipment. He was especially commended for his success in collecting a library of some 5000 volumes.

In the spring of 1838 he was back in St. Louis ready to begin his missionary work in earnest. In company with another priest he was sent to found a mission among the Potawatomies near Council Bluffs. It was here at St. Joseph's that Young Ignace and Left-handed Peter found him.

21 • *To the Flatheads at Last*

FATHER DE SMET VOLUNTEERED to answer the call from the mountains and become the first missionary to the Flatheads. Two priests were needed but since there was not another to spare De Smet alone was assigned the task of surveying the country to determine whether it was wise to plant a mission in such a distant place.

Full of enthusiasm, De Smet boarded a crowded steamer at St. Louis and after ten days arrived at Independence. Here he prepared to join a caravan of the American Fur Company with Captain Andrew Drips in command. In Father De Smet's personal party were six Canadian mule drivers, an Iroquois Indian named John Gray, an Englishman known as Romain and, lastly, Young Ignace, hunter *par excellence* and faithful friend.

After several weeks on the trail Father De Smet was attacked by a fever; he could not shake it off and it remained a close companion during most of the journey. Some days he felt a little better, on others he was utterly miserable. When he could no longer sit on his horse he would dismount and crawl into the cart. His own words tell how comfortable he was there:

> . . . After that I would go and lie in the cart on the boxes where I was jolted about like a malefactor. Very often we would have to cross deep and perpendicular ravines throwing me into the most singular positions; now my feet would be in the air, now I would find myself hidden like a thief between boxes and bundles, cold as an icicle or covered with sweat and burning like a stove.[24]

In spite of his illness and the discomforts of travel, Father De Smet made careful note of the country through which he was passing and described it in a style that was vivid and charming.

On June 30 the longest part of the trek had been made, for on that day the caravan pulled into the rendezvous. Thanks to Left-handed Peter's safe return, a Flathead delegation was waiting. As soon as the exhibitions were over the head men found Father De Smet and invited him to a council. As the first act the chief, who performed as master of ceremonies, leaned over and drew a small circle on the ground. Within this he put a piece of burning dung, then deliberately lit his pipe. With a solemnity befitting the occasion he offered the pipe in turn to the Great Spirit, to the sun, to the earth and to each of the cardinal points of the compass. While this was in progress all the head men sat like carved figures, motionless. As the calumet was passed each took it and went through identical movements.

Father De Smet received the pipe in his turn and when he had given a few puffs, he addressed the audience, which was quiet and expectant. Through an interpreter he explained the purpose of his visit to the mountains. God, he said, had created blackrobes to teach the holy law to all the nations of the earth and it was the duty of those who heard the voice to follow the word of God. There was continued silence while he explained the basic principles of the Christian way of life.

After the council broke up and the head men had held a consultation among themselves the spokesman returned with the decision of the chiefs. "Blackgown," he said, "your words have entered our hearts; they will never go out from them. We wish to know and practice the sublime law that you have just made known to us in the name of the Great Spirit whom we love. All our country is open to you." [25]

After four days of rest Father De Smet was ready to start from the Green River rendezvous to the Flathead country deeper in the Rocky Mountains. Their course took them across the tableland where the waters of the Snake River rise and into Jackson's Hole, a mountain valley with exquisite scenery. One day's travel through Pierre's Hole brought the little party to the main camp of the Flatheads and the Pend Oreilles. At the approach of the blackgown men, women and children rushed forward holding out their hands and telling him that the poles for his lodge had already been set up.

Gathered here was an encampment of about 1600. Father De Smet was conducted to the lodge of old Chief Big Face, who gave him a welcome in the name of the tribes. The priest, intending to stay a while and hold a mission, set up a simple ritual of worship for the Indians to practice mornings and evenings and arranged for certain periods of instruction. When the schedule was understood by the head men, one of them was given a bell for signaling the meetings. It was gratifying to Father De Smet to see how, after a few days, the Indians fell into the routine. At daybreak, the old chief would mount his horse and ride through the camp, waking up his people. "Wake up, my children," Big Face would cry.

"Speak to the Great Spirit. Tell him you love him, and want him to take pity on you. . . . See, the sun is coming. It's time to go to the river and wash. When the bell rings, go to the Father's lodge. Don't be late." Soon the encampment would be astir. The Indians were eager to hear the "Word" and would often go running to get a good seat in the lodge. Even the sick managed to persuade friends to carry them within sound of the priest's voice.

Father De Smet continued to address the people four times a day for about two weeks. With the aid of an excellent interpreter, Gabriel Prudhomme, he translated some prayers into the Flathead language. One day he announced that he would give a medal to the person who would be the first to recite without a mistake the Credo, the Ave, the Pater, the Ten Commandments and the Four Acts. The words had hardly left his lips when a chief stood up, saying, "Your medal, Father, belongs to me." And to prove it, the Indian recited all that he had been taught. For this accomplishment De Smet appointed the chief first assistant teacher of the catechism.

While holding this mission Father De Smet baptized some 600 persons. Others made requests but, since they did not seem ready, he told them to wait until the following year when resident missionaries would be with them. Among those baptized were two chiefs, a Flathead and a Pend Oreille, who were over eighty years old. When Walking Bear was told to make repentance for his sins, he said promptly, "I haven't got any sins. I've already asked the Great Spirit to pardon me." While the priest looked nonplused yet a little amused, Walking Bear continued," "I've never deliberately offended the Great Spirit in my life. Whenever I find anything evil in my heart, I immediately put it out."

Father De Smet admired the Flatheads in spite of some shortcomings. Gambling was their chief vice, but they promised to stop it when the blackgown explained that it was against God's commands. Theft and lying were uncommon and those who repeatedly disturbed the peace by quarreling were given suitable punishments. These Indians were teachable and the young people especially seemed to have keen minds. Being isolated, the tribe had not yet been corrupted by the vices of civilization.

When the mission ended the Indians started on their homeward march. Father De Smet traveled along, charmed as much by their carefree life as by the rough mountain scenery. The priest stopped short of going into the Bitterroot Valley, homeland of the Flatheads. Instead he decided to hurry back to St. Louis with a favorable report and recommendations for establishing a mountain mission. He explained his purpose to the Indians and, amid demonstrations of regret, set out from Three Forks in the present State of Montana. As far as Fort Alexander on the Yellowstone he had an escort of seventeen Flatheads. From there he went on through the hostile Blackfeet country with only two French-Canadian companions.

They crossed the tracks of the Crows, the Blackfeet, Gros Ventres, Assiniboines and Sioux, all of whom were famed for their tricks and their treachery. One entire day the travelers were followed at a distance by a band of Sioux. At noon, when they stopped to refresh themselves at a little spring, they were suddenly surrounded by warriors. De Smet arose and offered his hand, but the leading brave ignored it, saying shortly, "Why are you hiding in this gulch?"

With scores of fierce eyes upon him, Father De Smet made known that he had merely stopped to rest and take a drink.

"Who is he?" the Sioux demanded of the Canadian interpreter.

"He talks with the Great Spirit," said Gabriel Prudhomme. "He's a blackgown of the French."

The savage countenance relaxed as the brave motioned to his companions to put down their weapons. He then came forward to shake the hand that he had refused. Father De Smet made him a present of some twist tobacco and they sat down to smoke. The warrior chief invited the Father to spend the night in his village. He accepted, and was surprised to find an encampment of about a thousand persons. The priest invited the chief to eat supper with him. After the blessing the perplexed Indian turned to the interpreter and asked, "What's he talking about to his meat?"

"He's thanking the Great Spirit for letting us have food to eat," answered Prudhomme.[26]

Shortly after the meal twelve warriors appeared carrying a

large buffalo robe, which they spread out in front of De Smet's tent, meanwhile motioning to him to sit on it. Wondering, the priest followed directions, believing the performance to be a part of some ceremony. The corners of the robe were then siezed by four warriors in full regalia who with their burden marched behind the chief to the village. It was a kind of triumphal procession with the blackgown the center of interest, borne through the encampment for all eyes to see. A ludicrous sight, De Smet thought, as he struggled to keep from laughing.

In this manner the priest was carried to the lodge of the head chief, who rose and made a harangue praising the blackrobe. It should be the happiest day in the lives of the villagers, the sachem declared, because it was the first time they had ever seen a man who lived near to the Great Spirit.

After the chief's oration Father De Smet was requested to speak to the Great Spirit. During the blessing the savages held their hands raised high toward heaven. When it was finished, they lowered their hands to the earth.

"What do these movements mean?" De Smet asked through his interpreter.

Hands lifted to heaven, he was told, showed their dependance upon the Great Spirit for everything. Striking the ground indicated that they were miserable creatures, mere worms crawling at the feet of the all-powerful one.

Leaving the Sioux, Father De Smet traveled on unmolested, eventually coming to Fort Vermilion, where he embarked in a canoe for St. Louis.

There was general rejoicing when Pierre De Smet, in good health after his long bout with malaria, returned to give an enthusiastic account of his meeting with the Flatheads. Several of his associates caught the zeal for the Flathead cause and pledged their help in founding a permanent mission somewhere in the Rocky Mountains.

22 • *St. Mary's, the First Mountain Mission*

FILLED WITH EAGERNESS TO BE ON his way to the West again, Father De Smet went before his superiors with his plan for the Flathead mission. They heard him through, then shook their heads regretfully. There were not enough funds in the missionary chest to finance the proposed establishment.

After recovering from the rebuff De Smet went off to ponder the situation and what could be done about it. The Flatheads, he told himself, must not be disappointed. He would not admit defeat. Finally he went before his superiors with another plan. This time they gave permission for him to go to the Flatheads, provided he could raise the requisite amount of money. This was all he needed. With the help of friends and with confidence that God would support him in the cause, he set out.

He went first to New Orleans, stopping along the way wherever there were Catholic colonists. From there he journeyed to Philadelphia, never neglecting to make his appeal even in out-of-the-way pioneer places. In a few months, he was back again in St Louis, organizing a party for missionary work in the West. It was ready by April 1, 1841. God being willing, he would fulfill his promise to the Flatheads. And he was not going alone. As assistants, he had Father Nicholas Point, a Frenchman, and Father Gregory Mengarini, an Italian. Besides, there were three Brothers, recently from Belgium—Joseph Specht, Charles Huet and William Claessens.

By May 10 the missionary outfit had been assembled at Independence, Missouri. It consisted of the priests' mounts, several pack animals and a wagon and three carts, all drawn by oxen. It must have been hard on Father De Smet, scarcely rested from the return trip and the fund-raising campaign, to be traveling again over plain and mountain, journeying ceaselessly, counting endless miles. But his heart was with the Flatheads and wherever they lived, that place would be his goal.

The Flatheads had promised the previous summer that, on the first of July an escort would be waiting for the blackgown at the foot of the Wind River Mountains. They did not forget. At the appointed place and time ten lodges were pitched. Unluckily, Father De Smet's party was delayed two weeks. The Indians waited patiently till their provisions were almost exhausted, when they were forced to go on the hunt. De Smet was given this information at Fort Bridger, and immediately sent one of his hunters to notify the Flatheads of his arrival.

It was on the evening of the Feast of the Assumption that De Smet's party met the vanguard of the Flatheads. When the Indians saw not only one blackgown but several, they could only stare in amazement. Many teachers! This was too good to be true! For ten years they had been sending delegations in search of the white man's Book of Religion. For ten years they had lived in the twilight, waiting for the dawn of this day. Now it had come. Blackrobes stood before them. It was no dream to be driven away by the broad light of a summer morning.

The missionaries decided to stay at Fort Hall awhile to rest their animals and lay in a supply of food. Gabriel Prudhomme was sent to meet the main body of Flatheads, now in camp on the Beaverhead. Francis Ermatinger, Hudson's Bay agent at Fort Hall, welcomed the priests, sold them necessities at low cost and told them that the company looked with favor upon a Catholic mission in the mountains.

On August 29 the party began winding its way up the Snake River, across the continental divide and toward the source of the Beaverhead. As the priests came nearer the camp of the main body of Flatheads, Indian runners appeared with messages. One day, several chiefs who had been riding steadily for twenty-four hours met them. In the lead was Insula, or Little Chief, afterward baptized under the name of Michael. Next came the warrior, Bravest-of-the-brave, a superior horseman and the most handsome Indian De Smet had ever seen. He had sent his finest horse to Fort Hall with the stipulation that only the great blackrobe be allowed to ride the steed.

With this escort of chiefs, runners and hangers-on the missionary party moved on toward the main village of the Flatheads. When within a short distance of the encampment, they heard a medley of voices calling, "Paul! Paul!" This was Big Face's baptismal name. Soon they could see, towering above the crowd, the figure of the old chief who for some reason had been delayed. But his arrival gave occasion for another demonstration of welcome in honor of the blackrobes.

After resting a few days the whole body of Indians and whites pressed forward, finally arriving in the beautiful Bitterroot Valley. The missionaries went up the valley about twenty-eight miles, then stopped at what seemed to be an ideal location (between Fort Owen and Stevensville). This was to be the end of a long rugged trail, the place where Father De Smet's first Rocky Mountain mission was to be built.

On the first Sunday in October, the feast of the Rosary, the Jesuits took formal occupation of the promised land by planting the cross. The mission was to be dedicated to Our Lady of Mercy because the party had arrived on September 24, the day when the church gives special honor to the Blessed Mother.

No spot more beautiful could have been found for St. Mary's Mission. The buildings might be crude but there would always be the peaceful valley with the river flowing through and the mountains toward the sunrise and the sunset, pressing their heads against the clouds. But no time was to be lost, for it was apparent that winter in the Montana valleys came early. The ground was already freezing a little at night. Plainly no one could be idle if the chapel and a roof over their heads were to be provided before the snows fell.

Father De Smet and his assistants divided the labor among them. Father Mengarini, thirty years old, had been in the United States only a year. He would be employed chiefly with teaching duties. Father Point, who was forty-two, had left France in 1836. He was versed in law as well as theology and, in addition, was a skilled draftsman and an expert in pen sketching. Brother William Claessens, the chief carpenter, wielded hammer and saw as well as supervised all building activities. Everybody worked. With ax and brawn they cut down cottonwood trees, which grew abundantly by the river, trimmed them, cut them into lengths, then hauled the logs into position. The chapel and the dwelling house took form. Both buildings were chinked with mud inside and out and floored with large "shakes" nailed down with wooden pegs. The partitions were of deerskin, as were the small paneless windows. When these two buildings were completed there was still the stockade to erect, with bastions at two diagonal corners and a palisade about fifteen feet high.

Among traders, the Flatheads had a reputation of being well behaved, friendly people, living on good terms with all their neighbors except the Blackfeet, with whom they waged intermittent warfare. After several weeks of association with them the priests were strongly inclined toward a like opinion.

Insula, or Little Chief, took his religion seriously and wanted all his tribespeople to do the same. On one occasion a young girl was absent from prayers without a good cause, from his point of view. Little Chief sent for her, gave her a sound scolding and applied the cane rather freely. The Catholic manner of worship appealed to the Indians. Many developed a fondness for praying and singing canticles. Old Simeon was probably the most devout of them all. Sometimes when he woke in the night he would decide to get up and pray. First, he would stir up the fire to make his tent more comfortable. After making the sign of the cross he would pray a little, cross himself again, pray some more, smoke a little and then go back to his robe. At first, De Smet was puzzled about this night praying. Finally, it came to him that the Indians were taking literally one of his suggestions, "When you wake in the night, it is well to raise the heart to God."

The work of building and teaching went on together. Daybreak was the time for arising. Then, in order, came morning prayers, mass and breakfast. This was followed by an hour's instruction, after which came manual labor until about noon. There was catechism from two until about three-thirty and then work until night. The priests planned contests and rewards for children under thirteen in order to make the task of learning catechisms more pleasant. The young people came to look forward to Sundays, after the lesson, when they could indulge in sports directed by Father Mengarini. A favorite game was one in marksmanship. The Father would get near the center of a group of youths armed with bows and arrows. After giving the alert signal he would throw a ball high in the air, challenging any one to hit it. To his amazement and the delight of the onlookers the ball would frequently fall to earth pierced with a half dozen arrows.

Some of the Indians were not happy when they learned that the blackrobes regarded work as a virtue second in importance only to piety. The missionaries came to teach the red people to pray, yes, but also to work. Physical labor was necessary; further, it was a potent healer of disease as well as the most effective preventative of mischief. However, the savages soon fell into the routine of work as well as of worship. They learned how to make logs for building and how to make fences. In the spring they would be taught how to plow the ground and plant the seed that Father De Smet intended to buy from the Hudson's Bay Company's post at Fort Colville.

Father De Smet made careful preparations for this proposed trip to Colville because he intended to make it something more than mere business. He hoped to have contact with numerous Indians and to locate sites for possible future missions. Fort Colville was estimated to be about 300 miles distant and the season was getting late; nevertheless, the needs of winter had to be supplied and, in addition, tools, seeds and a start in cattle obtained if the mission were to be self-sufficient. He told the Flatheads of his intentions and asked for horses and a small escort in case he should be set upon by wandering Blackfeet. They responded by supplying seventeen horses and ten young braves.

De Smet left St. Mary's October 24. On the way he had the opportunity of preaching to a gathering of some 2000 Indians—Coeur d'Alenes, Pend Oreilles and Kalispells. He spent several days with them and baptized 190 persons.

At Fort Colville he was hospitably received by the factor, Archibald McDonald, and his Indian wife. The priest paid high tribute to the company's officials. He found that they always went far beyond what was expected in the way of courtesy, friendliness and generosity. Without his knowledge, McDonald and his wife slipped in among the provisions such little extras as tea, coffee, ham, candles and butter.

After being gone forty-three days De Smet returned to St. Mary's December 1, the feast of the Immaculate Conception. While he was away, Fathers Mengarini and Point had kept busy with mission duties. The Indians were really learning to work, they told De Smet, and as proof pointed to a pile of from two to three thousand rails. Instruction had been given regularly, since the time for baptism was approaching. It was the intention of the priests to legalize marriages on the same day. Eradicating polygamy, the Fathers found, was a harder task than stamping out gambling. Indians generally were reluctant to give up practices sanctified by tradition.

The buffalo hunt was an event that took precedence over everything else. The principal hunts took place three times a year, as a rule. Winter was the preferred time for then the fur was at its best and the robes made were of prime quality. This winter the Indians had delayed setting out until after their baptism. As a consequence food was scarce. The dogs were so hungry that they ate the thongs used for tying the horses.

Father Nicholas Point was to have his first experience in the chase. When the hunters started he rode at the head of some forty lodges and in the company of sixty Flathead warriors. They had not been many days on the trail when they fell in with huntsmen of various other tribes. Hunting in the dead of winter was not an experience to be sought by any but the toughened hunter. The weather was extremely cold. Storms frequently swept down on the encampment, almost burying it under drifting snow. In spite of everything the Flathead hunters obstinately stayed until a plentiful supply of meat had been taken.

One boisterous day when the air was as keen as a hunting knife Father Point was actually on the verge of freezing without realizing it. His companions noted the whiteness of his skin and the numbness which seemed to be getting control of him and hurried their teacher back to the camp.

In spite of the cold and the distractions of the hunt, the Indians worshiped much the same as they did back at St. Mary's. Sundays were kept religiously. At breakfast and at sunset the bell would ring for the Angelical salutation. Every morning found the huntsmen gathering at Father Point's lodge, which was so small that more than three-fourths of the congregation were obliged to stand out under the bitter sky.

The hunt was not without its dangers, not only from accidents, diseases and the ravages of winter but also from those traditional enemies the Blackfeet, whom Father De Smet believed to be "the most perfidious of all Indians." The Bannocks were a close second. Although the very name of "Blackfeet" was anathema to the Flatheads, there were decent representatives of the tribe who occasionally found their way to the Flathead camp. An example of such was the chief who had been baptized on Christmas Day under the name of Nicholas.

After the hardships of the hunt, Father Point was glad to be back in the safety and comforts of the mission. The plan of having a priest accompany the hunters was soon discontinued although in the beginning it had seemed a good one. The Fathers knew that when the Indians were left for long periods of time without religious supervision they soon returned to their old heathen practices. It was believed, too, that the presence of a priest would restrain their charges from barbarities inflicted on captives taken during a chance battle.

Notwithstanding these advantages, the position of a missionary during a buffalo hunt was a delicate one. The plains were not the private hunting estate of any one tribe but the open range where red men of many nations might meet, either in friendship or gory battle. If a priest were discovered in the camp of the enemy it was naturally supposed that he was in league with the foe. Such being the case, he would not be in the best position to proclaim God to all men. A priest should try to keep on neutral ground. The missionary also found that he could not prevent the torture of prisoners, especially if relatives and friends of his charges had suffered at the hands of the enemy. Father Point learned a good many things from first-hand experience—and on his first and only hunt. On the way out to the buffalo range, the Flatheads came upon a small band of Blackfeet and captured them. The prisoners appealed to the blackrobe for mercy. The priest took up the case with his Flatheads, pointing out that as Christians they were in duty bound to spare the enemy. They yielded reluctantly but some were angry with the priest for his interference.

On the first Christmas at St. Mary's Father De Smet added 150 baptisms and sanctioned thirty-two marriages. In all respects the Flatheads tried to comply with requirements. They came in large numbers to communion and as many as twenty at a time would appear for confession. A statue of the Blessed Mother was set up and all who passed would dutifully kneel for a moment of prayer. One old chief was baptized and admitted to communion in his eighty-second year. He did not live long after that. Seated beside the ancient red man shortly before death came, Father De Smet asked him if there were any faults which he cared to confess. "Faults?" the old one asked in hurt surprise. "It is my duty to teach others how to do good. How could I have any faults?"

In 1842 Father De Smet made a trip to Walla Walla for supplies. Shortly afterward, he made preparations to go to Europe to get funds and more recuits. The St. Mary's mission was going well and he had no hesitance in leaving it in the hands of his capable assistants. He hoped—with added helpers—to expand the mission work to other tribes of the mountains. He went by way of the Columbia River to Fort Vancouver, visiting St. Paul's on the way.

In the very beginning, Father Gregory Mengarini realized that example was always better than precept when it was a matter of teaching the natives. Accordingly he seized an ax and began to hew logs for the cabin. Some halfbreeds warned him that he would lose the respect of the people if he lowered himself by doing manual labor. The priest ignored the suggestion and was secretly pleased when a chief threw off his robe and asked for an ax. Seeing a head man at toil was an inspiration to the young men, who one by one began to take an interest in tools and what could be done with them.

When the first planting season came the Indians watched with curiosity an activity that seemed almost sacrilegious. Tearing up the face of the earth and ruining the grass, which was the only food for the ponies, seemed little short of criminal. And why? Just to bury a few seeds which would soon rot! They sat on the fence and watched skeptically. But when the plants came up and grew and matured, the natives looked with a new interest. Perhaps Father Point was right. Perhaps the earth would produce more if men cared for it. Maybe there would be more to eat for both red men and horses. The Indians came to like the garden produce, such as corn, potatoes, peas and carrots. They disliked onions, which made them cry like bantlings, and the greens, which they said were fit only for horse feed. One morning the gardener missed from his patch a half row of carrots and some onions. The second morning more carrots had mysteriously disappeared but the onions had been put back in their places.

Father Mengarini could swing an ax and he could also do a little with music. To provide activity and draw out native talent he organized a band for the young people. It was rather a conglomerate affair, he confessed; nevertheless, it was the admiration of all who listened to its performances. They had a flute, two accordions, a clarinet, a tambourine, piccolo, bass drum and cymbals. Father Mengarini said of his creation, "Our band, if weak in numbers, was certainly strong in lungs; for such as had instruments spared neither contortion of the face nor exertions of their organs of respiration to give volume to the music."[27]

The duties of Father Mengarini were wonderfully varied. While he listened to the music of his band he had to be thinking of ways by which the mission could be more self-sufficient. Flour was difficult to keep on hand. It was brought once a year from Fort Colville or Vancouver. Often the supply ran so low there was scarcely enough to make bread for the Lord's Supper. A grist mill was what was needed most. Yes, but to set up a grist mill there had to be skilled workmen. Brother Claessens was a mechanic. With able assistance, thought Mengarini, he might make this dream a reality. In time, he obtained the necessary help. When Father De Smet came back from Vancouver he brought a Canadian named Biledot, who was a millwright. Yet without grinding stones there still could be no mill.

In 1844 Father Anthony Ravalli came on the *Indefatigable*. It so happened that when Father Ravalli left Europe a merchant gave him a set of small buhrstones which came across seas with the priest. A pack horse carried them from Fort Vancouver to St. Mary's. These stones and the ingenuity of three men must be given the credit for the first grist mill in the present State of Montana. With this success to drive them on, the three men set to work to devise a sawmill, practically without materials. Four old wagon tires welded together and twisted and bent into proper form made the crank. Fashioning the saw was a more exacting operation. For this, a fifth tire was flattened out, tempered and filed and, lastly, toothed by means of a chisel. "Necessity is the mother of invention." The old saying was nowhere more applicable than at St. Mary's in those early days.

When winter came to the Bitterroot Valley and closed the mountain trails food was sometimes scarce at the mission. Father Mengarini suffered greatly from the cold. He declared sometimes that it was warmer out of doors than in the cabin, even with a fire burning. In the winter of 1842 he was afflicted with a persistent illness. He became weak and so thin as to be almost unrecognizable. When one young brave returned from the buffalo hunt, he asked, "Where has the young Father gone, and who is this old one who has come?"

Father Mengarini was becoming discouraged about his recovery when an old woman came with some boiled roots. "Eat," she commanded. Having no appetite, he was about to push the unsavory-looking dish away when she repeated, "Eat." Since there seemed to be no alternative, he forced himself to swallow the roots called *Lewisia rediviva* (bitter root) and after a while his vomiting ceased and the dizziness in his head began to disappear.

As Father Mengarini became better acquainted with the Indians and learned their language he began to question them about their beliefs. They recognized three creations. The first was destroyed by water, the second by fire. The third, also wicked, was saved by the pleas of Skomeltin, who promised that his people would do better if given another chance. The Flatheads knew no redeemer. A race of wicked giants once inhabited the world but were destroyed by a prairie wolf sent by Amotkin. These giants were called "people-killers" and were eventually changed to stone. The pagan Indians of Father Mengarini's day used to warn their children to hide their faces whenever they passed an overhanging rock so that the "people-killers" would not recognize them.

Father De Smet became a traveling missionary and an organizer of missions. When he came back on later visits to St. Mary's he always went away with glowing reports on the progress that was being made. The mills were turning out grist and lumber; the waters of the river were being directed toward the irrigation of gardens and orchards. By 1848 the farm had hogs, chickens and forty head of cattle. The number of buildings had increased to twelve, all constructed after the original pattern. Seen through De Smet's eyes, the major vices of the Indians had been eradicated: war and bloodshed had been greatly lessened; Christian love had supplanted hatred and revenge.

It was one thing, however, to be a visiting priest and quite another to be serving on the grounds day after day. Things were not always so peaceful as they appeared. From the beginning there were problems which had to be faced at every turn and with tact and courage. Unfortunately these did not grow less with the years; instead, they increased as others were added to complicate matters. There was always the menace of the Blackfeet—not out in the open but lurking in the shadows of the woods bordering the mission grounds. And farther out there were skirmishes between the Flatheads and their traditional enemies.

Some trouble that Father Mengarini had with his Flatheads caused an open rupture in 1847. Little Faro began assembling the people in his lodge, supposedly for prayer. Suspecting his motives, the priest scolded the Indian, thus making an enemy of him. Faro stirred up trouble and the Indians were promptly put under an interdict and denied mass until they repented and promised to behave themselves. Little Faro asked for pardon but there was some question about the sincerity of his repentance.

On the buffalo hunt following this episode the Indians indulged in the greatest of license. A faithful one among them reported to the priests that their conduct was worse than it ever had been before the coming of the blackgowns. Father Ravalli laid a large share of the blame for the backsliding on the influence of the undesirable white element that was settling the valley. These were principally French-Canadians and halfbreeds, former employees of the Hudson's Bay Company. A degraded lot without any religion, they expected to have material things given to them.

At this time the Mormons were moving into Utah and the area around Fort Hall. As soon as the Canadians learned of this they hurried across the mountains to trade ponies for cattle and goods of every sort. Some of the Flatheads trailed along after them. When they all came back trouble began. Without invitation the lawless Canadians came to winter their herds near the mission. Professing a desire to renew their connections with the Catholic religion, they loitered around, making no progress spiritually and expecting all kinds of favors.

It was a sore trial to the priests. The parasites demanded food and clothing as outright gifts. These could not be provided without ruining the mission's pinched economy and furthermore the priests felt no obligation to do so. When this was told to the hangers-on they at once began to circulate lies about the priests, designed to undermine the Indians' faith in their teachers. Besides, they flouted white standards of decency by boldly living with the Indian women.

The demoralizing effects of such an influence were soon noticeable in the natives. They became indifferent, spent more time on the hunt and made excuses for being absent from worship. The old love of life without restraints gradually took possession of many. The Flatheads next created an incident by shooting two Blackfeet who had been living peacefully near the mission and who had been well thought of by the priests. The relatives of the victims made threats to kill the priests. The leading Flatheads became aware of this but said nothing; instead, the greater number of them went on the buffalo hunt, leaving the mission under the protection of one old chief and two boys. Sensing the danger, Father Ravalli and Brother Claessens considered it prudent to gather into the inclosure the women and children, with as many horses as it would accommodate. This proved to be a wise decision. A band of Blackfeet fell upon the mission with whoops and shrieks but, not knowing how many might be within the defenses, dared not attack. They contented themselves with driving off some horses and shooting a boy who ventured outside the palisade.

The situation remained tense from this time forward. In fact, the death knell of the mission was already sounding. The Superior-General of missions recommended the closing of St. Mary's temporarily and in 1850 sent Father Joset to carry out orders. For the sum of $300 the mission property was leased to Major Owen, an independent trader, on condition that everything should be restored to the fathers if they returned within three years.

The workers who were at St. Mary's at the time of its closing were transferred to other locations. Father Ravalli went to the newer Sacred Heart mission at Coeur d'Alene and Father Mengarini to San Xavier's in the Willamette. Brother Claessens was assigned to accompany Father Joseph Joset to the Kalispell mission.

The priests had no sooner departed from the silent mission than the Flatheads began sorely to regret their loss. They were not, however, to be totally neglected. Priests from other stations served the flock by coming occasionally to instruct and say prayers. The little candle the Jesuits had lighted in the valley would be kept burning, if humanly possible. "Some day we may come back," said Father Ravalli as he closed the chapel door.

Those were sad, regretful years—those intervening years between the closing of St. Mary's, the first mountain mission, and its reopening in 1866. Sixteen years seemed a long punishment—a long time indeed—for the repentant Flatheads, who could do nothing but patiently wait for the return of their friends, the blackgowns.

23 • *The Sacred Heart of the Coeur d'Alenes*

THERE WAS A VALLEY, LOVELY and fertile, stretching westward from the Bitterroots. Clumps of pine and other conifers dotted its emerald expanse and in the center glittered a lake that looked all day at the sky. A river ran through. To the north, east and south rose mountains, night-capped in winter but blue-black when the suns of summer shone. Here lived the Coeur d'Alene or Pointed Heart Indians in their tepees made of poles, skins and grass. They did not cultivate the land but ate what nature provided: berries and roots from the woods and prairies, fish from the lake and river, game from the mountains. They feasted when there was an abundance, fasted when there was scarcity and gave little thought for the long tomorrow.

After the St. Mary's mission had been in operation about a year Father De Smet thought it was time to expand. Father Nicholas Point received the assignment to carry the cross to the Pointed Hearts. He was the typical Jesuit missionary, full of courage and zealous in soul-seeking. He had unlimited energy, deep sincerity but little buoyancy in his mood. Father De Smet could not help being impressed by his comrade's "sober and melancholy humor."

With a small escort of Flatheads, Father Point reached the land of the Coeur d'Alenes November 4, 1842. Since it was Friday, the day set apart for honoring the Sacred Heart, the mission was given the name, "Sacred Heart."

Father De Smet had met some of these Indians in his travels of the previous year and had been loud in his praise of their virtues and their potentialities. Father Point saw them in a different light. He found them altogether repellent in their filth, their vices and their heathenish practices. It nauseated him to see them using their hands for everything—fork, handkerchief, knife and spoon. When they ate they made revolting noises in their mouth, nose and windpipe. They had such a passion for gambling they would spend whole nights at a game. They were so lazy that nothing but the pangs of hunger would cause them to move. He found them "gluttonous, given to cheating, and to every mean vice." [28]

It was a dismal outlook for Father Point but maybe he could do something for these benighted ones. They were not a very large tribe. In 1805 Lewis and Clark estimated the number of Coeur d'Alenes to be about 2000, but in the days of Father Point they had been reduced by wars and smallpox to not many more than 300.

By spring the chapel and a cabin were finished and Father Point moved in. A few Indians came and settled down and were given plots of land to cultivate. Conditions among the natives improved, though slowly. These changes caused Father Point to take a different view of the Pointed Hearts. He found that they learned readily, practiced their religion and began to show real Christian virtues. Father Point bore the burden of the mission alone for a year, when assistants were sent, thanks to the efforts of Father De Smet in the East. Like the Protestants, the Catholics were compelled to go out and gather funds—bit by bit, from here and there. No missionary ever gathered more than did Pierre De Smet, who called himself "a beggar of God."

To the Coeur d'Alene mission came Father Peter De Vos, a man of about forty-six years of age and of frail health. With him was Father Adrian Hoecken, a young Hollander of twenty-eight. A third member of the reinforcement party was Brother McGean, carpenter and man of all work. When the new priests arrived Father Point was sent elsewhere to organize another mission. It then fell to Father Hoecken to take charge of the Sacred Hart and act as Superior. He had a most unpleasant time of it among the Pointed Hearts, due perhaps to a clash of personalities. The trouble all seemed to start over a sack of potatoes. The Indian who traded the potatoes to the mission tried to give only half measure, whereupon the Father said bluntly, "Very well. Keep the shirt and the potatoes, too." [29]

Another incident caused a rift so wide between the priest and his flock that it could not be bridged. Father Hoecken upheld an Indian girl who refused to accept the husband chosen by her parents. He tried to explain that the decision should be made by the woman concerned. The parents acquiesced but when the daughter then married a relative of the unpopular interpreter the natives seemed in the mood for a revolt. They became arrogant, stayed away from worship and hinted at further rebellion. They were subdued only by a strong threat to close the mission.

It was plain that Father Hoecken's work was done here so he was transferred and Father Nicholas Point returned to remain until 1845. The Indians soon settled down to the order that had previously been established. When Father Point was again called away to a new assignment the Sacred Heart welcomed Father Joseph Joset, sometimes called "the apostle of the Coeur d'Alenes." He became very fond of these "stiff-necked" people, and they of him. But something had to be done about the mission, he declared. It was in a poor location—unhealthful and infested with mosquitoes. Every spring the water flooded all the country around, almost isolating the mission post. At such times one could hardly approach the grounds, even on horseback.

It was Father Joset's responsibility to select a new site and build again. The one he chose was on an elevation overlooking the Coeur d'Alene River and about ten miles from the lake. This was to be known as the Old Mission, or Cataldo, after Father Joseph Cataldo. The mission grew. Buildings were added as needed. Little by little, land was brought under cultivation until a hundred or more acres were producing food and giving employment to many Indians. A large Pointed Heart village was located near by.

These Indians, however, were most unpredictable. While some were persuaded to accept a more or less settled way of life, the majority liked to wander at will and go on the war path at the slightest provocation. They were a sore trial to the priests, who more than once had to threaten to leave the mission in order to bring them to their senses. One evening at prayers a commotion like a sudden tornado shook the little congregation. Instantly the Father halted the service to make an investigation. He found that a woman had been stabbed by her former husband because she refused to live with him after he had remarried.

"Was this to be the end?" Father Joset asked himself. If such a deed could take place in the chapel, what greater crimes might be in the making? He remained isolated in his room for a while, keeping one boy to supply his wants and run errands. He sent a messenger to Father Hoecken, saying he believed the end had come and requesting him to send Indians to remove the mission property. The Sacred Heart would have to be closed. He could see no alternative.

But again they were spared. The chief was removed and another installed and the people pleaded with and admonished. In his heart Father Joset was glad they had been given another chance to make good. He loved his people and wanted them reclaimed. He would work even harder to make a settled, Christian way of life more appealing to these children of the forest. Before he had had time to get well started, however, he was transferred to Kettle Falls (in northeastern Washington) to organize a mission there.

Then in 1850 came Anthony Ravalli, who had arrived on the *Indefatigable* in 1844 and who had had some experience at St. Mary's. Ravalli was one of the most versatile of men. He had studied art, medicine, mechanics, the classics, philosophy and theology. He was a conspicuous figure in any company with his Roman nose, his sharply chiseled features and his sparkling humor. Now here he was in the midst of the capricious and sometimes unruly Pointed Hearts. As soon as he had looked the situation over, an idea was conceived in his mind: he would build a church for these people, one that would be a spiritual home. He would fashion it into a thing of beauty. With a hammer, a broadax, a small knife, pulleys and an auger, he set to work. His assistants were two Brothers and a few Indians who had to be instructed every step of the way.

Father Ravalli had given himself a stupendous assignment but he had the will to do it, and the warm encouragement of his Superior. Many willing Indians did the cutting, hauling and lifting of the timbers. Their wages amounted to a bowl of mush once a day and the only complaint was that too much food stuck to the cook's serving spoon. Working on the church was represented as a privilege as well as a Christian duty. It became a means of keeping some of the red men from roving. Even with the necessary interruptions, the church on Mission Hill, or "Skoot-Loty," was far enough along at the end of the year to permit the holding of services in it. Construction, though, went on slowly and piecemeal for in the wilderness needed materials were not easily available. After nine years it was still an unfinished structure, lacking doors, windows and a floor. It had, however, two beautiful altars and some handsome pictures. With his own skillful hands, Father Ravalli did the magnificent carvings on the altars, the window sills and the pillars.

Ravalli hoped that this church, long in the making, would be a symbol of unity for these nomadic people. For a while, it seemed that his hopes were to be realized. More and more Indians moved into the locality, settled down and began to show an interest in farming. This encouraging state of affairs, regrettably, was not destined to last long. Following the old urge to rove, many Indians began to lose interest in the life of the mission. They ceased to attend services and before long had drifted far away. Once again the Superior-General was faced with the problem of the Coeur d'Alenes. There was no use, he argued, in maintaining a mission for people who were gone most of the time; he began to take steps toward closing the post. At this critical moment, Father Joseph Joset, who always kept a watchful eye on the Pointed Hearts, made a fervent plea for them. "Let them have one last chance," he begged. That was his last request and it was granted.

The fact is pretty well established that Father Ravalli was in part to blame for the lack of interest on the part of his flock. He was a first-class builder and gave excellent medical care to his charges but he was not able to accomplish much in the line of teaching because the language remained a puzzle to him. He was transferred and Father Joset returned to the Sacred Heart to gather around him once again these wayward, yet likable Pointed Hearts.

But soon more trouble was brewing. The Indian wars that broke out in Washington Territory in 1855 spread to the eastern part of the area, finally involving the Coeur d'Alenes. Although

Father Joset pleaded and argued, his charges rode off on the warpath, joining forces with the Spokanes, the Yakimas and the Palouses against the United States Army. Father Joset followed along arguing peace as he traveled but he failed to prevent the Indian attack on Colonel Steptoe's troops marching north from Walla Walla in June 1858. After the wars were over, Colonel George Wright, who subdued the Indians, thanked Father Joset for his efforts to keep the peace.

For his part, Father Joset was low in spirit because the Coeur d'Alenes had profited so little from the toil and sacrifices of himself and other priests. Reluctantly, he agreed now with the Superior-General that the mission would have to be abandoned and the workers sent elsewhere.

As soon as they heard of the proposed closing of the Sacred Heart, both Colonel Wright and the road-builder, Lieutenant John Mullan, wrote to the Superior-General, pleading with him to give the "poor children" another opportunity to accept Christian civilization. This combined appeal brought results. The mission was continued, again on probation. From this time forward, however, things were to be different. The Pointed Hearts had had their lesson, which proved to be a lasting one. They came back to their devotions and their little lands, and ever afterward curbed their tendencies to wander in wild, irresponsible ways. But, declared the priests who had struggled here, there would have to be still another move. The Old Mission on "Skoot-Loty" would have to be abandoned and another built. Its very location was a drawback. There was not enough farmland surrounding it for the many natives who now wanted to settle down.

A further objection was that it was too isolated. Transportation was an almost unbearable burden. The round trip to Walla Walla required three months—a waste of strength and precious time. The produce of the mission had to be loaded onto wagons and taken to the river and transferred to rafts. The rafts were floated down the river to its mouth many miles below. Then a sail was set and Indian paddlers took the craft to the far southern extremity of Lake Coeur d'Alene. The next step was wagons again. While the raft was making its trip Indian helpers took the wagons to pieces and carried the parts on horseback around the lake, then put the vehicles together again at the end of the trail. The goods were finally loaded onto the wagons once more, and the journey to Walla Walla was continued. The supplies obtained at Walla Walla went through the same maneuvers, but in reverse order.

The priests set aside the sentimental appeals of "Skoot-Loty," and made the move with all of its inconvenience. The new mission was begun at De Smet, near the present Tensed, Idaho. One of the first buildings erected was a schoolhouse to accommodate the Sisters of Charity who were coming from Fort Vancouver. In the year of the removal, 1877, Chief Joseph's, or the Nez Perce, War broke out. This was a protest by the non-treaty Nez Perces against the reservation plans drawn up by the federal government. Naturally the priests were worried lest the Pointed Hearts again throw discretion to the winds and take the war trail on behalf of the Nez Perces, who made continuous appeals for assistance.

Rumor went to work, as it usually does in times of stress. When the report became current that the Coeur d'Alenes were going on the warpath the white settlers made a quick exodus to a place of safety. Here was an opportunity for the Indians to prove their character and they did so, to their everlasting credit. Instead of turning to pillage they protected the deserted farms of their white neighbors. When the war was over a vote of thanks signed by 107 settlers of the area was sent to Father Joseph Cataldo for keeping the northern tribes at peace.

The Coeur d'Alenes were now a different people. They lived in a land of plenty and were enjoying a measure of comfort and satisfaction. Warfare no longer had an appeal. The brave days of yore were becoming a memory. Priests came and went, returned, then left again. Their mission had lived through many changes and had survived threats of extinction. It was considered one of the most important of the mountain missions. Here at De Smet was established the first novitiate west of the Rocky Mountains. Father Joset died here in 1899, at the age of ninety, after having spent fifty-six years of his life in Indian service.

Indians as well as priests came and went in the life that flowed through the precincts of the Sacred Heart mission. Among them were the bad Indians, the indifferent, the vaccillating and the good, but there was none more deserving than Louise Sighouin. Louise had a brilliant conversion and seemed to understand the meaning of Christianity better than did the average Indian. She had two desires, which eventually became obsessions with her. One was to know the Great Spirit better and the other was to convert the pagans among her own tribe. She lived in poverty, prayed much and braved all manner of insults and dangers for the sake of her religion. She had the courage to face the greatest of all opponents, the medicine men, who imposed shamefully upon the people. They tried to counteract the good influences of the priests and Louise made herself valuable in helping the Fathers expose the fraudulent practices of these "jugglers."

Through the influence of this devout woman one of the medicine men was converted and baptized under the name of Isidore. Another, Peter Ignatius, had backslidden and had become a notorious gambler. Louise made up her mind to reclaim him. He lived a long two days' journey away but nothing was too hard for her. She made the trip to his lodge and by appealing to his good sense and pride was able to bring Chief Peter Ignatius back to his former honorable standing in the community.

Although her own health was far from good Louise went from lodge to lodge taking care of the sick; she became known throughout the tribe as "the good grandmother." Then she became a fanatic: she planted her garden seeds in the form of a cross, prayed long hours in the cemetery and saw frightening visions. When offenders were to be whipped by the chief she would go and beg to receive the punishment in their stead, saying that she wanted to emulate the sufferings of her Lord by bending her body under the cruel stripes.

Louise Sighouin did not live long. Said Father De Smet, "She walked in the ways of the Lord with a rapid step." Louise's coffin was made by her youngest son and all the children co-operated in digging the grave. Her husband Adolph, who was a cripple, had declared many times that if she died first and left him there would be no further reason for living. But before she passed away, Louise got a promise from him that he would live in a house close to the mission and remain true to God. The priest was finishing the last prayers over her remains when an Indian nearby ran from the lodge crying, "Sighoun—the good Sighoun is dead!" [30]

Before their conversion, said Father De Smet, the Pointed Hearts had been notorious for their idolatry and their "juggling." In fact, they entertained the most absurd superstitions until they found the true God. The first white man they ever saw wore a white coat and a black and white spotted shirt. In their ignorance the Indians believed the spotted shirt was the Great Manitou himself, the maker of the dread disease, smallpox. The coat, they thought, was the manitou of the snow. They believed that if they could possess both of these manitous their people would be forever free from the scourge of smallpox and that their winter hunts would always be aided by a snowfall which made it easy to track game.

The Indians offered to exchange several of their best horses for these manitous and the bargain was quickly made. The white coat and the spotted shirt continued to be objects of veneration for many years. In marching demonstrations these talismans were always given conspicuous positions. In smoking ceremonies the great medicine pipe would be offered to them with as much reverence as was shown to the earth, the water, fire and sun.

"But now we're different," the Coeur d'Alenes were fond of saying in later years. "God has been good to us."

24 • *St. Ignatius Among the Kalispells*

When Father De Smet returned from Europe in 1844 by way of the Columbia River he had in mind the plan for another mission in the Rocky Mountains—one for the Kalispells. He had met many of these Indians in his exploratory trips and was favorably impressed by their sincerity. He summoned Father Peter De Vos from St. Mary's to take charge and Father Adrian Hoecken, who had had trouble with the Coeur d'Alenes, to be an assistant.

The site chosen was in one of the prettiest and most fertile valleys in Montana, about fifty miles from St. Mary's. Not far to the northward lay Flathead Lake, about forty miles in length. There were few Indians living in the immediate vicinity but the openness of the country and the presence of good farming land would eventually attract many people. At least the Fathers hoped that this would be the case.

Building was begun promptly with Brother McGean as chief carpenter. By spring he had constructed, in the usual rough frontier style, a dwelling house, a chapel and a stable. In addition he had split 18,000 rails, and had fenced and put under the plow a good-sized field.

As soon as the Indians learned of the arrival of the blackgowns they began to trickle into the valley. When Easter came the Fathers gave thanks that their central location made possible the congregating of some thousand Indians for the holy services. Represented here at the time were Kalispells, Kootenais, Pend Oreilles and Flatheads.

Material improvements at St. Ignatius came slowly and painfully because of lack of funds and a shortage of workers. The grist mill was one of the most useful. A little later came the sawmill. Both were operated by power from a nearby stream. The water was diverted by means of a flume 1000 feet long and five feet wide, lined on the bottom and sides with tamarack timbers. Father Lawrence Palladino, stationed at St. Ignatius for six years in a later day, enlarged both mills and made other needed improvements. Though seemingly a toy affair, the whipsaw mill furnished all the timbers for the large church—100 feet long by forty wide—with its belfry rising to nearly 100 feet. The twelve columns of the nave were turned by hand. The most conspicuous feature of the interior was a life-sized crucifix carved by Father Anthony Ravalli.

These Indians were teachable and cooperative. When they

accepted Christianity it generally became a part of their being. Father Palladino found no "fair-weather Christians" among them. The sometimes frigid weather of Montana was never a factor in keeping them away from early mass. Under the direction of Father Joseph Menetrey they learned to sing in Latin the ordinary mass as well as some of the hymns of the benediction. They did this creditably but the Fathers thought that the congregation was somewhat "wild and savage like." To one of the visiting bishops it seemed "as if a dozen harmonious wolves were scattered among the congregation."

Preceding such special occasions as Christmas and Easter, the chiefs held what might be called an open court. At this time all those who had violated the law or the moral code of the tribe were brought before the assembly of the people. Frequently offenders who had not been formally indicted would go forward and ask for their punishment. At a signal from the head chief, the crowd would kneel briefly for prayer. When this was over the culprits would be examined and if found guilty would be punished on the spot. A buffalo robe would be spread and the offender told to lie prone upon it to receive his whipping. The number of lashes given depended upon the gravity of the crime. Young persons and women generally were given a light punishment.

The story was told about two Indians at St. Ignatius, one a Kalispell named Atol and the other a Blackfeet who had been adopted into the Kalispell tribe. These two had an argument over which was the greater offender. The Kalispell had left his wife to take another. The Blackfeet's wife had deserted him and he in turn had remarried. The question was which of these two men was more guilty. They took the matter to Father Palladino, who would have settled in favor of the Blackfeet if Atol had not pleaded his case so cleverly.

"Blackrobe," said Atol, "listen carefully and then decide."

Atol said he had been properly married by Father Menetrey to a woman of his tribe and that for the wedding feast the Father had given them a cabbage twice as large as their two heads put together. Atol himself cooked the cabbage and set it before his bride. She took several mouthfuls, each time spitting out the food and frowning angrily. Provoked, he looked her in the eyes and asked her why she was making such ugly faces.

"You shut up!" she replied saucily. "If I hadn't married you you would always be single, for no other woman in the village would have you."

"I got angry, Blackrobe," Atol continued. "Without saying another word I left her and the big cabbage and mounting my horse, went down to my people to get a wife to prove to my first wife that she had lied."

It was about three years after this that he came back to be whipped for his wrongdoing.

The practice of whipping did not originate with the missionaries as some people erroneously believe; it was used by various tribes of the West. The Kalispells believed that whipping wiped out guilt; because of this belief, the Fathers found it hard to convince the natives that they should confess the sins for which they were punished. In their heathen state they had used flogging as a punishment for slander, drunkenness, lying, theft, wife desertion and adultery. After they became Christians they added disorderly conduct in church to the list.

Father Palladino was sitting in the mission room one evening talking with Father Urban Grassi when an old Indian came in without bothering to knock. The priest asked him what he wanted. *"Ta-stem,"* the Indian answered, sitting down on the floor by the stove. "He says he doesn't want anything," Father Grassi explained. "But you'll see. He wants something but it may not come out for an hour."

The two priests went on with their conversation, ignoring the silent dark-skinned visitor. After a while the Indian said he wanted to make a confession and the Father moved his chair over closer. The penitent drew out from under his robe a little bundle of sticks bound together with a buckskin string. Untying the bundle, he took sticks of different lengths and placed them one by one before the priest. Here were the symbols of his sins—little, middle-sized and great—sins of thought, word and deed. The Indian made only a few grunts but Father Grassi understood. When confession was over, the Indian threw his sins into the fire and left.

"Many whites," commented Father Grassi, "cannot examine their consciences as this Indian did his."

The Indians were eager to remember the days of the week and were anxious that none of the great days of the church like Christmas and Easter go unrecognized. For a calendar they used a stick from twelve to eighteen inches in length, on which were cut notches—one for each ordinary day and a double one in the form of an X for Sundays. Before "going to buffalo" they would find out from the missionaries how many days would pass before the next Saint's Day so they would not overstay the time.

Those were great occasions when Archbishop Charles J. Seghers paid his visits to St. Ignatius, confirming a total of as many as 100 Indians. An incident of one visit caused the Archbishop great amusement. With the assistance of Father Joseph Cataldo he was examining some people for confirmation when an elderly Kalispell presented himself. Recognizing him as one who had already been confirmed, the Archbishop said, "Not you, my son. You have received the Holy Ghost already."

"Yes, great Blackrobe," answered the Indian, "but I lost him. He got drowned crossing the river." [31]

The Archbishop was not shocked at this apparent irreverence and was nonplused for only a moment. When the full meaning of the remark flashed upon him he had to repress an impulse to laugh. He had been in the habit of giving a small medal to every Indian confirmed in remembrance of the occasion. It was clear now what had happened. The old fellow had lost his while crossing the Pend Oreille River and was simply asking to have it replaced.

When St. Ignatius was about twenty years old, The Superior General of Missions decided that the educational program should be improved and expanded. Since prospects were brighter and more help available, a schoolhouse and living quarters for four teachers were constructed. The instructors were Sisters of Providence from Canada. At the head of the little group was Sister

Mary of the Infant Jesus; her companions were Sister Mary Edward, Sister Paul Miki and Sister Remi.

Arriving at Fort Vancouver July 11, 1864, they were soon ready to make the hardest part of the entire journey, the overland trip to the Rocky Mountains. Under the direction of Fathers Joseph Giorda and Gregory Gazzoli they reached Walla Walla without difficulty. This was the chief outfitting post for the mines and the missions of the interior. Besides the four Sisters, there were three Fathers and two Irishmen in charge of the prairie schooner, which carried the luggage as well as supplies for both St. Ignatius and the Sacred Heart missions.

Before the end of the first day the great ark of a wagon mired down in a mudhole. To pull it out required the combined strength of all the men and the mules. At the first encampment, Sister Paul Miki, more frail than the others, had no appetite for food. Without eating a bite she went to her bed on a blanket, with her saddle for a pillow. The following day, however, all the party, including Sister Paul, were in a gay mood.

There was need for sustained patience and good humor long before the mountains were reached. One night the horses got away and an entire day was lost in looking for them. The following day one of the Sisters was kicked by a horse, though not hard enough to cause serious injury. At the sandy camping place that night a windstorm came up and peppered the food with dirt. What was more annoying, a gale blew all night with such fury that the tents could hardly be kept staked to the ground. There was no sleep for anyone till along toward morning.

At the Spokane River the party was met by Chief Seltice of the Coeur d'Alenes, who went along as its escort for a day. Then the mountains were reached. At the Sacred Heart mission the Sisters were permitted two days of rest before resuming the horseback journey over trails so narrow that the animals could hardly find a safe place to put their feet. In spite of the hazards there were no accidents, and the party reached St. Ignatius on October 17. Here a uniquely different life opened up for the Sisters of Providence. In a crude, unfinished building they began the tasks of washing, scrubbing and baking in what was to be the first boarding school in the State of Montana. Indians of varying ages stood around as silent as mummies, no doubt wondering where these strange black-robed women came from.

The curriculum included simply studies in English, spelling, arithmetic, reading and writing. Part of the day was always devoted to cooking, dairy work, sewing, mending and—later on—practical gardening. The Fathers believed that training for the Indians should lean heavily toward the industrial side. Since the red man was opposed to manual labor for males he had to be taught its value and dignity. If he was to survive in a world dominated by energetic white men he would have to be given the kind of education that would enable him to be self-supporting.

For several years the girls' school was operated mainly on money secured by "begging expeditions," as the Sisters termed them. The nuns even visited the mines and combed the sparse settlements for miles around to get aid for their work.

It was hard to keep the boys' school going for the first four years and the program of necessity was meager. However, when the federal government began to subsidize the institution in 1874 the growth was steady and expansion on many lines was undertaken. The sawmill, the planer and the grist mill gave many opportunities to train boys in mechanics. Industrial arts included the trades of harnessmaker, cobbler and tinsmith. A printing press was brought from the East. In time, several books were published, among which were *A Manual of Prayer and Christian Doctrine* and a dictionary of the Kalispell language that could also be used by the Flatheads and several other tribes. Another useful publication was *Narratives from the Scriptures.* Of all the activities offered, the most fascinating for the Indian boys was saddlemaking—easy to understand, for the horse was their first love.

After its "Golden Age," St. Ignatius suffered reverses. The federal government discontinued the subsidy and from then on there was a constant struggle—soliciting, begging, praying—for its very existence. This new harsh day found Father Cataldo in his old age going from door to door in the interests of the school. He raised $3000 but it was still not enough.

There came three destructive fires: first, the boys' dormitory; then the whole establishment of the Sisters of Providence; and

—as if this were not enough—the Ursuline School, founded some time after the first boarding school, was reduced to ruins.

But St. Ignatius had something within itself that was indestructible. Like the fabled phoenix it rose from the ashes into new life, and became the nucleus of a larger community—always with a religious heart. It became the parent of other Montana missions which, though of vast importance, belong to a later period of time and to an area that was not Old Oregon.

25 • *The Jesuits at Spokane*

THE JESUITS WERE DEDICATED missionaries and they sowed by many waters. Father De Smet visited the homeland of the Spokane Indians on his first exploratory tour of 1842 and twenty years later, Fathers Joseph Caruana and Giorda made contact with the Indians at their fishing station near the falls. There was a large encampment where the Northern Pacific depot now stands but no sign of a white settler's cabin on either side of the river. On this occasion the Fathers baptized five adults and seventeen children.

The Spokane Indians were then living chiefly on Peone Prairie, named after Baptiste Peone, a 'breed. Father Cataldo humorously declared that Peone was one-fourth white, one-fourth Spokane and one-forth Kalispell. The Father could not recall what the other ingredient was, but of this he was certain—that Baptiste Peone came in quarters and that he was already a Christian.

It became Father Cataldo's assignment to start a mission at Spokane, if possible. Father Joseph Cataldo was born in Sicily in 1837. He was a pale, sickly youth when he asked for admission to the novitiate of the Society of Jesus at Palermo. He entered but ill health forced him to take a rest. After a few months he was back again to finish his studies. Eventually he came to Boston where he continued his studies in theology until he was transferred to Santa Clara, California.

Father Cataldo's one purpose in coming to America was to be a missionary to the Indians but his superiors were reluctant to recommend such a strenuous life for a consumptive. However, he persisted in his efforts to get an assignment until finally the General in Rome said, "Let him go to the mountains."

It was so ordered but when the Fathers saw the frail young man starting out they shook their heads. "He might live three months," said one. "Oh," said another, "with his persistence, he might possibly live a year." [32]

The consumptive priest survived the trip to Fort Vancouver and even the more difficult journey from Walla Walla to the Coeur d'Alene mission. Seven days on horseback were not enough to finish him off, although he arrived terribly fatigued. On the way he had been met by Chief Seltice (also spelled Seltis and Seltees), whose mother was a Spokane Indian. The chief talked earnestly with Father Cataldo about the need for a blackrobe to carry the word of God to the people at the Falls. Whether it was this meeting or something else, the fact was that Father Cataldo began to cherish a keen desire to be a missionary to the Spokanes. But he was assigned to the Sacred Heart for the present at least. After a few days of rest he began an intensive study of the Indian language under the guidance of Fathers Caruana and Gazzoli.

Although stationed among the Pointed Hearts, Father Cataldo was sent here and there to hold missions among other tribes. His opportunity to meet the Spokanes did not come until December 1866, when he and Father Paschal Tosi set out with an Indian guide. As they were nearing the end of the trip the guide led them to the top of a high hill and, pointing to the chasm below, said "Look!" They were surprised that an Indian had any appreciation of nature. For the first time they looked upon the spectacle of the Spokane River pouring its mighty volume of water over the precipice—Spokane Falls.

Near the falls were two camps of Indians—one of Coeur d'Alenes and the other of Spokanes, both concerned with salmon fishing. Father Cataldo first visited the Coeur d'Alenes, who readily responded to the invitation to mass and prayers. With the Spokanes it was different. "We're too busy with fish now," they said impatiently. "Come some other time and we'll listen to what you have to say about your religion."

Thus rebuffed, Cataldo approached Baptiste Peone about the matter. "Busy people can't listen to religion," he replied. "Too much fish now. Come some time when they don't have to work."

Father Cataldo returned later with the intention of building a house and staying among the Indians for a season of teaching. The Spokanes welcomed him with a great show of friendliness but with little inclination to help him build a cabin. For the immediate present he set up his tent near the largest encampment on Peone Prairie, close to the junction of the Little Spokane River and the main stream. No, he must not build a house without permission, Baptiste Peone told him. Only Chief Garry could give consent and he was away on a buffalo hunt that might keep him for five months.

Five months! Father Cataldo was in something of a dilemma. Peone, however, was not thinking of the priest's problem. He wanted Father Cataldo to stay and give instructions to himself and family. He had learned a part of the prayer, "Our Father," and was eager to learn the rest. The Father said he would gladly stay but he had to have a cabin, whereupon Peone replied, "I don't have the power to let you build a cabin. I'm only half Spokane. I'm just adopted into the tribe."

Peone seemed afraid of giving offense to Spokane Garry, who had been Christianized as a boy but who had not been practicing his religion very faithfully for many years. Yet he was a Protestant and he might not want the blackgowns on the premises. After more questioning, Father Cataldo learned that there was another chief who might be able to give the necessary permission.

After a delay of two weeks Cataldo, accompanied by Peone, went to the main Indian camp on the Little Spokane River. Old Chief Polotkin heard the request with patience, but said he feared Garry would be "mad" if anyone assumed power enough to give the priest permission to build a house. Baptiste spoke in behalf of the Father and tried to convince Polotkin that he certainly had the power to permit the missionary to stay for four months. While Polotkin hesitated Father Cataldo stated his proposal, saying in closing, "When the four months are up, I will go away, leaving the house in your possession. When Garry returns from Buffalo hunting, he will either be pleased or not. If he is pleased, very good; if he is not pleased, you just burn the house."

This was an easy way out, Polotkin probably thought, and gave consent. Now came plans for the construction of the house. Who would build it? "Not me," said Peone. "I'm too old, and you, Father have the lung sickness."

Father Cataldo had about made up his mind to build the house himself when Peone happened to think of the halfbreed Joe Pin, who might be persuaded to do the job. Jo was willing and with the help of some of his companions set to work felling trees and cutting logs. It did not take long to erect a crude cabin, chink the cracks, lay on a heavy mud roof and make a fireplace of rock and clay. Although hardly finished, it was dedicated to St. Michael on the Feast of the Immaculate Conception, December 8, 1866. This was the first place of Christian worship set up by the whites in Spokane. Here in the cabin, which served as chapel and dwelling house, Father Cataldo said mass. And here, in a comparatively short period of time, the conversion of the Upper Spokanes took place. As soon as Father Cataldo was established, Indians from distant parts of the valley came into the vicinity and camped.

The priest's day was a long one. Classes in religious instruction began shortly after breakfast and were resumed again immediately after dinner. He took time for only two meals a day. In the morning one of Peone's daughters would bring him a cup of coffee and in the evening he would prepare his own simple supper.

One day a delegation of older people led by Baptiste Peone came to their priest. "We are in hope to learn," said Peone, the spokesman, "but our minds can't keep up to the children."

"Very well," their teacher answered, "we'll have night school." Although this added a few more hours to his already long day, Father Cataldo did not mind because his assignment had to be completed in four months and he wanted it done as thoroughly as possible.

Father Cataldo was reluctant to leave such a promising field but he was obliged to obey his Superior and return to the Coeur d'Alenes. When the time came the Indians on Peone Prairie were greatly distressed and begged him to stay. The Father was amused at the psychology used by Baptiste Peone at the last religious meeting. After the congregation had dispersed, Peone called to the priest, "*Kuailks,* look behind the door!"

The Father obeyed. "Yes, Baptiste. . . . I see nothing."

"Again look!"

Cataldo looked but with the same result. When Peone insisted further, the priest smiled and said, "Perhaps there's somebody back there, Baptiste, but my eyes can't see him."

"You've guessed right, *Kuailks,*" Peone said emphatically. "The devil's behind that door. As soon as you go, he'll come out and tear down your good work." No doubt this was true, Father Cataldo thought. He promised to return if he could persuade the Superior that the need here was urgent.[23]

Before leaving, Father Cataldo gave instructions to Baptiste Peone to keep up the religious practices that had been started, especially that of calling the Indians together for prayers. Then he was off on the trail to the Old Mission, later to be called Cataldo in his honor. Although spring was approaching, the trail in some places was packed with snow five feet deep. In spite of his tubercular condition the Father survived this punishment, as he had lived through other hardships. His case was a strange one, he thought. If predictions had come true, he, Joseph Cataldo, S.J., would have been dead long ago. And here he still was, alive and working, and thirty years old!

During his long service among Indians of various tribes Father Cataldo acquired many nicknames. When he became lean and hard from his privations—shrunken and skinny as a mummy—the natives called him *chiluisse,* meaning "dried salmon." They could not understand what strange "medicine" drove that thin sickly-looking body.

After a fall from a horse that left him limping for a time his Indian friends began calling him "Broken Leg." After two more similar accidents he found himself answering to the name of *Kuailks Metatcopun,* meaning "blackrobe three times broken."

While Father Cataldo was working in other fields and going from place to place on peace missions, the Spokanes—people nearest his heart—were not neglected. Every winter a teacher came and spent some time instructing them. The first log cabin was destroyed by fire and in its place was erected a chapel as well as a dwelling house. The Catholics made so much headway in the conversion of the Spokane Indians that the Protestants became alarmed. Henry Harmon Spalding, now back at Lapwai, came to the Falls in 1875 and held a series of meetings which resulted in the baptism of several thousand people in the area.

The Jesuits then sought to counteract Spalding's successes by redoubling their efforts among the Spokanes. In that same year, 1875, Father Cataldo found time to return and supervise the erection of a boys' school building. The Fathers began to realize that the center of Catholic influence should be in the little town that was growing up by the Falls. By now the Indians had scattered and many were being taken care of by teachers in other missions. In 1881 Father Cataldo bought five lots in the village of Spokane Falls and the Jesuits promptly converted an old blacksmith shop into a church, which at first was attended by a dozen white people.

It was soon found that this shanty was far too small to accommodate the growing population, so the task of collecting funds to build a real church was begun. Then came a setback. Father Cataldo left for Europe and the zealous young priest who had shouldered the responsibilities died rather suddenly. But Heaven always seemed to raise up workers. Father Aloysius Jacquet now took over the job of finishing the drive for funds. He did not appoint an agent but went out himself, soliciting Protestants, Jews and unbelievers as well as Catholics, and always receiving a contribution. He was universally liked; no one resented the "black-gowned beggar."

One day Father Jacquet approached the officer in charge at Fort Sherman. To tease him, the officer said, "I'm not a Catholic, Father, and what do I care about your church?"

The priest flashed a smile and quickly replied, "Neither do I care for yours, Colonel, but I need money all the same." He got a twenty-dollar gold peice.[34]

Patience and unflagging labor had their reward and in the middle of the 1880s a fine new church, Our Lady of Lourdes, was dedicated. Later the Jesuits assisted the Sisters of the Holy Names in the building of their academy. The chief monument to the educational work of the Society of Jesus was Gonzaga, opened in September 1887, as a boarding school for boys. This school evolved into a college and finally, in the present day, a coeducational university.

Long before Jesuit activity became centered in Gonzaga, the Fathers from St. Michael's traveled near and far, carrying the consolation of the cross to isolated communities. A fine example of the priest-professor was Father Aloysius Jacquet, who spent most of the time in the saddle jogging over a country road to the settlements or the barracks or picking his way over a narrow trail to the mining camps of the Coeur d'Alenes—Burke, Wardner and Mullan.

One of the most colorful of these traveling missionaries of the pioneer period was Father Aloysius Folchi. Born of a noble Roman family, he entered the Jesuit order at the age of nineteen. In due course he found himself in the United States signing up as a missionary to the Indians of the Rocky Mountains. He labored in many small fields where he was universally loved for his humanitarianism, his humor, his sincerity and his simple piety. He was a familiar figure in all the little towns between Spokane and the Canadian border, in such places as Newport, Sandpoint and Chewelah. The older pioneers remember Father Folchi first of all for himself, secondly for his three bags and thirdly for his horse, Jack.

Wherever Father Folchi went, there went also the indispensable three bags: one for his vestments, one for his personal effects and the third for his toys. Children were his chief joy and concern and he could always gain an audience with them by hauling out the magic bag. Jack, the faithful horse, had his occasional whimsies and independent streaks. On one return trip Father Folchi accidentally dropped his spectacles and dismounted to look for them. After a short search he found them—but Jack in the meantime had walked on ahead, and no amount of persuasion could induce the beast either to return to his master or to wait for him to catch up. Jack chose to stay a few paces ahead of the Father for the whole of the seven intervening miles. But Father Folchi forgave his four-footed companion since such "temperamental flurries" were not common occurrences.

Inasmuch as Father Folchi's "vineyard," so to speak, was crossed by the Spokane Falls and Northern Railroad, he was allowed free passage on any of the trains and was permitted to flag either a passenger or a freight at his pleasure. Almost any place along the line, a small black-gowned figure might emerge from a country lane and signal a passing train. Every train carried opportunities for service and Father Folchi did not pass them by. Strong drink was habitual with railroad men so it became the Father's duty and pleasure to take them to task for this sin and, later, to administer the pledge.

Father Folchi might not be considered the greatest of the Jesuit missionaries but he gave magnificent service in small corners. He had no ambition for high places. Let him follow the byways to the homes of the humble and he was satisfied.

26 • *At Evening Time*

DURING THE TWENTY-YEAR PERIOD of the early missions some twenty-five priests organized and tended mission posts over the wide area of the "Inland Empire" and the Rocky Mountains. It is not for anyone to decide who was foremost among them, because each did the tasks assigned, dutifully and prayerfully, expecting no praise and receiving no monetary reward. In a sense Father De Smet towers above the others, not because of a greater devotion to duty but because he runs through the entire chapter of the early missionary period like a recurring theme. He was the trailblazer, the organizer; he became world-famous for his travels in the interests of Indian missions and for the charmingly written accounts of his experiences. If he had been assigned to a lonely station, confined by dull routine and narrow horizons, would he still have been the greatest among them?

Though Father De Smet was not perfect he was a sincere, godly servant, with ill will toward nobody. He had a genial, buoyant nature along with a keen sense of humor. He was kindly and affectionate and personally devoted to his family in Belgium, even after seas and years had separated him from the old hearthstone. He held himself aloof from the politics of his adopted country although the problems of slavery and the acquisition of new territories were of the deepest concern to him. People who admired his ability to keep free of bitter arguments said, "He thinks with his mouth shut."

The Indians were his first concern. For them he went over land and sea, winning for himself the reputation of being the most traveled missionary of any age. He went among the savages without fear, applying an unlearned psychology that won their complete confidence. He slept in their lodges. He ate their food even when its filth and vile odor grossly offended him. "The stomach of an Indian," he once wrote, "has always been a riddle to me." He was saddened by the federal government's Indian policy in the West. He believed that the natives were being too quickly pushed into the white man's civilization.

Father De Smet was not the typical missionary, technically speaking—not the teacher who took up residence among the native peoples. He was the promoter, the organizer, the locater, the propagandist in Europe, the most successful collector of funds ever to sail the Atlantic. He crossed the ocean nineteen times and made innumerable excursions over plains and mountains. He was chaplain in the United States Army in 1858 during the subjugation of the Indians in the Northwest, and was given the rank of major.

As a result of his tireless efforts the Middle-Columbia region became dotted with missions—some to be permanent, and others destined to close because of Indian troubles, lack of funds or scarcity of teachers. In 1846 he envisioned an Oregon conquered for Christ by the Jesuits. But in 1847 came the Whitman massacre, followed by several years of Indian unrest almost as devastating in their effects on missions as flood waters on a standing crop. When he made his last visit in 1863 he found the entire country in the process of being occupied by a worldly, grasping civilization that was ruining the hunting grounds, crowding the Indians onto poorer lands and forcing them into the straightjacket of the reservation system.

The leaders of the Protestant missions, as has been pointed out, had their critics. Father Pierre De Smet did not escape just because he was a Catholic and a Jesuit. Charges one after another were brought against him—charges which necessitated a well-considered defense. He was sensitive by nature and the pointed accusations wore him down. One of the first criticisms to be heard was that he was too expansive in his views. He planned on too large a scale, going beyond the bounds of good judgment in setting up in remote places missions that could not be well maintained. Fewer missions, well manned and adequately financed, would have been far better.

Further, he was charged with the offense against holy poverty and with spending money unwisely. When this point was reached Father De Smet was roused to resist these insinuations against him as a Jesuit and as a man. Accordingly, he forwarded to the Superior General an exact account of the mission funds that had been placed in his hands since 1840. He stated that he had made three journeyings into the mountains without spending a dollar apart from the modest sum he paid his guide. In addition he had traveled during the year just passed, 3000 miles in four months at a cost of only fifty dollars. When in Europe he always lived in almost a miserly fashion.

Another charge declared that he sometimes compromised the future of the missions by giving generously to the Indians and making promises which could not be fulfilled. His reports contained fantastic, overoptimistic statements that misled missionaries and caused them bitter disappointment when they arrived in the field. He indulged in "rhetorical flights to charm the reader" instead of picturing realistically what was in fact a bleak scene.

After an eloquent defense against all charges Father De Smet was finally exonerated. His health deteriorated as age crept on. He started out the strongest man in the St. Louis novitiate but it was not long until various ills began to plague him. He endured them all without complaint. When a missionary was once lamenting the hardships and the privations of his post, De Smet replied:

> I have been for years a wanderer in the desert. I was three years without receiving a letter from any quarter. I was two years in the mountains without tasting bread, salt, coffee, tea, sugar. I was for years without a roof, without a bed. I have been six months without a shirt on my back, and often have I passed whole days and nights without a morsel of anything to eat.[35]

As early as 1853 he found himself on the decline. His eyesight was getting poor and later he lost the hearing in one ear. His sojourn in Europe seems to have given him little relief. He suffered from some kind of affection of the throat, from erysipelas and from stomach trouble. A letter to relatives in Europe spoke of his being "broken down by all sorts of infirmities." He finally developed Bright's disease, which caused him to lose nearly a hundred pounds in weight.

Despite the privations of frontier life, most of the Jesuit priests lived out their allotted three score years and ten, and many went beyond. Father Joseph Joset attained the mellow age of ninety and died at De Smet, the Coeur d'Alene mission, his last charge. Father Cataldo, the "dried salmon," the "blackrobe three times broken," the supposed "consumptive," outlived his contemporaries and passed away at the age of ninety-one.[36]

Father De Smet's infirmities eventually called a halt to his physical activities. After this, he devoted his time to writing until death stilled his hand at the age of seventy-two. When taps sounded for him on that early morning in May 1873, the Society of Jesus lost one of its greatest soldiers and the red Indian lost one of his staunchest friends.

NOTES

1. Jason Lee's Diary, *Oregon Hist. Quarterly,* Vol. 27, 264
2, 3, 4, 5. C. J. Brosnan, *Jason Lee,* 12 ff.
6. Lee and Frost, *Ten Years in Oregon,* 173
7. Hines, *Missionary Hist. of the Pacific Northwest,* 244
8. *Ibid.,* 245
9. Clarke, S. A., *Pioneer Days of Oregon,* Vol. I, 365
10. Atwood, A. *The Conquerors,* 119
11. Wilkes, Charles, *Narrative of an Exploring Expedition,* Vol. 4, 344
12. Hines, *Missionary History,* 341
13. *Oregon Hist. Quarterly,* Vol. 37, 88
14. Gray, W. H., *History of Oregon,* 178
15. Drury, C., *Elkanah and Mary Walker,* 123
16. *Ibid.,* 139
17. *Ibid.,* 190
18. Drury, C., *Marcus Whitman,* 353
19. Cannon, Miles, *Waiilatpu,* 110
20. *Ibid.,* 54
21. Drury, C., *Henry Harmon Spalding,* 349
22. Blanchet, Francis, *Sketches,* 91
23. Bagley, Clarence, *Early Catholic Missions,* Vol. 2, 63
24. Chittenden, Hiram, *The American Fur Trade,* Vol. I, 203
25. *Ibid.,* 218
26. *Ibid.,* 252
27. Palladino, L., *Indian and White in the Northwest,* 52, 65, 78, 79
28. Bischoff, W., *The Jesuits in Old Oregon,* 39
29. *Ibid.,* 43
30. Chittenden, Vol. III, 1143
31. Palladino, L., *op. cit.,* 172

32. Weibel, G. F., *Reverend Joseph Cataldo,* 5
33. Crosby, L., "*Kuailks Metatcopun*" (Black-robe three times broken)
34. Bischoff, *op. cit.,* 172 ff.
35. Chittenden, H., Vol. I, 57.
36. Laveille, E., *Life of Father De Smet.*

BIBLIOGRAPHY

Allen, A. J. (Miss). *Ten Years in Oregon*. Ithaca, New York: Press of Andrus, Gauntlett and Company, 1850.

Atwood, A. *The Conquerors*. Cincinnati: Jennings and Graham; Endorsement of Washington State Historical Society, 1907.

Bagley, Clarence. *Early Catholic Missions in Oregon*. Seattle: Loman and Hanford, 1932.

Bancrof, Hubert Howe. *History of the Northwest Coast*. Vol. I, San Francisco: The History Company Publishers, 1886.

Bashford, James. *History of the Oregon Missions*. New York: The Abington Press, 1918.

Bischoff, William. *The Jesuits in Old Oregon*. Caldwell, Idaho: The Caxton Printers, Ltd., 1945.

Blanchet, Rev. Francis. *Historical Sketches of the Catholic Church in Oregon*. Portland, 1878.

Brosnan, C. J. *Jason Lee, Prophet of the New Oregon*. New York: Macmillan, 1932.

Cannon, Miles. *Waiilatou*. Boise, Capital News Job-Rooms, 1915.

Chittenden, H. M. *The American Fur Trade of the Far West*. Vol. I. New York: The Press of the Pioneers, 1935.

Chittenden, H. and Richardson, A. *Life, Letters and Travels of Pierre J. De Smet*. 4 vols. New York: F. P. Harper, 1905.

Clarke, S. A. *Pioneer Days of Oregon* (2 vols.). New York: Burr Printing House, 1905.

Crosby, Laurence. *"Kuailks Metatcopun" (Black-robe three times broken.)* Wallace, Idaho: The Wallace Times Press, 1925.

Davis, Rev. Wm. L. (S.J.) *A History of St. Ignatius Mission*. Spokane: Gonzaga Univ., 1954.

Delaney, Matilda Sager. *The Whitman Massacre*. Spokane, Wash.: Sponsored by the Esther Reed Chapter of D.A.R., 1920.

Drury, Clifford. *Henry Harmon Spalding*. Caldwell, Idaho: The Caxton Printers, Ltd., 1936.

Drury, Clifford. *Marcus Whitman, Pioneer and Martyr*. Caldwell, Idaho: The Caxton Printers, Ltd., 1937.

Drury, Clifford. *Elkanah and Mary Walker*. Caldwell, Idaho: The Caxton Printers, Ltd., 1940.

Drury, Clifford. *First White Woman Over the Rockies*. Glendale, California: A. H. Clarke Co., 1963.

Durham, Nelson. *Spokane and the Inland Empire*. Spokane, Chicago–Philadelphia: S. J. Clarke Publishing Company, 1912.

Eells, Myra. *Diary*. In Transactions of Oregon Pioneer Association, 1887–1894.

Eells, Myron. *History of the Indian Missions of the Pacific Coast*. Philadelphia: Amer. Sunday School Union, 1882.

Eells, Myron. *Father Eells*. Boston: Congregational Sunday School and Pub. Society, 1894.

Eells, Myron. *Marcus Whitman, Pathfinder and Patriot*. Seattle: Harriman and Company, 1909.

Elliot, T. S. *Coming of the White Women*. Oregon Historical Society, 1937.

Fuller, George. *History of the Pacific Northwest*. New York: Knopf, 1931.

Fuller, George. *The Inland Empire. Vol. II*. Spokane–Denver: H. G. Linderman, 1928.

Gatke, Robert. *Chronicles of Willamette*. Portland, Oregon: Binfords and Mort, 1943.

Gay, Theresa. *Life and Letters of Mrs. Jason Lee*. Portland, Oregon: The Metropolitan Press, 1936.

Gray, William H. *History of Oregon*. Portland, Oregon: Harris and Holman, 1870.

Hines, H. K. *Missionary History of the Pacific Northwest*. Portland, Oregon: Marsh Printing Company, 1899.

Hulbert, A., and Hulbert, D. *Marcus Whitman, Crusader*. Denver, Colorado: Stewart Commission of Colorado College and Denver Public Library, 1936.

Hulbert, A. *The Oregon Crusade*. Vol. V. Denver, Colorado: The Stewart Commission, 1935.

Jung, A. M. *Jesuit Missions among the American Tribes of the Rocky Mountains*. Spokane, Washington: Gonzaga University, 1925.

Kane, Paul. *Wanderings of an Artist.* Montreal, Canada: The Radisson Company, 1925.

Laveille, E. *Life of Father De Smet.* New York: P. J. Kennedy and Sona, 1915.

Lee, D. and Frost, J. H. *Ten Years in Oregon.* New York: J. Collard, Printer, 1844.

Lee, Jason. *Diary* Oregon Historical Quarterly, Vol. XXIV.

Lewis, W. S. *The Case of Spokane Garry.* Spokane: Spokane Historical Society. Vol. I, No. 1, 1917.

Lockley, Fred. *Oregon Trail Blazers.* New York: Knickerbocker Press, 1929.

Lyman, H. S. (Editor) *History of Oregon.* New York: The North Pacific Publishing Society, 1903.

Marshall, W. I. *History of the Whitman Saved Oregon Story.* Chicago: Blakely Printing Company, 1908.

Mc Beth, Kate. *The Nez Perces Since Lewis and Clark.* New York: Fleming and Revell Company, 1908.

McKee, Ruth Karr. *Mary Richardson Walker: Her Book.* Caldwell, Idaho: The Caxton Printers, Ltd., 1945.

McNamee, Sister Mary Dominica. *Willamette Interlude.* Palo Alto, Cal. Pacific Books, Publishers, 1959.

Mowry, W. A. *Marcus Whitman.* New York: Silver Burdett, 1901.

Nichols, Leona. *The Mantle of Elias.* Portland, Oregon: Binfords and Mort, 1941.

Nixon, O. W. *How Marcus Whitman Saved Oregon.* Chicago: Star Publishing Company, 1895.

O'Hara, Edwin V. *Catholic History of Oregon.* Portland, 1916.

Palladino, Lawrence B. *Indian and White in the Northwest.* Lancaster, Pennsylvania: Wickersham Pub. Company, 1922.

Parker, Samuel. *Journal of an Exploring Tour Beyond the Rocky Mountains.* Ithaca, New York: Mack, Andrus and Woodruff, Printers, 1840.

Penrose, Stephen. *Whitman, an Unfinished Story.* Walla Walla, Washington, 1935.

Richardson, M. M. *The Whitman Mission.* Walla Walla, Washington: The Whitman Publishing Company, 1940.

Sisters of the Holy Names of Jesus and Mary. *Gleanings of Fifty Years.* (1859–1909). Portland, Oregon: Catholic Church in Oreg., 1909.

Snowden, Clinton. *History of Washington.* New York: The Century History Company, 1909.

Spalding, H. and A. B. Smith, *Diaries and Letters Relating to the Nez*

Perce Mission (1838–1842). Glendale, Cal.: Arthur H. Clarke Co., 1958.

Spencer and Pollard. *History of the State of Washington.* The American Historical Society, Inc., 1937.

Townsend, John K. *Narrative of a Journey Across the Rocky Mountains to the Columbia River.* Philadelphia: H. Perkins, 1839.

Victor, Frances. *River of the West.* Hartford, Connecticut: Columbian Book Company, 1871.

Warren, Eliza Spalding. *Memories of the West.* (The Spaldings.) Portland, Oregon: Press of the Marsh Printing Company, 1916.

Weibel, G. F. *Reverend Joseph Cataldo.* (Short sketch. Reprint from Gonzaga University Quarterly.) 1928.

Wilkes, Charles. *Narrative of an Exploring Expedition.* 4 vols. Vol. IV. Philadelphia, Pennsylvania: Lea and Blanchard, 1845.

Whitman, Narcissa. *Diary,* in Transactions of Oregon Pioneer Association, 1887–1894.

Williams, Joseph. *Tour of Oregon, 1841–1842.* Manchester, New Hampshire: Standard Book Company, 1844.

INDEX